THE WORST HARD TIME

BOOKS BY TIMOTHY EGAN

The Winemaker's Daughter

Lasso the Wind: Away to the New West

Breaking Blue

*The Good Rain: Across Time
and Terrain in the Pacific Northwest*

THE
WORST HARD TIME

The Untold Story of Those Who Survived

the Great American Dust Bowl

Timothy Egan

 MARINER CLASSICS

Boston • *New York*

First Mariner Books edition 2006

Copyright © 2006 by Timothy Egan

Mariner Books
An Imprint of HarperCollins Publishers, registered in the United States of America and/or other jurisdictions.

Visit our Web site: www.marinerbooks.com.

Library of Congress Cataloging-in-Publication Data
Egan, Timothy.
The worst hard time : the untold story of those who survived the great American dust bowl / Timothy Egan.
p. cm.
ISBN-13: 978-0-618-34697-4
ISBN-10: 0-618-34697-X
1. Dust Bowl Era, 1931–1939. 2. Droughts — Great Plains — History — 20th century. 3. Dust storms — Great Plains — History — 20th century. 4. Depressions — 1929 — Great Plains. 5. Great Plains — History — 20th century. 6. Great Plains — Social conditions — 20th century. I. Title.

F595.E38 2006
978'.032—DC22   2005008057

ISBN-13: 978-0-618-77347-3 (pbk.)
ISBN-10: 0-618-77347-9 (pbk.)

Book design by Melissa Lotfy

Map by Jacques Chazaud

PRINTED IN THE UNITED STATES OF AMERICA

23 24 25 26 27 LBC 39 38 37 36 35

PHOTO CREDITS: Western History Collections, University of Oklahoma Libraries: pp. 18, 25, 36, 39, 41, 213, and 216; Library of Congress, Prints & Photographs Division, FSA/OWI Collection: p. vi, LC-USZ62-11491; p. 23, LC-USF34-034129-D DLC; p. 100, LC-USF34-004223-E DLC; p. 140, LC-DIG-FSA-8B38341; p. 163, LC-USF34-004078-E; p. 195, LC-USF34-004051-E; p. 208, LC-USZ62-47982 DLC; p. 249, LC-USF34-004053-E-DLC; p. 250, LC-USF34-004091-E; p. 251, LC-USF34-005244-E DLC; Denver Public Library, Western History Collection: pp. 201 and 205.

To my dad, raised by his widowed mother during the darkest years of the Great Depression, four to a bedroom. Among many things he picked up from her was this skill: never let the kids see you sweat.

"Between the earth and that sky I felt erased, blotted out."

—WILLA CATHER

Contents

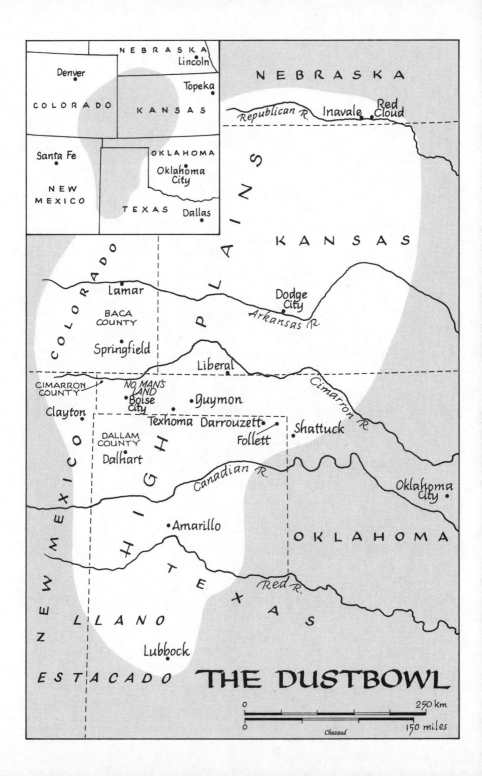

Introduction:
Live Through This

O N THOSE DAYS when the wind stops blowing across the face of the southern plains, the land falls into a silence that scares people in the way that a big house can haunt after the lights go out and no one else is there. It scares them because the land is too much, too empty, claustrophobic in its immensity. It scares them because they feel lost, with nothing to cling to, disoriented. Not a tree, anywhere. Not a slice of shade. Not a river dancing away, life in its blood. Not a bump of high ground to break the horizon, give some perspective, spell the monotone of flatness. It scares them because they wonder what is next. It scared Coronado, looking for cities of gold in 1541. It scared the Anglo traders who cut a trail from Independence to Santa Fe, after they dared let go of the lifeline of the Cimarron River in hopes of shaving a few days off a seven-week trek. It even scared some of the Comanche as they chased bison over the grass. It scared the Germans from Russia and the Scots-Irish from Alabama — the Last Chancers, exiled twice over, looking to build a hovel from overturned sod, even if that dirt house was crawling with centipedes and snakes, and leaked mud on the children when thunderheads broke.

It still scares people driving cars named Expedition and Outlander. It scares them because of the forced intimacy with a place that gives nothing back to a stranger, a place where the land and its weather — probably the most violent and extreme on earth — demand only one thing: humility.

Throughout the Great Plains, a visitor passes more nothing than something. Or so it seems. An hour goes by on the same straight line and then up pops a town on a map — Twitty, Texas, or Inavale, Nebraska. The town has slipped away, dying at some point without funeral or proper burial.

In other places, scraps of life are frozen in death at midstride, as Lot's wife was petrified to salt while fleeing to higher ground. Here is a wood-framed shack buried by sand, with only the roof joists still visible. In the distance is a copse of skeletal trees, the bones of orchards dried to a brittleness like charcoal. And is that a schoolhouse, with just the chimney and two walls still standing? Then you see fence posts, the nubs sticking out of sterile brown earth. Once, the posts enclosed an idea that something could come from a shank of the southern plains to make life better than it was in a place that an Ehrlich, an O'Leary, or a Montoya had left. The fence posts rose six feet or more out of the ground. They are buried now but for the nubs that poke through layers of dust.

In those cedar posts and collapsed homes is the story of this place: how the greatest grassland in the world was turned inside out, how the crust blew away, raged up in the sky and showered down a suffocating blackness off and on for most of a decade. In parts of Nebraska, Kansas, Colorado, New Mexico, Oklahoma, and Texas, it seemed on many days as if a curtain were being drawn across a vast stage at world's end. The land convulsed in a way that had never been seen before, and it did so at a time when one out of every four adults was out of work. The people who live here now, the ones who never left, are still trying to make sense of why the earth turned on them. Much as they love this place, their doubts run deep. Was it a mistake to hang on? Will they be the last generation to inhabit the southern plains? And some feel deep shame — for the land's failure, and their part in it. Outside Inavale not long ago, an old woman was found burning a Dust Bowl diary written by her husband. Her neighbor was astonished: why destroy such an intimate family record? The horror, the woman explained, was not worth sharing. She wanted it gone forever.

Fence tops lead to small farms, some still pulsing with life, and lead further to towns that service what is left of the homestead sections. Here is Springfield, standing for another day in Baca County, in the far southeast corner of Colorado, with Kansas on its eastern side, the No Man's Land of the Oklahoma Panhandle to the south, a piece of New Mexico in another corner. For sale signs. A mini-mart. A turkey buzzard perched on a tower near city hall. Springfield is the county seat for Baca, which has about four thousand people spread over its wrinkled emptiness — fewer than two people per square mile. A hundred years ago, a county with population density this low was classified as "frontier." By that definition, there is far more frontier now in this part of the world than in the day of the sod house. The town has the High Plains look, that slow-death shudder. They have not tried to dress it up or put makeup on battered storefronts. It is what it is. No flashing banners. No pretense.

A few blocks off Main Street is a house of sturdy stone. A bang on the door brings a small, brittle woman to the porch.

"I'm looking for Isaac Osteen."

"Ike?" Her voice is from somewhere long ago. "You want Ike?"

"Sure."

"He's up on the ladder, fixing the roof. Out back."

The roof is steep-pitched, a challenge for the nimble. Ike Osteen is eighty-six years old. He scrambles to the edge, a twenty-five-foot drop to the ground.

"Hello, there," he says. He is springy still, with liquid blue eyes, a full head of silver hair.

"Morning."

"You wanna talk about this drouth."

It is never *drought* in the southern plains.

All around him, the land is drying up again, a few years into the new century. The snow never came to many parts of the Rockies this year, and where it did fall, there is nothing left. The white reservoir of mountain snowpack — feeding the Arkansas River, the Cimarron, the little dribs and drabs pulled from high peaks to the prairie — is anemic. To some people, most of them too young to know better, this dead dry spell is like another era. A second Dust Bowl, they say.

"Nobody who lived through the Dirty Thirties believes that," says Ike, one foot prodding for the ladder. "Just wasn't any comparison."

One of nine kids, Ike Osteen grew up in a dugout. A dugout is just that — a home dug into the hide of the prairie. The floor was dirt. Above ground, the walls were plank boards, with no insulation on the inside and black tarpaper on the outside. Every spring, Ike's mother poured boiling water over the walls to kill fresh-hatched bugs. The family heated the dugout with cow chips, which burned in an old stove and left a turd smell slow to dissipate. The toilet was outside, a hole in the ground. Water was hauled in from a deeper hole in the ground. Ike's mother was Irish; he is not sure about his father's side.

"I was born in America, that's as far as I need to go."

His father had followed the old Santa Fe Trail in 1909, the year Congress tried to induce settlement in one of the final frontiers of the public domain — the arid, western half of the Great Plains — with a homestead act that doubled the amount of land a person could prove-up and own to 320 acres. The last homestead act was a desperate move, promoted by railroad companies and prairie state senators, to get people to inhabit a place that had never held anything more than a few native hunting camps and some thirteenth-century Indian villages.

The Osteens were following a rumor: there was supposed to be a dam going up on the Cimarron River in No Man's Land that needed hired hands.

"They got down there with their horses and wagon, and they were told there weren't any jobs. But people said, If you like this area, you can get 320 acres for the asking. They looked around over the border into Colorado and said, Well here's a perfectly flat piece of ground and there aren't any rocks on it. It was nothing but prairie grass. They dug down with a shovel. Saw it wasn't sand. The sod went down deep. Let's homestead this."

Ike's father died at the age of forty-six. He left behind a widowed mother of nine in a cramped hole in the ground in the middle of the

High Plains. The Osteens had the wind and 320 acres of land. The wind powered a windmill, which pumped water 140 feet up from the Ogallala Aquifer. The water was piped into small storage tanks. Cattle drank from the tanks and fattened easily on the rich grass. That was all you needed to stay alive: water and grass. If the wind ever stopped blowing for long, the Osteens fell into that fear that comes when the land goes mute. Without the wind, there was no water, no cattle, no life. The cows produced milk and thick cream. The cream was brought into town and swapped straight up for flour, coffee, sugar, a jar of hooch. The family had hens in a coop, laying a regular supply of eggs, and a .22 caliber rifle.

In 1929, the start of the Great Depression, the boys rode a mule to school. For the next nine years, Ike would see Baca County go mad. Earlier, the land had been overturned in a great speculative frenzy to make money in an unsustainable wheat market. After a big run-up, prices crashed. The rains disappeared — not just for a season but for years on end. With no sod to hold the earth in place, the soil calcified and started to blow. Dust clouds boiled up, ten thousand feet or more in the sky, and rolled like moving mountains — a force of their own. When the dust fell, it penetrated everything: hair, nose, throat, kitchen, bedroom, well. A scoop shovel was needed just to clean the house in the morning. The eeriest thing was the darkness. People tied themselves to ropes before going to a barn just a few hundred feet away, like a walk in space, tethered to the life support center. Chickens roosted in midafternoon.

"There'd be days, you couldn't see your hand in front a' your face," Osteen says, using the exact words that other people from his generation use. They know some people do not believe them, just as many in the East did not believe the initial accounts of predatory dust until a storm in May 1934 carried the windblown shards of the Great Plains over much of the nation. In Chicago, twelve million tons of dust fell. New York, Washington — even ships at sea, three hundred miles off the Atlantic coast — were blanketed in brown.

Cattle went blind and suffocated. When farmers cut them open, they found stomachs stuffed with fine sand. Horses ran madly against the storms. Children coughed and gagged, dying of something the doctors called "dust pneumonia." In desperation, some families gave away their children. The instinctive act of hugging a loved one or shaking someone's hand could knock two people down, for the static electricity from the dusters was so strong. Ike Osteen's life spans the flu epidemic of 1918, the worst depression in American history, and a world war that ripped apart the globe. Nothing compares to the black dusters of the 1930s, he says, a time when the simplest thing in life — taking a breath — was a threat.

Up the road from Baca County, the fence posts lead to another witness, Jeanne Clark. She narrows her eyes in the hard prairie sunlight, stirred by memory. Her constant companion, an oxygen cylinder, is by her side on a wheeled cart. She is alone in the place where she spent most of her life. It is so hard to laugh, and Jeanne Clark, whose personality is like seltzer water, has always liked to laugh. Her lungs, scarred from dust pneumonia, hold a small part of the story. When doctors first examined her lungs they thought she surely had suffered from tuberculosis. No, sir. It was the black dusters of the 1930s.

"I still have terrible nightmares," she says.

Jeanne's mother, Louise Walton, was a Broadway dancer and actress, a lively, high-stepping woman who seemed headed for the big time after landing a role in "The George White Scandal." But the late nights and hard living of New York took a toll on her. Her health broke down; her breathing became erratic. Doctors prescribed a remedy: go west, to the southern plains, go west to breathe. She took the train from New York, traveling through Chicago, St. Louis, Topeka, Garden City. When at last she landed in Lamar, Colorado, it was as if she had left the planet. There was no green. No lights at night. No buzz of purpose or industry. God, it was flat. Like a brown ocean. A stranger asked Louise: "Why are you here?"

"For the air," she said. "For the air."

The prescription, geography as therapy, had worked for others. Since the late nineteenth century, the western plains had been a haven for "lungers," as pilgrims with respiratory ailments were called. It was not just Doc Holliday, the killer and homeschooled dentist, who came to Kansas to remedy his tuberculosis. Every good-sized town in the arid belt had a sanatorium offering various amenities. For a while, Colorado City was so full of English-accented patients fleeing the foul industrial air of urban Britain that it was known as Little London. A doctor met Louise Walton at the train station and directed her to the nicest building in town, the hospital.

Over several years, Louise's health did improve. Her energy came back. She married a rancher and had a little girl, Jeanne. The Broadway dancer, the rancher, and their young daughter were just starting to build a life in the flatlands when the sky turned lethal. By 1934, the soil was like fine-sifted flour, and the heat made it a danger to go outside many days. In Vinita, Oklahoma, the temperature soared above 100 degrees for thirty-five consecutive days. On the thirty-sixth day, it reached 117. It was a time without air conditioning, of course, a time without even electricity for most farmers in the southern plains.

On the skin, the dust was like a nail file, a grit strong enough to hurt. People rubbed Vaseline in their nostrils as a filter. The Red Cross handed out respiratory masks to schools. Families put wet towels beneath their doors and covered their windows with bed sheets, fresh-dampened nightly. The sheets turned a muddy brown. At school, Jeanne Clark, the New York dancer's daughter, went through dust drills. When the storms hit, they usually came without warning. Weather forecasting, with no pictures from high above, relied on changes in atmospheric pressure, but such measures rarely picked up galloping earth. Dusters went undetected until they rolled into a neighboring town and a phone link was set in motion.

"The principal would call everyone out of class and say, 'Go home! Go home now. And hurry!'"

A Sunday in mid-April 1935 dawned quiet, windless, and bright. In the afternoon, the sky went purple — as if it were sick — and the temperature plunged. People looked northwest and saw a ragged-topped formation on the move, covering the horizon. The air crackled with electricity. *Snap. Snap. Snap.* Birds screeched and dashed for cover. As the black wall approached, car radios clicked off, overwhelmed by the static. Ignitions shorted out. Waves of sand, like ocean water rising over a ship's prow, swept over roads. Cars went into ditches. A train derailed.

Jeanne Clark had been outside playing when her mother called to her, panic in her voice.

"It was like I was caught in a whirlpool," she says. "All of a sudden it got completely dark. I couldn't see a thing."

That was Black Sunday, April 14, 1935, day of the worst duster of them all. The storm carried twice as much dirt as was dug out of the earth to create the Panama Canal. The canal took seven years to dig; the storm lasted a single afternoon. More than 300,000 tons of Great Plains topsoil was airborne that day. For weeks afterward, eight-year-old Jeanne Clark could not stop coughing. She was taken to the hospital, where dozens of other children, as well as many elderly patients, were spitting up fine particles. The doctor diagnosed Jeanne with dust pneumonia, the brown plague, and said she might not live for long. Jeanne's mother had trouble believing the doctor's words. She had come here for the air, and now her little girl was dying of it.

Down south, at the high western edge of the plains, a wind-bent cowboy feeds a horse in a field near the house he built in Dalhart, Texas. The breeze is up again in the Panhandle, blowing tumbleweeds against a fence, tossing around cottonwood leaves. Melt White walks with the slow, stiff gait of a horseman in his later years.

"Need some rain," he says.

White remembers when the rain merchants came through town in the Dirty Thirties. Dalhart took up a collection and paid a man named Tex Thornton to induce moisture from the sky. The grass was gone by then. Thornton set off his pyrotechnics, dynamiting the sky, just as he promised. Still the dry days dragged on, one white sky after another.

Nearly all the people who Melt White grew up with are gone now. It was in Dalhart that some of the leading citizens of the Texas Panhandle vowed to make a last stand, promising they would never leave town. If nature is out of whack, then we'll fight with everything we got, they said at town meetings. On Sundays, a mob of people with clubs herded rabbits into a corral and smashed their skulls. The skies, for a time, were blotted with great clouds of grasshoppers. To kill the hoppers, the townsfolk mixed a blend of arsenic, molasses, and bran, and spread it over the land, aided by the National Guard. Melt White was sickened by the rabbit drives, the plagues of hoppers, a town of random death and no comfort from the sky. The land was broken.

"God didn't create this land around here to be plowed up," says White. "He created it for Indians and buffalo. Folks raped this land. Raped it bad."

When the dusters blew so hard that even charter members of the Last Man Club started to move away, the White family stayed put. They were stuck, without money or prospects, children underfoot. Bam White got sick and Melt took over some of his father's family raising duties; it was hard. He was a kid with a temper. He got into a lot of fights. The other kids teased him about his skin, which seemed too full of the sun, even in winter. One Sunday, Melt asked visiting relatives how the family came to be. You shush, boy, he was told. Melt kept at it. Finally, an aunt told about the Apache and Cherokee in him. She said he should never tell anybody — keep it inside the family.

"It's a disgrace to be part Indian," he says. "That's what she said."

But from then on, White understood some of the anger inside him. This cowboy was an Indian, and he was not going to leave town. But what if somebody found out his secret?

At its peak, the Dust Bowl covered one hundred million acres. Dusters swept over the northern prairie as well, but the epicenter was the southern plains. An area the size of Pennsylvania was in ruin and on the run. More than a quarter-million people fled the Dust Bowl in the 1930s. Looking around now, it may seem that most people just hurried through the southern plains or left in horror. Not true. John Steinbeck told part of the story, about getting out, moving somewhere green. Those were the Exodusters. But Steinbeck's exiles were from eastern Oklahoma, near Arkansas — mostly tenant farmers ruined by the collapse of the economy. The families in the heart of the black blizzards were further west, in towns like Guymon and Boise City in Oklahoma, or Dalhart and Follett in Texas, or Rolla and Kismet in Kansas. Not much was heard about the people who stayed behind, for lack of money or lack of sense, the people who hunkered down out of loyalty or stubbornness, who believed in tomorrow because it was all they had in the bank. Yet most people living in the center of the Dust Bowl, about two thirds of the population in 1930, never left during that hard decade.

It was a lost world then; it is a lost world now. The government treats it like throwaway land, the place where Indians were betrayed, where Japanese Americans were forced into internment camps during World War II, where German POWs were imprisoned. The only growth industries now are pigs and prisons. Over the last half-century, towns have collapsed and entire counties have been all but abandoned to the old and the dying. Hurricanes that buried city blocks farther south, tornadoes that knocked down everything in their paths, grassfires that burned from one horizon to the other — all have come and gone through the southern plains. But nothing has matched the black blizzards. American meteorologists rated the Dust Bowl the number one weather event of the twentieth century. And as they go over the scars of the land, historians say it was the nation's worst prolonged environmental disaster.

"In no other instance was there greater or more sustained damage to the American land," the historian Donald Worster wrote.

Afterward, some farmers got religion: they treated the land with greater respect, forming soil conservation districts, restoring some of the grass, and vowing never to repeat the mistakes that led to the collapse of the natural world around them and the death of the children breathing its air. Many of the promises lasted barely a generation, and by the time the global farm commodities era was at hand, the Dust Bowl was a distant war, forgotten in a new rush to spin gold from straw.

For now, the narrative of those times is not just buried among the fence posts and mummified homesteads. People who lived through the whole thing — the great town-building, farm-fattening, family establishing prosperity of the 1920s, followed by the back hand of nature in the next decade, when all of life played out as if filmed in grainy black-and-white — are with us still, shelters of living memory. But before the last witnesses fade away, they have a story to tell.

I

PROMISE
The Great Plowup

1901–1930

1

The Wanderer

T HEY HAD BEEN on the road for six days, a clan of five bouncing along in a tired wagon, when Bam White woke to some bad
news. One of his horses was dead. It was the nineteenth-century equivalent of a flat tire, except this was the winter of 1926. The
Whites had no money. They were moving from the high desert chill of
Las Animas, Colorado, to Littlefield, Texas, south of Amarillo, to start
anew. Bam White was a ranch hand, a lover of horses and empty skies,
at a time when the cowboy was becoming a museum piece in Texas
and an icon in Hollywood. Within a year, Charles Lindbergh would
cross the ocean in his monoplane, and a white man in blackface
would speak from the screen of a motion picture show. The great
ranches had been fenced, platted, subdivided, upturned, and were going out to city builders, oil drillers, and sodbusters. The least-popu-
lated part of Texas was open for business and riding high in the Roaring Twenties. Overnight, new towns were rising, bustling with banks,
opera houses, electric streetlights, and restaurants serving seafood
sent by train from Galveston. With his handlebar mustache, bowlegs,
and raisin-skinned face, Bam White was a man high-centered in the
wrong century. The plan was to get to Littlefield, where the winters
were not as bad as Colorado, and see if one of the new fancy-pantsers
might need a ranch hand with a quick mind. Word was, a family could
always pick cotton as well.

Now they were stuck in No Man's Land, a long strip of geographic afterthought in the far western end of the Oklahoma Panhandle, just a sneeze from Texas. After sunrise, Bam White had a talk with his remaining horses. He checked their hooves, which were worn and uneven, and looked into their eyes, trying to find a measure of his animals. They felt bony to the touch, emaciated by the march south and dwindling rations of feed. The family was not yet halfway into their exodus. Ahead were 209 miles of road over the high, dry roof of Texas, across the Canadian river, bypassing dozens of budding Panhandle hamlets: Wildorado, Lazbuddie, Flagg, Earth, Circle, Muleshoe, Progress, Circle Back.

If you all can give me another two or three days, White told his horses, we'll rest you good. Get me to Amarillo, at least.

Bam's wife, Lizzie, hated the feel of No Man's Land. The chill, hurried along by the wind, made it impossible to stay warm. The land was so threadbare. It was here that the Great Plains tilted, barely susceptible to most eyes, rising to nearly a mile above sea level at the western edge. The family considered dumping the organ, their prized possession. They could sell it in Boise City and make just enough to pick up another horse. They asked around: ten dollars was the going rate for an heirloom organ — not enough to buy a horse. Anyway, Bam White could not bring himself to give it up. Some of the best memories, through the hardest of years, came with music pumped from that box. They would push on to Texas, twenty miles away, moving a lot slower. After burying their dead horse, they headed south.

Through No Man's Land, the family wheeled past fields that had just been turned, the grass upside down. People in sputtering cars roared by, honking, hooting at the cowboy family in the horse-drawn wagon, churning up dust in their faces. The children kept asking if they were getting any closer to Texas and if it would look different from this long strip of Oklahoma. They seldom saw a tree in Cimarron County. There wasn't even grass for the horse team; the sod that hadn't been turned was frozen and brown. Windmills broke the plain, next to dugouts and sod houses and still-forming villages. Resting for a long spell at midday, the children played around a buffalo wallow, the ground mashed. *Cimarron* is a Mexican hybrid word, descended from the Apache who spent many nights in these same buffalo wallows. It means "wanderer."

A few miles to the southeast, archaeologists were just starting to sort through a lost village, a place where natives, seven hundred years earlier, built a small urban complex near the Canadian River, the only reliable running water in the region. People had lived there for nearly two centuries and left only a few cryptic clues as to how they survived. When Francisco Vásquez de Coronado marched through the High Plains in 1541, trailing cattle, soldiers, and priests in pursuit of precious metals, he found only a handful of villages along the Arkansas River, the homes made of intertwined grass, and certainly no cities of gold as he was expecting. His entrada was a bust. Indians on foot passed through, following bison. Some of Bam White's distant forefathers — the Querechos, ancestors of the Apache — may have been among them. The Spanish brought horses, which had the same effect on the Plains Indian economy as railroads did on Anglo villages in the Midwest. The tribes grew bigger and more powerful, and were able to travel vast distances to hunt and trade. For most of the 1700s, the Apache dominated the Panhandle. Then came the Comanche, the Lords of the Plains. They migrated out of eastern Wyoming, Shoshone people who had lived in the upper Platte River drainage. With horses, the Comanche moved south, hunting and raiding over a huge swath of the southern plains, parts of present-day Kansas, Colorado, Oklahoma, Texas, and New Mexico. At their peak in the mid-1700s, they numbered about twenty thousand. To the few whites who saw them in the days before homesteading, the Comanche looked like they sprang fully formed from the prairie grass.

"They are the most extraordinary horsemen that I have seen yet in all my travels," said the artist George Catlin, who accompanied the cavalry on a reconnaissance mission to the southern plains in 1834.

The Comanche were polygamous, which pleased many a fur trader adopted into the tribe. Naked, a Comanche woman was a mural unto herself, with a range of narrative tattoos all over her body. From afar, the Indians communicated with hand signals, part of a sign language developed to get around the wind's theft of their shouts. The Comanche bred horses and mules — the most reliable currency of the 1800s — and traded them with California-bound gold-seekers and Santa Fe–bound merchants. In between, they fought Texans. The Comanche hated Texans more than any other group of people.

Starting around 1840, the Texas Rangers were organized by the Republic of Texas to go after the Indians. A mounted Comanche was the most effective warrior of the plains. The Comanche were difficult targets but even better on offense. Years of hunting bison from horses at full speed gave them skills that made for an initial advantage over the Rangers. Once engaged in battle, they charged with a great, rhythmic whoop — like a football cheer. After a raid and some rest, they would charge again, this time wearing their stolen booty, even women's dresses and bonnets. They were proud after killing Texans.

"They made sorrow come into our camps, and we went out like buffalo bulls when the cows are attacked," said Comanche leader Ten Bears in 1867. "When we found them we killed them, and their scalps hang in our lodges. The white women cried, and our women laughed. The Comanches are not weak and blind like the pups of a dog when seven sleeps old."

The Comanche buried their dead soldiers on a hill, if they could find one, and then killed the warriors' horses as well. Bison gave them just about everything they needed: clothes, shelter, tools, and of course a protein source that could be dried, smoked, and stewed. Some tepees required twenty bison skins, stretched and stitched together, and weighed 250 pounds, which was light enough to be portable. The animal stomachs were dried and used as food containers or water holders. Even tendons were put to good use, as bowstrings. To supplement the diet, there were wild plums, grapes, and currants growing in spring-fed creases of the flatland, and antelope, sage grouse, wild turkeys, and prairie chickens, though many Comanche thought it was unclean to eat a bird.

The tribe had an agreement signed by the president of the United States and ratified by Congress, the Medicine Lodge Treaty of 1867, which promised the Comanche, Kiowa, Kiowa-Apache, and other tribes hunting rights to much of the Great American Desert, the area south of the Arkansas River. At the time, there was no more disparaged piece of ground in the coast-to-coast vision of manifest destiny. The nesters and sodbusters pouring into the post–Civil War West could have the wetter parts of the plains, east of the one-hundredth meridian and beyond the Texas Caprock Escarpment. To the Indians would go the land that nobody wanted: the arid grasslands in the west. Early on, Comanchero traders called the heart of this area "el Llano Estacado" — the Staked Plains. It got its name because it was so flat and featureless that people drove stakes into the ground to provide guidance; otherwise, a person could get lost in the eternity of flat. The Staked Plains were reserved for the natives who hunted bison.

At the treaty signing, Ten Bears tried to explain why Indians could love the High Plains.

"I was born upon the prairie where the wind blew free, and there was nothing to break the light of the sun. I was born where there were no enclosures, and where everything drew free breath. I want to die there, and not within walls . . . The white man has taken the country we loved and we only wish to wander on the prairie until we die."

Within a few years of the signing, Anglo hunters invaded the treaty land. They killed bison by the millions, stockpiling hides and horns for a lucrative trade back east. Seven million pounds of bison tongues were shipped out of Dodge City, Kansas, in a single two-year period, 1872–1873, a time when one government agent estimated the killing at twenty-five million. Bones, bleaching in the sun in great piles at railroad terminals, were used for fertilizer, selling for up to ten dollars a ton. Among the gluttons for killing was a professional buffalo hunter named Tom Nixon, who said he had once killed 120 animals in forty minutes.

Texans ignored the Medicine Lodge Treaty outright, saying Texas land belonged to Texans, dating to the days of the Republic, and could not be offered up as part of the American public domain. With the bison diminishing, the Indians went after Anglo stock herds. Led by Quanah Parker and other leaders, the Comanche also attacked the trading post at Adobe Walls, just north of the Canadian River. Parker was regal-looking and charismatic, with soft features that made him appear almost feminine. His first name meant Sweet Smell, which is believed to have come from his mother, a Texan kidnapped at age nine and raised as a Comanche. She married into the tribe and raised three children, including Sweet Smell. After Cynthia Parker had lived twenty-four years as an Indian, the Texas Rangers kidnapped her back and killed her husband, Chief Peta Nocona. She begged to be returned to the Indians, but the Rangers would not let her go home.

The Red River War of 1874–1875 broke the Comanche. In one battle, in Palo Duro Canyon, six Army columns descended on an Indian encampment, catching them by surprise. The natives fled. The Army slaughtered 1,048 horses, leaving the Lords of the Plains without their mounts for the remainder of the war. On foot and starving, they were no match for General Philip Sheridan and his industrial-age weaponry. The natives were sent to various camps in the Indian Territory of Oklahoma, and some of their leaders were imprisoned in Florida. In his later years, Sweet Smell married seven women and built a large house. He founded a native religion based on vision quests through the hallucinogens peyote and mescal, a practice the Supreme Court ultimately upheld as a protected form of worship. The last bison were killed within five years after the Comanche Nation was routed and moved off the Llano Estacado. Just a few years earlier, there had been bison herds that covered fifty square miles. Bison were the Indians'

Comanche Indian camp, Oklahoma, winter, late 1860s or early 1870s

commissary, and the remnants of the great southern herd had been run off the ground, every one of them, as a way to ensure that no Indian would ever wander the Texas Panhandle.

"For the sake of a lasting peace," General Sheridan told the Texas Legislature in 1875, the Anglos should "kill, skin and sell until the buffaloes are exterminated. Then your prairie can be covered with speckled cattle and the festive cowboy . . . forerunner of an advanced civilization."

The animals left behind sun-crisped turds, which the nesters used to heat their dugouts and soddies, until they too ran out.

Empty of bison and Indians, the prairie was a lonely place; it had taken barely ten years to eliminate them. In victory, the American government was not sure what to do with the land.

"The High Plains continues to be the most alluring body of unoccupied land in the United States, and will remain such until the best means of their utilization have been worked out," the United States Geological Survey wrote in a report at the dawn of the twentieth century.

At the Texas border, the White family crossed into the XIT ranch — or rather, what was left of it. Virtually all his life Bam White had heard stories of the Eden of Texas, the fabled land of waist-high bluestem, of short, resilient buffalo turf, and the nutrient-rich grama, part of what Coronado had called "an immensity of grass." Horizon to horizon, buffalo heaven, and a cattleman's dream, the XIT had been part of the New World's magical endowment — grasslands covering 21 percent of the United States and Canada, the largest single ecosystem on the continent outside the boreal forest. In Texas alone, grasslands covered two thirds of the state, with more than 470 native species. Virtually all of the Panhandle, nearly twenty million acres, was grass. In the spring, the carpet flowered amid the green, and as wind blew, it looked like music on the ground. To see a piece of it in 1926, even in winter dormancy, could delight a tomorrow man like Bam White, who loved sky and earth in endless projection.

The temperature warmed just before dusk, and the sky boiled up, thunderheads coming out of the east. It was too early in the year yet for clouds to be throwing down lightning and hail, but it happened enough that people took precautions when warning signs appeared overhead. Bam fretted about his horses. They looked sad-eyed and road-worn. Like most cowboys in the High Plains, he preferred darker horses, chocolate-colored or leathery brown, on a belief that they were less likely to attract lightning. One of his horses was lighter, not quite beige, just light enough to bring a thunderbolt down on it. Bam had never actually seen a light-haired horse combust at the touch of lightning, but he had heard plenty of stories. A friend of his had seen a cow struck dead by a sky-spark. Bam looked around: there were no rock overhangs or little arroyos such as they had passed through up north. Well, hell — what did those XIT cowboys used to do? If those boys could get through a thunder-boomer without shelter, Bam White could do the same.

Everybody in Texas had a story about the XIT. It was the ranch that built the state capitol, the granddaddy of them all. Fifteen years after the end of the Civil War, Texas wanted the biggest statehouse in the union, a palace of polished red granite. To pay for the new stone showpiece, the state offered up three million acres in the distant Panhandle to anybody willing to construct the building. After the tribes were routed, Charles Goodnight had moved a herd of 1,600 cattle down from Colorado to Palo Duro Canyon. The grass then was free; it attracted other nomadic Anglo beef-drivers and speculators from two continents. In 1882, a company out of Chicago organized the Capitol Syndicate, and this group of investors took title to three million acres in return for agreeing to build the capitol. It would cost about $3.7 million, which meant the land went for $1.23 an acre. The syndicate drew some big British investors into the deal, among them the Earl of Aberdeen and several members of Parliament. By then, the Great Plains cattle market was the talk of many a Tory cocktail hour. Books such as *How to Get Rich on the Plains* explained how any investor could double his money in five years.

The ranch land was empty. No people. No bison. No roads. No farms. Just grass — three million acres of it.

"Those salubrious seasons at the end of the Eighties made that country appear a paradise," wrote one early rancher, Wesley L. Hockett.

At dusk, when the sky burned pink against the expanse of sod, a cowboy could be moved to tears, it was so pretty. Much of the XIT was in the heart of the Llano Estacado, where the Comanche had roamed. And like the Comanche, the cowboys developed their own sign language to communicate over distances. The syndicate stocked the grassland with cattle, erected windmills in order to pump water up for the animals, and fenced it. Barbed wire was invented in 1874, and by the early 1880s ranchers were stringing it across the plains, closing off the free grass. In 1887, there were 150,000 head of cattle on the XIT ranch and 781 miles of fence. It was soon the biggest ranch in the world under fence.

The XIT was lord of the Panhandle. Not just the landowner, but also the law. They formed vigilante posses to chase down people who encroached on the ranch or stole cattle, and spread poison to kill wolves and other animals with a taste for XIT calves. When railroad feeder lines came to the ranch, the cattle shipping points were made into towns, which brought merchants, ministers, and other hustlers of body and soul. It was a good life for a cowboy, earning about thirty dollars a month fixing fences, riding herd, eating chow at sunset. A black cowboy, or Mexican, had more trouble. A man everybody called Nigger Jim Perry was the lone black cow puncher on the XIT.

"If it weren't for this old black face of mine," said Perry, "I'd be foreman."

The XIT prohibited gambling, drinking of alcohol, and shooting anything without permission. Outside the ranch borders, little rail towns sprang up with a different set of laws. One of those was Dalhart, which was born in 1901 at the intersection of two rail lines, one going north to Denver, the other east to Liberal, Kansas. In Dalhart, an XIT cowboy could get a drink, lose a month's salary in a card game, and get laid at a shack known simply as the Cathouse.

But even with the finest grass in the world, with 325 windmills sucking water up from the vast underground aquifer, with the elimination of predators, with several thousand miles of barbed wire, and with martial-law control over rustlers, the biggest ranch in Texas had trouble making a profit. The open range, on the neighboring plains states, was stocked with far too many cattle, causing prices to crash. The weather might display seven different moods in a year, and six of them were life-threatening. Droughts, blizzards, grass fires, hailstorms, flash floods, and tornadoes tormented the XIT. A few good years, with good prices, would be followed by too many horrid years and massive die-offs from drought or winter freeze-ups, making shareholders wonder what this cursed piece of the Panhandle was good for anyway. Bison have poor eyesight and tend to be clannish, but they are the greatest thermo-regulators ever adapted to the plains, able to withstand temperatures of 110 degrees in summer, and 30 below zero in winter. But cattle are fragile. The winter of 1885–1886 nearly wiped out cattle herds in the southern plains, and a second season of fatal cold the next year did the same thing up north. Cowboys said they could walk the drift line, where snow piled up along fences north of the Canadian River, for four hundred miles, into New Mexico, and never step off a dead animal.

With the British investors pressing for a better return on their piece of unloved and nearly uninhabited Texas, the syndicate turned to real estate. The problem was how to sell land that only an herbivore with hooves could love. Parts of the XIT were scenic: little pastures near a spring, red rock and small canyons to break the ironing board of the High Plains. There was some timber in the draws, but not enough for fuel or building material. What fell from the sky was insufficient to grow traditional crops. And the rate of evaporation made what rain that did fall seem like much less. It takes twenty-two inches in the Panhandle to deposit the same moisture as fifteen inches would leave in the Upper Mississippi Valley. The native plants that take hold, like mesquite, send roots down as far as 150 feet.

And then there was the larger image problem.

Great American Desert. It was Stephen Long, trying to find something of value in the treeless wilderness, who first used those words in 1820, later printed on maps that guided schooners west. It would stay as cartographic fact until after the Civil War, when the Great American Desert became the Great Plains. Zebulon Pike, scouting the

Man standing in unplowed native grass, Baca County, Colorado

southern half of the Louisiana Purchase in 1806 for Thomas Jefferson, had compared it to the African Sahara in his report to the president. Jefferson was crushed. He feared it would take one hundred generations to settle the blank space on the map. It was a vast empty sea, invariably described as featureless and frightening by the Americans who traveled through it.

"A desolate waste of uninhabited solitude," wrote Robert Marcy, after exploring the headwaters of the Red River. Marcy had the same opinion of the region as did Long, the influential American explorer who followed Pike. After conducting an extensive survey, Long wrote in 1820 the words that still make him seem unusually prophetic:

"In regard to this extensive section of the country, I do not hesitate in giving the opinion that it is almost wholly uninhabitable by a people depending upon agriculture for their subsistence."

The answer to the syndicate's problem was aggressive salesmanship. Why, this wasteland could be England or Missouri, if plowed in the right way. Brochures were distributed in Europe, the American

South, and at major ports of entry to the U.S.: "500,000 acres offered for sale as farm homes" and cheap, as well, the land selling for thirteen dollars an acre. Twice a month, agents for the syndicate rounded up five hundred people and put them on a train from Kansas City for the Texas Panhandle to see for themselves. The train ride was free.

Speculators who bought from the syndicate turned around and added to the claims. "Riches in the soil, prosperity in the air, progress everywhere. An Empire in the making!" was a slogan of W. P. Soash, a real estate man from Iowa who bought big pieces of the XIT and sold them off. "Get a farm in Texas while land is cheap — where every man is a landlord!"

To prove the agriculture-worthy potential of the Llano Estacado, the syndicate set up experimental farms, demonstrating to immigrants how they could make a go of it on the Texas flatlands. They worked with government men from the Department of Agriculture. Well, sure, it rained less than twenty inches a year, which was the accepted threshold for growing a crop without irrigation, but through the miracle of dry farming a fellow could turn this land to gold. Put a windmill in, and up comes water for your hogs, chickens, and garden. And dryland wheat, it didn't need irrigation. Just plant in the fall, when a little moisture would bring the sprouts up, let it go dormant in the winter, and then wait for spring rains to get the crop going again. Harvest in summer. Any three-toed fool could do it, the agents said. As for the overturned ground, use the dust for mulch, farmers were advised; it will hold the ground in place and keep evaporation down. That's what Hardy Campbell, the apostle of dry farming from Lincoln, Nebraska, preached — and the government put a stamp on his philosophy through their agriculture office in the Panhandle. No nester was without *Campbell's Soil Culture Manual,* a how-to book with homilies that all but guaranteed prosperity. What's more, the commotion created by the act of plowing itself would bring additional rain, causing atmospheric disturbances. Rain follows the plow? Damn right! The Santa Fe Railroad printed an official-looking progress map, showing the rain line — twenty inches or more, annually — moving west about eighteen miles a year with new towns tied to the railroad.

Mounted cowboys, Oklahoma-Texas border, 1885

With scientific certainty, steam from the trains was said to cause the skies to weep.

Seasoned XIT ranch hands scoffed at such claims; the demo projects were a scam, cowboys said. They warned anybody who would listen that the Panhandle was no place to break the sod. Dust mulch? How was that supposed to hold moisture in the ground, with the wind blowing steady at thirty clicks an hour? The land was high and cold, with little drainage, and nearly treeless in its entirety. As for rainfall, the average in the county was about sixteen inches a year, not enough, by any traditional standards, to sustain a crop. At Dalhart, the elevation was 4,600 feet. A blue norther would come down from Canada through the Rockies and shake a person to their bones. The Panhandle was good for one thing only: growing grass — God's grass, the native carpet of plenty. Most of the land was short buffalo grass, which, even in the driest, most wind-lacerated of years, held the ground in place. This turf had supported the southern half of the great American bison herd, up to thirty million animals at one point.

The best side is up, the cowboys said time and again — for chrissakes don't plow it under. Nesters and cowboys hated each other; each side thought the other was trying to run the other off the land. Homesteaders were ridiculed as bonnet-wearing pilgrims, sodbusters, eyeballers, drylanders, howlers, and religious wackos. Cowboys were hedonists on horseback, always drunk, sex-starved. The cattle-chasers were consistent in one way, at least. They tried telling nesters what folks at the XIT had passed on for years, an aphorism for the High Plains:

"Miles to water, miles to wood, and only six inches to hell."

The syndicate had bondholders in London to satisfy. By 1912, the last of the XIT cattle were off the land, and the ground that was leveraged to build the state capitol of Texas had ceased to function as a working ranch. Four years later, Charlie Goodnight held what he called "the last buffalo hunt" on his ranch in Palo Duro Canyon. More than ten thousand people showed up to watch the old cowboy chase an imported buffalo, a limp choreography. When Bam White and his family crossed over into Texas in 1926, only 450,000 acres were unplowed of the original three-million-acre XIT.

The family spent the next night in north Dallam County, a day's ride from Dalhart. The thunderheads had missed them, passing farther east. Bam White rose in the winter darkness and gave his horse team another pep talk.

We're in Texas now, keep on a-going, one leg at a time. You got us outta Colorado. You got us outta Oklahoma. Now get us through Texas to Littlefield, and a new home.

They had crossed into one of the highest parts of the High Plains, where the wind had its way with anything that dared poke its head out of the ground, and it was flatter even than Oklahoma. Lizzie White wondered again why *anyone* — white, brown, or red — would choose to live in this country, the coldest part of Texas. Even the half-moon, icy at night, looked more hospitable than this hard ground. As they said on the XIT, only barbed wire stood between the High Plains and the North Pole.

The Whites arrived in Dalhart on February 26, 1926. Bam found a place to camp at the edge of town and took to fretting again. Littlefield was still 176 miles to the south. The family was down to the last of their dried food, and they didn't know a soul. It was not the first time a family with significant Indian blood had returned to the old treaty lands. Comanche, Kiowa, and Apache who had drifted back lived a shadowed existence, dressed like whites, going by names like "Indian Joe" and "Indian Gary." As long as they stayed largely invisible, nobody paid much attention to them. Indians were not citizens yet. They could be forcefully removed to a reservation. Any hint of their earlier presence was gone, erased for the new tomorrow. Dalhart had no history beyond the XIT; what came before was viewed as having little merit.

"The northern Panhandle was settled by a group of fine pioneer people and its citizens are of the highest type of Anglo Saxon ancestry," the *Dalhart Texan* declared shortly after the Whites rolled into town.

But the new citizens of this new town were refugees, each in their own way. Bam went to have a look around. Train whistles blew at regular intervals. The railroads were still offering bargain fares to lure pilgrims to the prairie, though the good land had been taken. The town looked like dice on a brown felt table, the houses wood-framed and bare-ribbed — as tentative as a daydream. Dalhart's first residents had planted locust trees, but most of them did not last in the hard wind, between drought and freeze. Chinese elms were doing a little better. The town was birthed by railroad men and was never under the thumb of the XIT. Like the rest of the Panhandle, its frontier was *now*, in the first three decades of the twentieth century. While the northern plains were losing people disenchanted with the long winters and ruinous cycles of drought and freeze, the southern plains were in hormonal midadolescence. There was oil gushing and news of wildcatters making a killing spread far and wide. The oil drew a new kind of prospector to go with the nesters and wheat speculators tearing up the grassland. Nearly thirty towns were born in the Panhandle between 1910 and 1930.

Much of Texas took its prohibition seriously. Not Dalhart. It took its whiskey seriously, in part because some of the finest corn liquor in America was coming out of the High Plains. Up north, in Cimarron County, Oklahoma, and Baca County, Colorado, farmers had been growing corn for whisk brooms, but then the vacuum cleaner, in just a few years, ruined the market for broomcorn. Prohibition saved the broomcorn farmers, making grain more valuable as alcohol than the dried stalks had ever been for sweeping. A single still near the Osteen family homestead up in Baca County was turning out a barrel of corn whiskey a day, every day, nearly every year of Prohibition. Some farmers made five hundred dollars a week. At the peak of Prohibition, five counties in a three-state region of the High Plains shipped fifty thousand gallons a week to distant cities.

"This is a period of fast times," a Dalhart businessman, Jim Pigman, wrote in his diary, "and much drinking of poor liquor."

Just a few strides from the railroad switch tower, Bam White came upon a curious sight: a two-story sanitarium. It was the only hospital for hundreds of miles. On one side of the sanitarium was a tobacco ad — a big, red-and-white snorting bull promoting Bull Durham Smoking Tobacco. Inside was a specimen room, with pickled fetuses, tumors, an enlarged liver, goiters, and a heart. The liver had belonged to a saloonkeeper in the days before Prohibition. It was grayish green and huge, and served as a visual aid — an example of what can happen to someone who poured too much corn whiskey down his gullet. Presiding over the sanitarium was a tobacco-spitting, black-bearded man of the South, Dr. George Waller Dawson. The Doc always wore a dark Stetson, though he was said to take it off during surgery, and kept a brass spittoon nearby for his tobacco habit. He chewed through child delivery and lung surgery, it didn't matter. His wife, Willie Catherine, was the finest-looking woman in the Panhandle. That wasn't just Doc Dawson's opinion; in 1923, she won a diamond ring as prize for being voted the most beautiful woman at a Panhandle Fourth of July celebration.

"My Willie," the Doc called the missus. She had dark eyes, an aquiline nose, and a powerful taste for literature. Willie kept the accounting books of the sanitarium and also served as anesthesiologist. She was the only person who could run the solitary x-ray machine for a few hundred miles in any direction. The Doc and his Willie were always busy cutting open cowboys and splicing nesters back together after they had been sliced by barbed wire, thrown from a horse, or knocked down by a windmill pump. They patched bones, yanked gallstones, and cut away shanks of infected flesh from people who insisted on paying them with animals, live and dead. In one month alone, the Doc and Willie performed sixty-three operations. A Kentuckian, Dawson had come to Texas for his health. He had persistent respiratory problems and legs that would sometimes freeze up on him, a kind of paralysis that puzzled the Kentucky medical community. The High Plains was the cure. He arrived in 1907, planning to start a ranch and live off his investments. In time, he hoped to breathe like a normal man and lavish attention on the lovely Willie. But he lost nearly everything two years later in a market collapse. His second chance was found in the two-story brick building in Dalhart, well north of his ranch. He opened the sanitarium in 1912.

By the late 1920s, Dr. Dawson intended to cut back on his medical work and try once more to make a go of it on the land. The money in farming was so easy, just there for the taking. Despite all his years of practicing medicine, the Doc had saved up very little for his retirement. The nest egg would be in the land. He had purchased a couple of sections and was going to try his luck at cotton or wheat. Wheat was supposed to be the simplest way to bring riches from the ground. Doc Dawson would take some time off from running the hospital and see if he could coax something from the Staked Plains to free him of the rubbing alcohol and the pickled organs. It was their last best chance, he told his family.

Bam White walked past the sanitarium and on down Denrock, the main street of Dalhart. The cowboy passed the Felton Opera House, two stories tall with fine Victorian trim, then a clothing store, with window displays of new dress shirts and silk ties. This was Herzstein's; as far as anyone knew, they were the only Jews in Dalhart. Streetlights, with wicks that had to be lit every night, dangled from cords strung to poles. A bustle of people played cards and jawboned over grain prices inside a new-looking, yellow-brick hotel, the DeSoto. The DeSoto was first class: solid walnut doors, a bathtub and toilet in every room, along with a telephone. A guest could dial 126 and get a reservation to see a girl at the place just west of Dalhart. It didn't have a name, just the Number 126 house. Next door to the DeSoto was the moving picture establishment, the Mission Theater. None of Bam White's children had ever seen a movie.

Crews came by with sprinklers to wet down the streets, but dust still kicked up with every carriage and car that passed by. The town felt somewhat tentative; a mighty breath or a twister could blow everything down, collapsing all the pretty painted sticks. Talking to folks, Bam White found out real quick who owned Dalhart. That would be Uncle Dick Coon, the well-fed gentleman sitting there at the DeSoto with his cards in one hand and a hand-rolled cigarette in the other. He owned the DeSoto, the Mission Theater, just about every business on Denrock. You watch Uncle Dick for just a few minutes, folks said, and you would see him flash a hundred-dollar bill from his pocket. Three months of cowboy wages pinched between two fingers. Bam White had never seen a hundred dollar bill till he came through Dalhart.

The C-note was Uncle Dick's heater, his blanket. As a child, Dick Coon's family was often broke. The corrosive poverty hurt so much it defined the rest of his life. As long as Uncle Dick could touch his C-note, he had no fear in life. And he had certainly known fear. Dick Coon was fortunate to live through the Galveston hurricane of 1900, the worst single natural disaster in American history. He lost everything in Galveston but was never bitter. His life had been spared, while six thousand people lost theirs. Dick Coon didn't plan on getting rich in Dalhart; didn't even plan on staying in the High Plains. In 1902, he had been passing through Dalhart, making a train connection to Houston, when he fell under the spell of one of the syndicate's real estate agents. He heard enough to buy his own piece of the old XIT. The ranching went well, but the real money was in town building.

Back from his tour of town, Bam White found Lizzie in a panic and the children looking at him like they'd just had the life scared out of them. What is it?

Dead horse.

Again?

Dead. Check for yourself, daddy.

Bam White's horse was flat on its side, the body cold, rotted teeth exposed. She was dead all right. Now Bam was without enough of a team to make it another step. The family had no means to buy another horse, and it had been hard enough traveling from Boise City to Dalhart. Well, then, it must be a sign, Bam said to the kids — maybe he was born for this XIT country anyhow. There have got to be plenty of jobs in this new town, even on a gentleman's ranch.

Marooned, Bam made his decision on the spot: the family would stay in Dalhart. A guy in town had told him about opportunities in the newly plowed fields. This town was going places. It had a shine, a face full of ambition. The fields were turning fast, making money for anybody with a pulse and a plow. The way White looked at Dalhart was the way Doc Dawson and Uncle Dick looked at their homes in the Panhandle: as the last best chance to do something right, to get a small piece of the world and make it work. The wanderer would settle in and see what the earth would bring him in what had been the world's greatest grassland.

2

No Man's Land

I F DALHART WAS A PLACE where dreams took flight on the last snort of a dying horse, the next huddle of humans up the road was a town where just the opposite happened. Hope died the first time people laid eyes on Boise City, Oklahoma. It was founded on fraud. Even the name itself was a lie. *Boy-City,* the promoters pronounced it, from the French words *le bois* — trees. Except there was not a single tree in Boise City. Nor was there a city. But that didn't stop the Southwestern Immigration and Development Company from selling lots, at forty-five dollars apiece, in a phantom town in the newly opened Panhandle of Oklahoma. The company sent fliers all over the country, showing a town as ripe as a peach two days into its blush. The brochures sketched a Boise City with elegantly aged trees lining the streets, a tower of cold, clean water gushing from an artesian well in the center of town, and houses any banker would be proud to call home. The streets were paved. Businesses were chock-a-block on Main Street. Three railroads were building lines to Boise City, the company said, and a fourth was on the way. You could grow cotton, corn, or wheat on rich land just outside the city limits. Hurry — sites are going fast. A fiction, all of it. But the story helped them sell three thousand town lots in 1908, one year after Oklahoma became the forty-sixth state.

When the lucky buyers showed up to see their share of the shining new city on the designated opening day, they were shocked. Women

came in full-length white dresses and men in polished boots. If anyone from the development company had been around, the life would
have been choked out of them by the best-dressed mob on the plains.
On Boise City's imaginary streets, the buyers found stakes in the
ground and flags flapping in the wind. No railroads. No tracks. No
plans for railroads. No fine houses. No businesses. The artesian well
was a stockman's crude tank next to a windmill, full of flies. Worst of
all, the company did not even own the land it had sold.

The developers were arrested for fraud. *Lurid* was the word the
government used to describe the lies of the town developers, J. E.
Stanley and A. J. Kline. After a two-week trial, the pair was found
guilty and sent to Leavenworth Federal Penitentiary. Kline died in his
cell — a lesson apparently not passed on in the annals of American
real estate.

Boise City, without trees, railroad, or bankers' homes, somehow
took shape nonetheless. It was closer to Colorado's capital of Denver,
299 miles north, than it was to its own statehouse in Oklahoma City,
340 miles to the east. But the founding principle of feisty fraud carried
over long enough for the site to win designation as the Cimarron
County seat, despite murder threats from rival towns. By 1920, Boise
City had 250 residents, and the big county at the far end of No Man's
Land was approaching 3,500 people.

Hyperbole in service of Western settlement was certainly not limited to town developers. Railroads, banks, politicians, and newspaper
editors all played a variation of the scheme — selling a windblown
piece of ground that was supposed to increase in value as more people saw a fledgling town emerging from a larva of forlorn dirt. But
Kline and Stanley were among the few people ever convicted of lying
about the High Plains. The flattest, driest, most wind-raked, least ara-
ble part of the United States was transformed by government incentive, private showmanship, and human desire from the Great American Desert into Eden with a haircut. Settlement was a dare, on a grand
scale, to see if people could defy common sense. During a Fourth of
July celebration in 1928 at the highest point in Oklahoma, the 4,973-
foot-high tabletop of Black Mesa, in the far northwest corner, the fea-

tured speaker, state senator W. J. Rizen, said, "The Panhandle of Oklahoma is destined to be the greatest wheat-growing country in the world."

No Man's Land had been one of the last places in the United States where a person could hide, and nobody cared enough to come look for them, or to get lost, never to be found again. For nearly 350 years after Coronado marched through, the land remained unwanted.

"Not a single landmark is to be seen for forty miles — scarcely a visible eminence by which to direct one's course," wrote Josiah Gregg while traveling between the Arkansas and Cimarron Rivers in 1831. Gregg was a meticulous note-taker, but he was exaggerating. The land bunches up at the western edge, near Black Mesa, and a few stunted piñon and cedar trees grow in the north-facing draws there. Gregg told a story about Captain William Becknell, the first to try a shortcut from the Santa Fe Trail in 1822 and angle through No Man's Land. Becknell and his thirty men ran out of water and wandered, near death, till they killed a bison and cut open its stomach, drinking fluids from the animal's insides to save themselves. For additional hydration, they cut the ears of their mules and drank the blood, Gregg wrote.

Five flags had flown over No Man's Land. Spain was the first to claim it, but two expeditions and reports from traders reinforced the view that the land was best left to the "humped-back cows" and their pursuers, the Comanche, Kiowa, and Apache. Spain gave the territory to Napoleon. The French flag flew for all of twenty days, until the emperor turned around and sold it to the United States as part of the Louisiana Purchase. A subsequent survey put the land in Mexico's hands, an extension of their rule over Texas in 1819. Seventeen years later, the newly independent Republic of Texas claimed all territory north to Colorado. But when Texas was admitted to the Union in 1845, it was on the condition that no new slave territory would rise above 36.5 degrees in latitude, the old Missouri Compromise line. That left an orphaned rectangle, 35 miles wide and 210 miles long, that was not attached to any territory or state in the West, and it got its name, No Man's Land. The eastern boundary, at the one hundredth meridian, was where the plains turned unlivably arid, unfit for Jefferson's farmer-townbuilders.

In the late nineteenth century, one corner of the Panhandle served as a roost for outlaws, thieves, and killers. The Coe Gang was known for dressing like Indians while attacking wagon trains on the Cimarron Cutoff. The Santa Fe Railroad pushed a line as far as Liberal, Kansas, on the Panhandle border, in 1888. Kansas was dry. And so a place called Beer City sprang up just across the state line: a hive of bars, brothels, gambling houses, smuggling dens, and town developers on the run. The first settlement in No Man's Land, Beer City lasted barely two years before it was carted away in pieces. Law, taxes, and land title companies finally came to the Panhandle in 1890, when the long, undesired stretch was stitched to Oklahoma Territory.

The name *Oklahoma* is a combination of two Choctaw words — *okla*, which means "people," and *humma*, the word for "red." The red people lost the land in real estate stampedes that produced instant towns — Oklahoma City, Norman, and Guthrie among them. But the great land rushes never made it out to the Panhandle. No Man's Land was settled, finally, when there was no other land left to take.

It was a hard place to love; a tableau for mischief and sudden death from the sky or up from the ground. Hazel Lucas, a daring little girl with straw-colored hair, first saw the grasslands near the end of a family journey to claim a homestead. Hazel got up on the tips of her toes in the horse-drawn wagon to stare into an abyss of beige. It was as empty as the back end of a day, a wilderness of flat. The family clawed a hole in the side of the prairie just south of Boise City. It was not the promised land Hazel had imagined, but it had . . . possibility. She was thrilled to be at the beginning of a grand adventure, the first wave of humans to try to mate with this land. She also felt scared, because it was so foreign. The lure was price, her daddy said. This land was the only bargain left in America. The XIT property, just thirty miles to the south, could cost a family nearly $10,000 for a half-section. Here it was free, though there was not much left to claim. By 1910, almost two hundred million acres nationwide had been patented by homesteaders, more than half of it in the Great Plains. Hazel missed trees. She wanted just one sturdy elm with a branch strong enough to hold a swing. And she didn't want to live in a hole in the ground, with the snakes and tarantulas, and sleeping so near to the stink of burning cow manure. Nor did she want to live in a sod house, the prairie grass stacked like ice blocks of an igloo. Soddies leaked. Friends who had been in the Panhandle long enough to make their peace with it told the Lucas folks that if a person wore out two pair of shoes in this country, they would never leave. You just had to give this land some time to make it work.

Hazel's family arrived in No Man's Land in 1914, the peak year for homesteads in the twentieth century — 53,000 claims made throughout the Great Plains. Every man a landlord! But people were already fleeing the northern plains, barely five years after passage of the Enlarged Homestead Act. The northern exodus should have been a warning that the attempt to cover the prairie with "speckled cattle and festive cowboys," as General Sheridan had said, was a mistake. Places like Choteau County, Montana, lost half their population between 1910 and 1930, while Cimarron County, Oklahoma, grew by 70 percent and Dallam County, Texas (home of Dalhart), doubled its population during the same time. The killer winters — temperatures of minus forty in Montana froze farm animals in place — were not a

Family and their sod house, No Man's Land, date unknown

problem in the southern plains, people told themselves. Just get your piece of the grassland and go to it.

The federal government was so anxious to settle No Man's Land that they offered free train rides to pilgrims looking to prove up a piece of dry land, just as XIT realtors had done. The slogan was "Health, Wealth, and Opportunity." Hazel's father, William Carlyle, known as Carlie, built a dugout in 1915 for his family and started plowing the grass on his half-section, a patch of sandy loam. The home was twenty-two feet long by fourteen feet wide — 308 square feet for a family of seven.

Without a windmill, the Lucas family would not have lasted a day, nor would much of the High Plains been settled. Windmills came west with the railroads, which needed large amounts of water to cool the engines and generate steam. It was a Yankee mechanic, Daniel Halladay, who fashioned a smaller version of bigger Dutch windmills. The Union Pacific Railroad was his first big customer. Eventually, a nester could buy a windmill kit for about seventy-five dollars. Some people hit water at thirty feet, others had to go three times as deep. Some dug the hole by hand, a grueling task, prone to cave-ins; others used steam or horse-powered drills. Once the aquifer was breached, a single wooden-towered windmill could furnish enough water for most farming needs on a full section of land. The pumps broke down often, and parts were hard to come by. But nesters were convinced they had tapped into a vein of life-giving fluid that would never give out. Don't just look at the grass and sky, they were advised; imagine a vast lake just below the surface.

"No purer water ever came out of the ground," a real estate brochure circulating through the Panhandle in 1908 claimed. "The supply is inexhaustible."

In trying to come to terms with a strange land, perhaps the biggest fear was fire. The combination of wind, heat, lightning, and combustible grass was nature's perfect recipe for fire. One day the grass could look sweet and green, spread across the face of No Man's Land. Another day it would be a roaring flank of smoke and flame, marching toward the dugout. Hazel Lucas was petrified of prairie fires, and for good reason. A few years before the family arrived, a lightning bolt lit up a field in New Mexico, igniting a fire that swept across the High Plains of Texas and Oklahoma. It burned everything in its wake for two hundred miles. Fire was part of the prairie ecosystem, a way for the land to regenerate itself, clean out excess insect populations, and allow the grass to be renewed. The year after a fire, the grass never looked healthier. Cattle, planted on the land for only a few years, tried fleeing the big fires, but they were often burned or trampled to death. Nesters frantically dug trenches or berms around their homes, hoping to create buffer lines. Sometimes a rolling blaze skipped over a dugout; other times it snuffed the roof and smoked out everything else. Pushed by the winds, a prairie fire moved so quickly it was difficult for a person on horseback to outrun it.

But some people felt immune. Once, a preacher joined a postal carrier making his rounds in No Man's Land. The sky turned black and lightning flashed. Bolts struck the ground and electrified barbed-wire fences. The preacher cowered for cover. The carrier told him to relax. "God isn't that awful," he said. "Lightning will never strike a mailman or a preacher." Within ten years, God would change moods.

When it wasn't fire, it was another element on the run in No Man's Land. The year the Lucas family arrived in the Panhandle, the worst flood in young Cimarron County's history terrorized a string of ranches and homesteads. Most of the year, the Cimarron River skulks meekly away to the east, a barely discernible trickle in midsummer. But in the spring of 1914, after a week of steady rains, the Cimarron jumped its banks and went on a rampage. The flood knocked out a dam that had just been completed, carried a thirteen-room ranch house into the river, and washed away numerous homes. Two children drowned.

Even the entertainment could be traumatic. People would gather at makeshift rodeo stands near Boise City on Saturday afternoons to watch the cow dip. Cattle were herded into a chute and down into a vat of water. Once they hit the water, they were drowned by two cowboys, on either side of the vat, who held their heads down while the beeves bucked. Some of the children didn't like it — an amusement ride with sudden death at the end.

The Lucas family stayed through the fires, the floods, and the pe-

culiar social life because the land was starting to pay. Not as grassland
for cattle, but as crop-producing dirt. Carlie dug up part of his half-
section using a horse-drawn walking plow and planted it in wheat and
corn. The Great War, starting in 1914, meant a fortune was about to be
made in the most denigrated part of America, all of the dryland wheat
belt. Turn the ground, Lucas was advised, as fast as you can.

Within a few years, the family built a home above ground, rising
from their dugout in line with thousands of other prospectors of
wheat. They bought lumber, nails, siding, and roofing material from
the rail town of Texhoma, forty miles southeast, and went about
building a frame house, with living room, kitchen, bedrooms, fruit cellar, trim, shingles, and large windows. The door faced south, a neces-
sity in No Man's Land to keep the northers from blowing cold into
the new abode. Framing timber around the bright Oklahoma sky, the
Lucas family dreamed of space enough to play music and cook without bumping into each other, or falling to sleep at night without having to scan the floor for snakes. But just as the new house was starting
to take shape, a musclebound blow arrived one spring afternoon,
strong enough to knock a person down. They fled into the old dugout
next door. The wind screeched, tugging at the new house. It was a
steady roar, not a gale. On the morning of the second day, they heard

Dugout homestead, Blaine County, Oklahoma Territory, 1894

the awful clank of crumbling timbers. Hazel Lucas poked her head above the dugout and saw in a swirl of dust and wood chips that their new home was being carried upward and away with the wind. The storm took the entire house. After four days, the family went searching the prairie, looking for pieces of their home.

For all the horror, the land was not without its magic. The first Anglos in the Panhandle used to recite a little ditty:

> *I like this country fine*
> *I think it's awfully good.*
> *For the wind pumps all the water*
> *And the cow chops all the wood.*

After a rain- or hailstorm had rumbled through, the sky was open and embracing, the breeze only a soft whisper against the songs of meadowlarks and cooing of doves. A prairie chicken doing its mating dance, its full-breasted plumage in a heave of sexual pride, was a thing to see. So was a pronghorn antelope coming through the grass, bouncing out of a wallow. Robin's egg blue was the color of mornings without fear. At night, you could see the stars behind the stars. Infinity was never an abstraction on the High Plains.

Hazel Lucas would ride her horse Pecos over the prairie to visit with the James boys, one of the last big ranching families, whose spread touched parts of Texas and Oklahoma. There was Walter and Mettie and their kids Andy, Jesse, Peachey, Joe Bob, Newt, and Fannie Sue. The boys could ride, rope, and cuss better than anyone in Boise City, and the stories they told made a girl feel she was being allowed into a secret — and vanishing — world. Andy was a bit of a mysterious presence and had a swagger that drew people to him. He would disappear for five days at a time, then show up suddenly in Boise City.

"Where you been, Andy?" Hazel asked him.

"Riding fence."

"What'd ya eat out there?"

"Grasshoppers."

"How do you eat a grasshopper?"

"Just snap off his head, light a match, and stick it up his ass."

"Yeah? How's that taste?"

"Mighty crunchy."

For the rest of her life, whenever Hazel saw Andy James, she would say to him, "Mighty crunchy."

Hazel also learned to play basketball outside, wearing the black sateen bloomers of the Cimarron County High School girls team. The coach's Model-T was kept at courtside, to chase balls once the wind got a hold of them, or to light the court after dusk. Hazel was barely sixteen when she went to see the first track meet held in Cimarron County. She could not take her eyes off a fleet-footed boy who won several races. She had the crush bad on that good-looking kid, Charlie Shaw, who was tall, about six-foot-five inches. You could tell, all the Lucas cousins said, by the way they looked at each other that something was doing between them.

In the fall of 1922, Hazel saddled up Pecos and rode off to a one-room, wood-frame building sitting alone in the grassland: the schoolhouse. It was Hazel's first job. She had to be there before the bell rang — five-and-a-half miles by horseback each way — to haul in drinking water from the well, to sweep dirt from the floor, and shoo hornets and flies from inside. The school had thirty-nine students in eight grades, and the person who had to teach them all, Hazel Lucas, was seventeen years old. In its first years, the schoolhouse lacked desks.

Sod schoolhouse, Texas-Oklahoma Panhandle, 1889

Fruit crates, or planks nailed to stumps, did the job. After school, Hazel had to do the janitor work and get the next day's kindling — dry weeds or sun-toasted cow manure.

When the winds kicked up as always or a twitching sky threatened hail, she felt like she was back in the dugout, cramped and gasping for space. But when it was nice, she took the children outside and staged horse races. She taught them basketball. Once, she loaded up players in a wagon and galloped off four miles to play another team. But the sky turned ugly, growled, and broke in a fit of hail. The children started to cry. One horse panicked and bolted. Kids jumped from the wagon, hail storming down on them. Hazel Lucas leaped from the carriage seat to the back of the panicked horse, seized the bridle, and rode the horse to calm.

All the while, she wondered about a life far away, in one of the bustling cities of the Midwest, or just a place where the routine of a day was not so full of random death. The *Kansas City Star* arrived by mail in Boise City once a week, and Hazel got a sense of how fast America was moving: flappers, gangsters, and stunts — two men tried to play airborne tennis while standing, strapped, to the wings of a biplane. In Cimarron County, most people didn't even have electricity, and many still lived in earthen dugouts or soddies.

But no group of people took a more dramatic leap in lifestyle or prosperity, in such a short time, than wheat farmers on the Great Plains. In less than ten years, they went from subsistence living to small business-class wealth, from working a few hard acres with horses and hand tools to being masters of wheat estates, directing harvests with wondrous new machines, at a profit margin in some cases that was ten times the cost of production. In 1910, the price of wheat stood at eighty cents a bushel, good enough for anyone who had outwitted a few dry years to make enough money to get through another year and even put something away. Five years later, with world grain supplies pinched by the Great War, the price had more than doubled. Farmers increased production by 50 percent. When the Turkish navy blocked the Dardenelles, they did a favor for dryland wheat farmers that no one could have imagined. Europe had relied on Russia for export grain. With Russian shipments blocked, the United States stepped in, and issued a proclamation to the plains: plant more wheat to win the war. And for the first time, the government guaranteed the price, at two dollars a bushel, through the war, backed by the wartime food administrator, a multimillionaire public servant named Herbert Hoover. Wheat was no longer a staple of a small family farmer but a commodity with a price guarantee and a global market.

When he first came to No Man's Land, Carlie Lucas had hoped to make just enough from his half-section to feed his family. But within a few years of arriving, he was part of the great frenzy to turn over ground and get out as much wheat as possible to sell abroad. If he could produce fifteen bushels an acre on his half-section, that meant 4,800 bushels at harvest. It cost him about thirty-five cents per bushel to grow. At a selling price of two dollars a bushel, his profit was nearly eight thousand dollars a year. In 1917, this was a fortune. A factory worker on the Ford assembly line made only five dollars a day, about one-eighth the take-home pay of a prosperous wheat farmer. Imagine doing thirty bushels an acre, or double. And Hardy Campbell, through his epistles on dry farming, said any yeoman could do fifty bushels an acre, even without adequate rain. Still, this was something audacious. People had been farming since Biblical times, and never had any nation set out to produce so much grain on ground that suggested otherwise. If the farmers of the High Plains were laying the foundation for a time bomb that would shatter the natural world, any voices that implied such a thing were muted.

"The real difficulty of the semi-arid belt is not the lack of rain," wrote Hardy Campbell in his *Manual*, which sold for $2.50, "but the loss of too much by evaporation, and this can be largely controlled by proper cultivation."

What had been an anchored infinity of grassland just a generation earlier became a patchwork of broken ground. In 1917, about forty-five million acres of wheat were harvested nationwide. In 1919, over seventy-five million acres were put into production — up nearly 70 percent. And the expansion would continue in the decade after the war, even as there was no need for it. It was one of the occasional episodes in human history when fortunes were said to go only one way.

"The uncertainties of 1919 were over," wrote F. Scott Fitzgerald, the most insightful chronicler of the hubris of the 1920s. "America was going on the greatest, gaudiest spree in history."

For a young family casting about for a way to make good money out of nearly nothing to start, the dryland wheat game looked like an easy gamble.

Indeed. The self-described wheat queen of Kansas, Ida Watkins, told everyone she made a profit of $75,000 on her two thousand acres of bony soil in 1926 — bigger than the salary of any baseball player but Babe Ruth, more money than the president of the United States made.

Hazel Lucas married the boy she had fallen for, Charles Shaw, when she was eighteen. They were both schoolteachers, but Charles wanted to try something else. They left the Panhandle for Ohio in the spring of 1929, driving up through the Midwest in their Model-T Ford. At one point, the young couple from a county without a stoplight found themselves in downtown St. Louis with a broken car, in a river of traffic. Horns honked, people cursed, and Charles and Hazel looked at each other and laughed. They made their way to Cincinnati, where Charles studied mortuary science. Hazel took to the city. She visited Cincy's National Zoo, parks, museums. By the end of summer, the Shaws were low on money, and they decided that Hazel should return to Oklahoma while Charles stayed on at the school. She had arranged for another teaching job, which came with extra duties as a school bus driver. Hazel took the train home, arriving in early September 1929, a time when the country was in a fever of fast moneymaking, and the Oklahoma Panhandle was busting its britches. Hazel was going to get a teacher's job that paid enough to save some money. She wanted to start a family, too. Stepping off the train in Texhoma, she walked a few steps away from the tracks and spun around, staring out in every direction at the big land, the soft light, with the smell of wheat loading from elevators. The sky, the horizon, the earth itself had no end. She knew she belonged in No Man's Land; the lonely prairie felt *right*.

Women were scarce in No Man's Land, so much so that a newspaper advertisement was placed in the *St. Louis Post-Dispatch* by sixty-five "lonely men with dugouts and a willingness to work." One of the bachelors, Will Crawford, lived alone in his hole in the ground outside Boise City. He had come west from Missouri on the free train, but he had never found a bride and did not do much to prove up his land. Crawford was a rare sight: a fat man on the prairie. He was fatter than any man in three states, it was said. When children tried to guess his weight, he would never reveal the exact amount — somewhere between 300 and 700 pounds, he said. A farmhand, Will worked for all the food he could eat.

The fat man sat for lunch at the table of his neighbors one day, consuming a meal of sausages, potato soup, and canned tomatoes. When he was done, he reached into the front pocket of his bib overalls and produced a slip of paper.

What to think of this? He showed them the note:

"Wanted, a real man. Sadie White, 419 Locust, Wichita, Kansas."

Crawford's overalls were so big they had to be ordered special through the general store, which received them from the clothing factory in Wichita. Sadie worked in the factory and had been taken by the size of the garment. Will was curious about the note but afraid to write back; the postmaster's office was in the general store, and they might intercept the letter and tease him. He summoned all his courage and wrote to Sadie White, sending the letter from another location, in Texhoma. Months passed. Then during the wheat harvest, the big man was spitting watermelon seeds through his mustache after an enormous dinner, when he mentioned that he might build a house next to his dugout. It seemed odd; he had never before shown much ambition beyond what to have for lunch. Will complained that his dirt-floored hole just wasn't comfortable. Over the fall months, he built a basement with cement walls, and two rooms aboveground. He shingled the roof and painted the outside walls a bright color. Then Will disappeared for a week. When he returned, all of Cimarron County was clucking at the news: Big Will Crawford was married. He had taken a train to Wichita, and there he met and married Sadie White, the woman who had sewn the note in the biggest pair of overalls she ever made in the factory. They took up in the fat man's new house and made a go of it until the land dried up in the 1930s and the death dusters came and stilled the lives of people in No Man's Land.

Will's closest neighbors were the Folkers, a family that came to No Man's Land with him on the free train. Fred Folkers, and his college-educated wife, Katherine, had left a rocky, fallow hillside in Missouri for the free dirt of the Oklahoma Panhandle. To Katherine, it was a prairie prison. Many nights, she cried herself to sleep; this place was so empty. The Folkers proved up a full section, 640 acres, planting trees and plowing the ground. The orchard was Fred's favorite creation, the trees sprouting pink in the spring, bearing heavy fruit in the fall. When he first put dozens of spindly, pathetic-looking sticks in the Panhandle dirt, the idea that this bundle of branches would ever mature to a huddle of thick-waisted fruit trees was preposterous. He planted cherry and peach trees, plum and apple, and, off to one side, berries that grow best in the maritime climate of the Pacific Northwest — huckleberries, gooseberries, currants. It did not matter that early spring and most of summer could pass with nary a teardrop from above; the Folkers had their underground lake, all that water brought to the surface by windmill pumps. The only way to irrigate his orchard was for Frederick to carry pails of water back and forth from his well to fruit trees.

The Folkers had arrived with very little, like other nesters fleeing an Old World of senseless wars or a New World with a landless future. In No Man's Land, they were first-generation aristocracy. It was the same in Dalhart and Boise City and Texhoma, in Shattuck and Liberal and Garden City. People were establishing country clubs for the new farmer-businessmen, stringing electric lights through towns and building swimming pools, one bigger than the other. By sheer will, they would force green on the dry land. The caution of John Wesley Powell, the one-armed Civil War veteran who warned against trying to stamp squares of traditional farms on the High Plains, was thrown to the wind. "No part of it can be redeemed for agriculture except by irrigation," Powell had written in his 1878 *Report on the Arid Region of the United States*. To do so, he concluded, would be destructive.

Hah! In time, when the trees grew, and the town squares started to wear the years with a proper fit, there was no reason it couldn't look like Bloomington, Indiana, or Marion, Ohio, or so the proud home-steaders thought. In Garden City, Kansas, they dug a hole in the ground, 337 feet long by 218 feet wide, poured cement for weeks on end, and filled it with water. It was the world's biggest swimming pool, they boasted, in a place that had only a weak spring a few years earlier. About the same time, a man named John R. Brinkley ran for governor of Kansas, promising to bring a lake to every county in the state.

With a horse-drawn plow, Fred Folkers produced barely enough to stay afloat. What changed everything for him, and other dryland farmers, was the tractor. In the 1830s, it took fifty-eight hours of work to plant and harvest a single acre. By 1930, it took only three hours for the same job. No longer did Fred Folkers or Carlie Lucas have to cut their wheat with a mule-drawn header, stacking it in piles to be threshed later. A tractor did the work of ten horses. With his new combine, Folkers could cut and thresh the grain in one swoop, using just a fraction of the labor. Folkers bought an International 22-36 tractor, a Case combine, and a one-way plow — a twelve-foot Grand Detour. The one-way plow would later be cursed as the tool that destroyed the plains because of its efficiency at ripping up grass. But for now it was a technological miracle. Folkers plowed nearly his entire square mile, and then paid to rent nearby property and ripped up that grass as well. By the late 1920s, his harvest was up to ten thousand bushels of wheat — a small mountain of grain. What's more, there was now an easy way to get the wheat of Fred Folkers and Carlie Lucas to the rest of the world. In 1925, a train finally arrived in Boise City, almost twenty years after the fantasy locomotives of the Southwestern Immigration and Development Company were promised.

Up in eastern Montana, towns that had been built thirty years earlier with the arrival of the railroad were folding. The northern plains homestead experiment was a bust, and no amount of government incentive or railroad promotional schemes could keep it going. But here in the southern plains, the rail lines were just coming to blank spots on the map. Folkers had to haul his wheat only a few miles to a grain elevator in Boise City and off it went — to Chicago, New York, Europe.

The phantom town built on fraud, Boise City, was growing with every harvest. People gave up their horse-drawn wagons for Model-Ts, even if there were not enough roads to get around. Most of the year, people drove right over the hardened prairie. Here was a new Baptist church, a new Presbyterian church, a Catholic church for the Mexicans who lived out near the Lujan ranch. A clothier from just across the border, in Clayton, New Mexico, came to town and took orders for suits and dresses. Herzstein was the name. Simon Herzstein took two trips a year to New York and returned with outfits that could make a prairie couple look like a pair of dandies from the picture shows. He gave out shoe brushes to his customers, stamped with the words: "If it's from Herzstein's, it's correct."

With tractors came mortgages. For a long time, banks had refused to lend to farmers west of the ninety-eighth meridian. It was fool's country, a devil's land of drought and dust. But a handful of wet years in the new century showed that caution was unwarranted. John Johnson's First State Bank in Boise City loaned money all over the county, as people gladly committed their property to paper to get more money to plow more grass and put more wheat in the ground. A new courthouse, with Roman columns, rose on the site of the little stockman's windmill that had posed as an artesian fountain in 1908. By 1929, Boise City had a theater, a hotel, a bookstore, a bank, a newspaper, a creamery, a few cafes, and a telephone office where people would call into an operator, asking to be hooked up to a neighbor. After a few minutes of hollering back and forth about idle gossip, they were.

Flush with their newfound money, the Folkers invested in even bigger dreams. They made plans to take on more ground in booming No Man's Land. They ordered appliances from the Sears and Roebuck catalogue — the store even sold a complete house, which could be assembled from a kit — and put harvest money in the bank. Fred bought dresses for Katherine and his daughter, Faye. And finally, they built a big-shouldered house to replace the crumbling shack in which Katherine had cried herself to sleep so many nights over the last ten years. To the children, the shack had always seemed to be haunted. At night, Faye and her brothers heard scratching and clawing in the walls, like a ghost with long nails trying to get at them. It was centipedes, nesting in the walls. Faye could never sleep when the centipedes were at work. The shack was nothing but a heap of upright splinters: one-by-ten-inch planks nailed to two-by-four-inch studs, with wallpaper on the inside and tarpaper on the outside. For insulation, newspapers were pasted to the walls. Some nesters even arranged the papers in neat, horizontal rows, so they could read the fading news stories. When the sound of scratching inside the walls got too bad, Katherine grabbed her flat iron and took to the walls. As the centipedes died under the crush of her iron, they made a hissing sound.

While the new house was still under construction, the Folkers lost the old house in a hailstorm — softball-sized, in the lexicon of sporting goods used to describe prairie roof-breakers. Nobody mourned the shack's collapse. The family now had two bedrooms, a living room, a big kitchen with a kerosene cook stove, and a basement large enough to hold a winter's supply of coal. For Faye's tenth birthday, in 1928, the family took her into Boise City to window-shop. She was bright and creative, with the kind of ambition that left people thinking she would probably not stay long in the flatlands.

Take a look at that piano, Faye's daddy told her, passing a furniture store. Happy birthday — it's yours. The piano cost three hundred dollars — ten dollars down, ten dollars a month. With the piano came a teacher, who charged fifty cents a lesson. The same year, Frederick Folkers went to the car dealership, in Liberal, Kansas, and came home with a spanking new 1928 Dodge — a beauty, with four doors and room enough to carry the whole family. They parked the Dodge out in front of the new house and snapped a picture. The centipede scratching, the hissing of an iron on insect legs, was replaced by piano music that drifted out of the Folkers's new house and settled on fruit trees and the fresh-plowed fields of No Man's Land.

In all the High Plains, a kind of giddiness took hold. There were big dances on Saturday nights, farmers jumping to a prairie jitterbug, the bootleg hooch flowing free. Cimarron County, the far end of No Man's Land, had 5,408 people by the end of the 1920s, and Boise City was a town of twelve hundred. People who had come to the Panhandle wanting only to own a small piece of something now realized that through easy loans, they could own a large piece of anything, and with tractors and threshers they could do the work of a wagonload of field hands. Occasionally, Fred Folkers said it all seemed to be happening too fast. Christ Almighty, the grasslands were being erased from the Great Plains, going the way of the bison and the Indian. If this ground were not meant for grass, what was it for? But maybe rains did follow the plow after all. Sure, Boise City was nothing but a criminal's dream at first, but now it had a railroad station, a new courthouse, a tractor dealership, a couple of nice places to eat, and a few grain towers, all surrounded by broken fields of golden wheat. There could be some truth to the pitch that the front line of civilization kicked water from the sky, because the 1920s brought wet years. The recent past told another story though. Droughts in the 1870s and 1890s had dissuaded other sodbusters from trying to turn the soil. But the railroad men and pamphleteers had promised that the simple act of tearing up the prairie sod would cause atmospheric disturbances, enough to vary weather patterns. Now that the prairie sod was fully torn up — by God, here was the rain.

People were pouring into town, taking up rooms at the Crystal Hotel — suitcase farmers who had no intention of ever settling there. They wanted only to rent out a tractor and a piece of ground for a few days, drop some winter wheat into the fresh-turned fold, and come back next summer for the payoff. It was a game of chance called "trying to hit a crop." One suitcase farmer broke thirty-two thousand acres in southeast Kansas in 1921. Four years later, he plowed twice that amount. The banks seldom said no. After Congress passed the Federal Farm Loan Act in 1916, every town with a well and a sheriff had itself a farmland bank — an institution! — offering forty-year loans at six percent interest. Borrow five thousand dollars and payments were less than thirty-five dollars a month. Any man with a John Deere and a half-section could cover that nut. If it was hubris, or "tempting fate" as some of the church ladies said, well, the United

States government did not see it that way. The government had already issued its official view of the rapid churning of ancient prairie sod.

"The soil is the one indestructible, immutable asset that the nation possesses," the Federal Bureau of Soils proclaimed as the grasslands were transformed. "It is the one resource that cannot be exhausted, that cannot be used up."

3

Creating Dalhart

B AM WHITE FOUND a shack outside of Dalhart, and the man
who owned it said he could put his family up there, grow
anything he dared on the ground nearby, and split the pro-
ceeds with him. Sharecropping was better than wandering south in a
wagon with half a team of horses, so the cowboy decided to give
Dalhart a good long chance, even if crop-grubbing was no life for a
man of the open range. It seemed a shame that the old XIT grasslands
were still being carved up, but cattle weren't paying, and the ranches
were disappearing by the day. The rains came steadily in the spring in
those years, 1926 through 1929, and with wet years, everyone forgot
about the dry ones and said the weather had changed — permanently
— for the better. It was also said you could grow anything on land that
had been so accursed. The family raised turnips, some weighing three
pounds or more, which seemed to belong on the High Plains. The
Whites loaded up their wagon and took the root vegetables to town,
where they sold them to the grocer; it gave them just enough, after
paying the landlord his share, to free Bam White for a few days to play
the fiddle or scout again for ranch jobs. There were three kids between him and Lizzie. While living in Dalhart, they had had a baby
girl, but she looked bad when she greeted her first minute, not breathing at all, purple. She was stillborn. Lizzie White could not shake the
feeling that this land was no good for them, and maybe they should
have kept moving south. But Bam White was a tomorrow man who fit

right into this Next Year Country. Even as they buried the stillborn baby, White's gut told him this town was going somewhere.

Optimism was contagious. Dalhart had a country club now, out past the steam laundry on a dirt road next to the Rock Island Railroad tracks. Further out, beyond the baseball park, the Number 126 house was roaring night and day. Girls came in from Denver and Dallas, sidled up nice or danced a tune to the player piano before slipping away to one of the two big rooms where a man could get a poke and be on his way. Boots on or off, both were options at the Number 126 house. They sold beer that didn't taste like warm spit and let a customer sometimes take two girls for the price of one if he was a regular and didn't smell like field manure.

Doc Dawson bought himself another two sections of land and thought about planting it in cotton. Cotton was supposed to pay even more than wheat. It dusted some in those years — sandstorms, which were tolerated as one of the little snit-fits of the prairie. The sandstorms were light-colored and never seemed a threat, but they could blow for days, tearing up the eyes and fouling the tractor engine. When John Dawson came home from college in 1926, the Doc took him out to his land and told the boy how this country was going to make them rich. He stooped over, ran the dirt through his hands, gave it a good sniff. But the cotton never took hold, and after two failed crops, the Doc despaired that he did not have anything to show for his share of the richest land on earth when everyone else on the High Plains was building a pile, either from oil or wheat or from fleecing the people who came scouting for oil or prospecting in wheat. Even that damn movie man down near Lubbock was setting himself up to make a fortune. Hickman Price came to the Panhandle and said, well, if it's factory farms that are going to make the wheat pay here, let's get to it. He had made his money in films, but here, he told people, there were even bigger riches available. By 1929, he had fifty-four square miles, nearly 35,000 acres, wheat coming off the land like Model-Ts. It was the Henry Ford model brought to agriculture, he bragged, econ-o-me of scale. Do the math, friend. The movie man said he could produce his wheat for forty cents a bushel, and if it sold for $1.30, he could bring in upwards of a million dollars a year. In five years' time, from 1924 to 1929, acreage in the Texas Panhandle that was plowed under for wheat grew from 876,000 to 2.5 million — a 300 percent increase.

The boys down at DeSoto's, Uncle Dick Coon and all his card-playing cronies, told the Doc he should stop fooling around with cotton, and don't even try the oil biz — just get himself a couple good years of wheat while the price was still decent. Maybe prices would fall, but they would have to take a mighty plunge in order for a wheat man not to make anything.

Even the last cowboys were giving up on grass. The James boys had been forced by bankruptcy to sell off a big section of their ranch outside Dalhart. They held onto another piece in the 1920s, between Boise City and Dalhart, but word had it that the land would soon be up for sale, in small lots. In desperation, Andy James tried to hit a vein of oil, to find one strike that would keep the family on the ranch. They borrowed again from a bank that already had taken back much of the ranch and hired out a drill that went down, two hundred, five hundred, a thousand, fifteen hundred, eighteen hundred feet until the drill bit snapped and still no oil to save the James boys. Bam White wandered over to the James ranch, watching with other cowboys as the last place to run cattle on a big range of God's best sod went to the bankers. Bam never made it past second grade, but his instinctual smarts told him it was not right — all this good grass going under — and he wondered how it had come to this for a cowboy in the country meant for men on horses. Andy James looked so sad then, a broken man in a time of fast fortunes. He shook his head and wiped his brow, his face all leathered from the sun and wind, his powerful shoulders held stiff, and sometimes just said nothing at all. Or he kicked the ground and cursed, looking out at the tractors tearing up the grassland, even in the darkness, using headlights.

This grass was never meant to be plowed, James told his fellow cowboys, drinking black coffee that the boys would lace on occasion with hooch. It wasn't never supposed to be nested or cut up. Cattle could fatten so easy on the bluestem, and it was a shame it couldn't pay anymore. A goddamn shame. The grass was pure biomass; an acre, without help, could bring a rancher two thousand pounds of forage for his cattle, a single section added up to more than a million pounds of nature's finest food for herbivores. A decade earlier, at the start of the Great War, the James brothers had the biggest working ranch left in the Panhandle, over 250,000 acres spread north into Cimarron County and west into New Mexico. But even then the end was drawing near, with beef prices falling on surplus cattle after the plains was stocked with too many animals. The cattle era had lasted not even as long as the Comanche run of the land after their treaty was signed. People felt sorry for Andy James; he was heading out with history's backwash, poor son of a buck.

Uncle Dick Coon still kept a hundred-dollar bill inside one pocket, but he was making so much money the C-note was like small change. On his land outside of town, Uncle Dick raised prized bulls, for show and breeding. Inside of town, he owned the finest buildings on the main street, Denrock, including all the places that kept the juices flowing, like the DeSoto and a drugstore where pharmacists filled prescriptions for whiskey. Medicinal whiskey. The DeSoto Hotel was processing fine-dressed pilgrims faster than Uncle Dick could keep the floors polished. White-gloved doormen greeted visitors who came to smell money as it was being minted.

Into this confident, muscle-flexing town in 1929 walked John L. McCarty. He looked like a young Orson Welles, dark-haired, intense and athletic, with a silver tongue that translated even better on paper. He bought the *Dalhart Texan,* became its editor and publisher, and made plans to turn it into the loudest, most influential daily newspaper in the Texas Panhandle. McCarty saw himself as a town builder with a pen. He was twenty-eight, and Dalhart had just over four thousand people. The town and the editor were born the same year. Less than fifty years earlier, the Census found zero population — not a single soul! — living in the four counties of the Texas Panhandle's far corner. Now the Rock Island Railroad emptied newcomers every week from the East, and the Fort Worth & Denver line brought them in from points north and south. They were coming by wagon, car, railroad. Even airplanes were landing on a strip of dirt outside Dalhart.

McCarty tried to rouse Dalhart's townsfolk to greatness. These folks were strong men and women, lucky to be living in a town still wet around the edges, a town born to big things. McCarty loved the Felton Opera House, the fine food they served at the DeSoto, the suits he could buy through Herzstein's, the boys who tipped their hats to him at the Cozy Corner, the ladies who mentioned in forced modesty their latest trips to the Gulf or California for write-ups on page two of the *Texan*. He was the loudest cheerleader at baseball games, where the Dalhart nine took on Clayton, Boise City, or Dumas; their failure was a civic letdown. He felt personally responsible for Dalhart's future. He could sound like a booster with blinders, but McCarty had some literary flourishes and was judicious in citing classical scholars or gimcrackery from American wise men. About once a week, his column ran next to Will Rogers on page one of the *Texan*, and folks told him he was the better writer. McCarty was no flimflam man, but rather someone who bought into the vision of Dalhart, City on the High Plains.

People came to the High Plains now because they had missed out on earlier land grabs, land rushes, land betrayals, and land auctions. They had missed the best homestead land, the best stolen Indian land, the best railroad grant land, the land that was quickly taken in the first Homestead Act of 1862 and the Enlarged Homestead Act of 1909. What had started with a rousing slogan that thousands marched to in the 1856 presidential campaign of John Fremont — "Free Soil, Free Men, Fremont!" — was down to the ugliest dirt in the country. Already much of the earlier homestead land, planted in wheat or corn, was worn out, not producing as it once did. Of the roughly two hundred million acres homesteaded on the Great Plains between 1880 and 1925, nearly half was considered marginal for farming. But even by the 1920s, there was still a chance for a family to make history: people who had descended from a beaten-down part of the world, people whose daddy had been a serf, a sharecropper, a tenant, and even slaves, castaways, rejects, white trash, and Mexicans could own a piece of earth. "Every man a landlord" meant something. Historians had been herded into thinking that the American frontier was closed after the 1890 census, that western movement had effectively ended just before the close of the last century, that settlement had been tried and failed in the Great American Desert. But they overlooked the southern plains, the pass-through country. In the first thirty years of the twentieth century, it got a second look.

"The last frontier of agriculture," the government called it in 1923. Southern families, field hands, Scots-Irish and Welsh usually, came in steady waves, fleeing exhausted land for a prairie untouched. The Scots-Irish had left Ireland and the north of Britain in the eighteenth century and settled on thin soil on either side of the Appalachian spine before spreading out to the South and Midwest. They were cannon fodder in the Civil War, many left landless. People from the new cities of Oklahoma, out of work when oil prices plummeted, came as well. Mexicans were drawn by jobs on irrigated beet farms in Kansas and Colorado. When young men started looking around Kentucky or Arkansas in 1910 and were told there was nothing for them but a life laboring for someone else, they pointed to the Texas Panhandle or No Man's Land of Oklahoma and said goodbye, see ya on the farm. My farm. And more than any other group, they came from a faraway part of Russia: thousands of people who had been adrift for centuries, thrown to the wind. When they arrived in Omaha or Kansas City, the scouts, land merchants, and railroad colonists sent them on to the High Plains.

It was a different story up in the northern plains, where people were cursing the railroads for perpetuating a fraud that broke many a family. They had taken a gamble, stripped away the grass, put in grain outside places like Miles City, Montana, and Marmarth, North Dakota. Then came a few dry years, a killer winter or two, and the wheat glut from the rest of the plains. Just like that, life was gone, main streets shuttered, homesteads left to Front Range chinooks. Some towns along the northern railroad lines folded barely a generation after they were hatched. But in the southern plains, people welcomed the railroads with open arms and big festivities, as if nothing had happened up north. History might repeat itself, but few bothered to make such a warning.

Through his column, John McCarty exhorted Dalhart to take no small steps, praising visionaries like Uncle Dick Coon. They needed a real hospital. They needed a second auto dealer, a second bank. Riding outside of town on his newspaper rounds, watching as clouds of dirt trailed the tractors tearing up the old Llano Estacado, it did not matter to McCarty that there was not a river or stream anywhere to be seen, that there was not a lake or any surface water.

"Americans are nearer to the final triumph over poverty than ever before in the history of the land," said the new president, Herbert Hoover, who took office in 1929. He had won in a landslide, breaking the Democratic hold on the solid South, taking the prairie states with him.

The tractors rolled on, the grass yanked up, a million acres a year, turned and pulverized; in just five years, 1925 to 1930, another 5.2 million acres of native sod went under the plow in the southern plains — an area the size of two Yellowstone National Parks. This was in addition to nearly twenty million acres of prairie that had already been turned. Only four small farms existed in Dallam County, Texas, in 1901, covering barely a thousand acres; by 1930, a third of the county was in cultivation.

"This is the best damned country God's sun ever shone upon," McCarty declared in the pages of the *Texan,* and among those who nodded in agreement were people trying to learn the English language by reading the newspaper. The Germans from Russia knew what it was like to live in a place where God's sun gave out.

4

High Plains Deutsch

B Y THE SUMMER OF 1929, the United States had a food surplus, and every town along the rail lines of the southern plains sprouted a tower of unsold wheat, stacked in piles outside grain elevators. There was a glut in Europe as well, after Russia resumed exporting its wheat. As trains approached Liberal, Guymon, Texhoma, Boise City, or Dalhart on the straight lines across the High Plains, the wheat mounds were the first things to appear on the horizon, towers of grain that nobody wanted. It was a sign of prosperity but also a warning of things to come. The balance was tipping. Prices headed down, below $1.50 a bushel, then below a dollar, then seventy-five cents a bushel — a third of the market high point from just a few years earlier. Farmers had two choices: they could cut back, hoping supplies would tighten and prices would rise, or they could plant more as a way to make the same money on higher output. Across the southern plains, the response was overwhelming: the farmers tore up more grass. They had debts to meet on those 6 percent notes, debts for new tractors, plows, combines, and land purchased or rented on credit. The only way for someone who made ten thousand dollars in 1925 to duplicate his earnings in 1929 was to plant twice the amount. And so the tractors took to the buffalo grass like never before, digging up nearly fifty thousand acres a day in the southern plains in the final years before the land started to break people. What had been prairie turf for thirty-five thousand years was peeled off in a swift de-carpeting that remade the panhandles of Texas and Oklahoma, big parts of

Kansas, Nebraska, and southeast Colorado. There was no worse time to plow up the grassland than in the fall, when it would be exposed for months, subject to the winds of late winter and early spring — the blow season. To leave that much land naked was a gamble, and many farmers knew it.

The price of wheat may have been falling, but it could not spoil one American story. George Alexander Ehrlich sat at a wedding table in September 1929 and told his grandchildren what it had been like in the bad years on the Volga River in Russia, in the village of Tcherbagovka. Some of his nine children were around him as well. They were at church in Shattuck, Oklahoma, the one place where a person named Schoenhals or Hofferber did not have to pretend to be somebody else. Shattuck is just across the Texas state line, about seventy-five miles east of Dalhart. Ehrlich spoke with the accent that had evolved in a generation's time in the panhandles: a very old style of German, with a sprinkling of Russian, spiced with the dialect of Texas-Oklahoma, where two syllables were never used when one would do. Save your breath, folks said: you might need it someday. Yep.

He told his family about being chained to horses in barns in the Russian countryside. George used to travel with his father, a leather tanner, learning the trade. One of the tricks his father taught him was a way to deter horse thieves. At night, George and his father locked the horses' legs to their ankles. They slept that way in the barn, horses and Ehrlichs, bound by shackles. George would have followed his father's footsteps into the tanning trade if it were not for the draft notice he received from the Russian czar on his sixteenth birthday. The Ehrlichs knew what happened once a boy left the village: he was never seen again. Often, the czar's army would not even do the family the service of sending a death notice. To avoid this service, they would have to leave Russia. In 1890, the Ehrlichs boarded a ship out of Hamburg, an immigrant boat with enough supplies to last twenty days. It was supposed to take only two weeks to get to New York. Midway into the voyage, a wind came up with sideways rain and high waves, rising in heaving swells, forty feet, swamping the boat. They had sailed into a late season typhoon, and it played with the ship as if it were a bathtub toy: it was knocked and tossed and slapped. All hands retreated to a lower cabin, where they cowered, listening to the wood beams strain and the winds scream and the ship fall apart. Don't worry, the captain said, the deck is sealed; the boat is unsinkable. On the second day of the storm, the ship's mast snapped and crashed into the water, but it did not break clean. The boat listed. The mast was snagged in the ocean, tipping the immigrants' ship at such an angle that water poured in and swamped the deck. The captain sent out an SOS and told everyone to prepare for death.

As George told this story — the founding narrative of the Ehrlichs in the New World of Oklahoma — more of his children came around to his table, and they were joined by other adults as well. The older people knew the story, but it was worth hearing again, the way George told it. They poured wine and quaffed beer and ate the spicy, smoked sausages. More food, everyone. For five days in advance, the women of Shattuck, Oklahoma, had been cooking for this wedding, and the scent of fresh-made wurst and strudel drifted out the church to the fields. In the German settlements on the High Plains, there was no more defiant celebration of group survival than a wedding. The rest of the year, the Anglos could make fun of their clothes, the sheriff could call them in for questioning, the merchants could refuse them entry into stores, the children could mock their accents, the farmers could laugh at their planting methods, and other immigrants could deride them as "Rooshians." But the wedding day on this Sunday in September 1929 belonged to the Germans from Russia. Through an improbable journey of 166 years, they had bounced from southern Germany to the Volga River region of Russia to the Cherokee Outlet of Oklahoma. The *Russlanddeutschen* were not Russian nor were they fully German. Hardened by long exile, state cruelty, and official ridicule, they wanted only to be left alone. The treeless expanse of the southern plains was one of the few places in the United States that looked like home.

"A queer looking set they are," the *Hays City Sentinel* in Kansas had described some Volga Germans as they passed through, a generation earlier, surely one of the most exotic species on the Great Plains. "They are here; they are there; and at every corner they may be seen jabbering about this and that and no one knows what. Their presence is unmistakable; for where they are, there is also something else — a smell so pungent and potent as to make a strong man weak."

At the wedding, women served a dish of cabbage that had been shredded by wooden kraut cutters, mixed with ground pork and onion, wrapped in bread dough, and baked. Another table was laden with Kase noodle, made with thick cottage cheese and onion tops. Butterball soup was steaming and rich. A pig's skull had been rendered, boiled again, and transformed into hog's head cheese. Chickens were roasted; tubers peeled, boiled, crowded into tanks of potato salad. The women milled their own grain and from that, using eggs from their henhouses and milk from their barns, baked dozens of cakes and pies. They brought stewed apples and pickled watermelons as well. Men did not cook. Men made beer — strong, thick, yeasty. Men made wine, using grapes that arrived by train from California or were grown on arbors on a protected side of a barn. Men killed pigs and made sausage, the organs chopped with salt, pepper, and garlic, stuffed into casings of large intestines and smoked.

These nesters preferred high-top *filzstiefel* shoes with soft interior linings to cowboy boots, and featherbeds to American mattresses. No house was without schnapps and wurst. In church they sang *"Gott is de liebe"* and made such a month-long fuss over Christmas that customs in America changed as well. They were a culture frozen in place in 1763 and transplanted whole to the Great Plains. Without them, it is possible that wheat never would have been planted on the dry side of the plains. For when they boarded ships for America, the Germans from Russia carried with them seeds of turkey red — a hard winter wheat — and incidental thistle sewn into the pockets of their vests. It meant survival, an heirloom packet worth more than currency. The turkey red, short-stemmed and resistant to cold and drought, took so well to the land beyond the ninety-eighth meridian that agronomists were forced to rethink the predominant view that the Great American Desert was unsuited for agriculture. In Russia, it was the crop that allowed the Germans to move out of the valleys and onto the higher, drier farming ground of the steppe. The thistle came by accident, but it grew so fast it soon owned the West. In the Old World, thistle was called *perekati-pole,* which meant "roll-across-the-field." In America, it was known as tumbleweed.

The Russlanddeutschen held onto their religion, their food, their dress, their rituals, their epic family narratives, and their seeds of grain. In America, they learned about baseball, jazz, the tractor, and the bank loan.

They were known as tough-nutted pacifists, a migratory people whose defining characteristic was draft-dodging. The German Mennonites from near the Black Sea, conscientious objectors from the beginning, certainly were opposed to war on principle. But many of the other Germans from Russia would kill without flinching, showing their warrior skills in American uniforms when they shot their own former countrymen during the two world wars in the twentieth century. What they would not do is fight for the Russian czar or — worse — fight for the Bolsheviks. They had a promise, dating to a manifesto of July 22, 1763, by Catherine the Great, offering homestead land, tax breaks, cultural autonomy, and no military conscription. When the promise was broken 110 years later, they closed up entire villages and fled to America. Catherine, they always felt, was one of them, a German-born empress who married into Russian nobility just after she turned fifteen. By the age of thirty-three, she had dethroned her husband, Peter, and became ruler of Russia. A forceful monarch, Catherine reigned for nearly forty years and was as crucial — indirectly — to settlement of the American Great Plains as the railroad.

Catherine believed that Russia could use fewer Russians and more Germans. A German peasant was not as slovenly as a Russian peasant. Early on, she worried about the frontier on both sides of the middle Volga River, near the cities of Samara and Saratov, in what was then southeastern Russia. She wanted a buffer against Mongols, Turks, and Kirghiz, who roamed and raided the steppe territory much in the way that Apache and Comanche controlled the High Plains. Agricultural colonies, even with people who were not Russian, would bring stability. Catherine's manifesto promised free land, no taxes for the first thirty years of a colony, and no military service for male heads of family and their descendants. The manifesto was aimed at all of Western Europe except Jews, who were expressly prohibited from accepting the offer. In the poor villages of southern Germany, where families were broken by the bloodshed and poverty of the Seven Years' War, Catherine's representatives found their colonizers.

"We need people," Catherine said, "to make, if possible, the wilderness swarm like a beehive."

Americans like to think that theirs was the first country to open its land to the tired, poor, and opportunistic, to grant religious freedom and property to those who had been tossed aside in older lands. But well before manifest destiny carried tides of pilgrims to the American West, Russia offered its own Big Rock Candy Mountain — a treeless, wind-buffed mantle of ground that could have been the High Plains but for the big river in its midst. In the Volga region, every adult male could claim about thirty acres, and that land would go back to the community upon death of the owner. No taxes would be levied for thirty years. No military service. No restrictions on religion.

"Polygamy would be of great use in increasing the population," Catherine offered, a suggestion the Germans never followed up on until some of them joined the Mormon church a century later. Dozens of villages sprang up in the middle and lower Volga. They were obsessive about keeping dirt from the house; cleanliness was the highest of virtues. If someone spit watermelon seeds onto the street, a punishment of ten lashes followed. Laws required the villages to be clean, the streets swept at least once a week. Each married couple had to plant twenty trees. Upon marrying, the young couple lived with the bride's family until land was reallotted upon the patriarch's death. Their blood enemy were the Kirghiz, a Tartar tribe whose members had grazed their livestock on the steppe, and later honed plundering into a warrior art.

The Kirghiz sacked Schasselwa on the Volga in 1771, riding into town in full war cry, faces painted, lances forward. They burned the church, raped women young and old, grabbed babies from their mothers. Houses were torched, plundered, and the granaries emptied of their food. The kidnapped women and boys were sold as slaves in Asia. To this day, a good ole boy in the Oklahoma Panhandle named

Schmidt or Heinrich can turn ashen and clench-fisted at the mention of Schasselwa. It burns in the memory of a Volga German as Little Big Horn embitters a Sioux or mention of Cromwell's march through Ireland can inflame a Gaelic soul.

By 1863, a century after Catherine's manifesto, there were nearly a quarter-million Germans living on either side of the Volga River. Another group, primarily German Mennonites, had populated higher ground near the Black Sea. Between obsessive street cleaning and house sweeping, the Germans sang. On cold Russian nights, song warmed the stone walls of churches, and it was one of the things that most impressed outsiders. What the colonists on the Volga would not do is become Russian, and this ultimately led to their exile. Russians had grown increasingly resentful of the Germans in their midst, with their snug villages, big harvests, nationalistic pride, and continued exemption from military service. Why special privileges for them?

In 1872, Czar Alexander II revoked Catherine's promises, declaring that German-speaking Russians had to give up their language and sign up for the army. He raised taxes and took away exclusive licenses to brew beer. Both were fighting causes. For American railroads, fighting constant debt and the fallout of a speculative bubble, the czar's orders could not have been more fortuitous. Drought and a grasshopper plague ravaged the American Plains in the early 1870s.

"In God we trust, in Kansas we bust" was the slogan on banners draped on wagons of people who had tried to grow something and had given up. On marginal lands in Kansas and Nebraska, farmers were walking away and denouncing the railroads for promoting fraud. Facing bankruptcy, the railroads found their salvation on the steppes of southern Russia. Their agents in the immigration racket had some experience with Germans and saw them as good clients: they traveled in groups, paid on time, and were considered hard working and thrifty. Some railroads practiced selective ethnic shopping. Burlington printed brochures in German, for example, but not French or Italian. At the same time, reconnaissance groups of Germans were returning to the Volga with firsthand accounts of the land in the middle of America. They liked what they had seen of the Canadian prairie, the Dakotas, and all the way down the plains into the Indian Territory of

Oklahoma. It was brutally hot, when it wasn't cold enough to freeze eyelids shut. It was treeless, windswept, and free. The Promised Land — all over again, just like Russia.

Beginning in 1873, villages folded up and left for the Great Plains. Katherinenstadt, Pfeifer, Schoenchen, and others became near ghost towns. The Germans boarded small boats on the Volga to Saratov. From there, it was a train ride to a North Sea port where they took immigrant vessels to New York, Baltimore, or Galveston and boarded trains for the flatlands. In American ports, many were amazed to see a black person for the first time. Some Germans arrived with little more than a yellowed picture of Catherine the Great and a note pinned to their coat, indicating a family or destination. Before long, in places like Lincoln, Nebraska, or Ellis County, Kansas, more German was heard in the streets than English. In the 1870s, about 12,000 Russian Germans came to Kansas; within fifty years, 303,000 would populate the Great Plains. Often the new towns were given the name of the villages they had left behind. In Kansas, Germans established Liebenthal, Herzog, Catherine, Munjor, Pfeifer, and Schoenchen, which meant "a little something lovely."

"No one thinks of drouth and grasshoppers — everyone is happy and energetic," the *Chicago Tribune* reported in a typical dispatch on the kinetic Germans in 1876. They plowed the grass and planted turkey red on land that others had not dared to farm. What struck some of the American yeomen about these Russian Germans was that they liked to sing, and they kept the floors of their simple houses clean enough to dine on. Dust inside the house was something they would not tolerate.

George Ehrlich turned eighteen on his journey across the Atlantic in 1890. As he continued with his story at the wedding, he told about his emotions on the immigrant boat: scared, yes — a week into the sailing, he regretted leaving home. His money was strapped to a lower leg, and all his possessions fit into one bag. Part of his family had gone one way to Ellis County in an earlier migration, while others stayed behind, hoping they could hide from the czar's conscription police. George received his draft notice at the same time that a terrible drought hit the Volga region, another nudge to go to America. When the wind of the hurricane got ahold of the ship's mast and dragged it into the water, he thought he would never see American soil. The mast was broken about ten inches from the bottom. The longer it dragged in the water, the more the ship listed. The typhoon raged, seas engorged, wind and heavy rain clawing at the ship. Another SOS went out. Nothing in response. They were all going to drown in the mid-Atlantic. Another German — George knew him only as a Catholic boy — offered to crawl out on the mast and try to saw it off. The Captain said it would kill him, but if the boy wanted to give it a try — Godspeed. They tethered the boy to a rope, handed him a saw, and sent him on his way. He shimmied out, the sea heaving, salt spray sweeping over him, inching along the downed mast. When he was far enough along the beam, he started sawing. He cut through rope cables and oak until his hands were numb. At last, the mast broke away. As the beam fell to the sea, the boat righted itself. Now the Captain ordered all the immigrants to bail. The ship had only one working propeller; the other was broken by a cable that had snapped in the storm. The boat limped on, steadily west, away from the grip of the typhoon. In New York, it was announced as lost at sea.

Almost two months after leaving Hamburg, the immigrants arrived in New York Harbor, their food gone, many of them desperately ill. George Ehrlich landed in America on New Year's Day, 1891.

Back at the wedding, it was time for toasts. To Catherine the Great, of course. And to America. They raised glasses of schnapps and the spritzy white wine made by the Germans in Oklahoma and thanked God for their good fortune. The accordions and dulcimers came out. They danced the Hochzeit, which was like the fox trot, only faster. The wheat harvest was going to be the biggest ever. In Shattuck and just across the border in the Texas towns of Follett and Darrouzett, the Volga Germans were shedding some of the thrift their forebears had practiced, buying new tractors, Fordsons and Titans, taking out loans from banks to get still more land. Plant more wheat. Fast!

After arriving in the plains, George Ehrlich had stayed with relatives in LeHigh, looking for work. While there, he missed the rush of

1893 in Oklahoma, when the Cherokee Strip was opened and more than 100,000 people dashed to claim a piece of six million acres of formerly Indian ground. Six years later, Ehrlich heard there were still a few sections left in the old Indian Territory, well west of the good land. For many Germans in Kansas, this was the final chance to get a share of America. In the fall of 1900, George and twenty other men traveled from Kansas to Shattuck, scouting for free land. Close to town, everything was taken, staked by Smiths and Richardsons and Winters and Sherills. George took off on foot, heading for a distant rise to the west.

"I'll throw my hat in the air if I find what I like," he said. "If not, I'm going back to Kansas." George walked toward the rise. At the base of the small hill, six miles out of town, he found thick grass, rippling in the wind, and a pronghorn antelope grazing. He put his claim on a quarter-section of rich grass at the base of the hill. *Paradise,* he called it.

Back in Kansas, George made his peace with his family and prepared to leave, along with hundreds of other Germans. They rounded up their cattle, their chickens, their horses, packed kraut cutters and Bibles, accordions and songbooks. The train was stuffed with farm animals and Bekkers, Borns, Spomers, Haffners — so full that the conductor ordered several people off. It would not move with the weight, he said. Some of the children were hiding under the skirts of their mothers to avoid being counted. They pleaded: this was their last hope. They had fled from places in the world that most Americans did not know existed — could not find on a map — and still were without a home. Oklahoma was their last chance, as Dalhart was to the cowboy Bam White, as No Man's Land was to the Lucas and Folkers families.

When the train arrived in Shattuck, the Germans were stunned by what they saw. Oklahoma looked like hell. The land was black and charred. The air was full of smoke, the smell putrid. Across the way, the grass of what was to be their new farms was burned, and for miles on the horizon there was nothing but sharp, black bristles. The Indians — mainly Cherokee — who had been promised this land for eternity had left in a fiery fury. They had been betrayed at least three times by the American government. This latest land grab, which opened some of the last chunks of Cherokee Nation territory to homesteading, was agreed to by several tribal leaders, who accepted a promise of 160 acres a person in return for giving up the larger land base. But other Indians thought they were robbed. The Comanche felt the same way. Their small reservation was opened to settlement at the same time, leaving the Lords of the Plains with little but brochures from the government on how to become farmers. As the Indians walked away from the land, they burned everything in their wake, torching the grass. Maybe it would scare the Germans back to Russia.

On this bewhiskered and blackened land, the Volga Germans would try to recreate what they had in Russia. The second day in Shattuck, a blizzard hit Oklahoma. It snowed for two days. The Germans camped near the train station but their animals strayed into the storm. They spent the next week collecting the beasts, but some died in the chill, with no grass to eat. Shopkeepers in Shattuck refused to sell to the Germans; others tried to pass an ordinance prohibiting the language from being spoken in the city limits. It seemed odd to the Anglo ranchers that these singing, beer-making, strangely dressed people hurried about their business as if predestined to the southern plains.

But the new German villages on the Oklahoma prairie were no stranger than other colonies of outcasts popping up on the High Plains. Oslo, Texas, a few miles to the west, was supposed to be Norway in brown. Oslo was founded by Anders L. Mordt, late of Kristiania, Norway. Scandinavians belonged in the Dakotas, people told Mordt when he showed up in Guymon, Oklahoma, in 1909 and set up his land office. Mordt had other ideas. He vowed to build one of the biggest Norwegian colonies in the United States on empty ground just across the Texas border. He secured a hundred sections on a site he promised would soon have a rail line running through it, and he bought advertisements in Norwegian language newspapers in the United States. "Buy now before the price goes up," went one advertisement in a 1909 issue of *Skandivaven*. "Plenty of rain and the grains look good." The Norsemen came, about two hundred families. They erected a schoolhouse and a Lutheran church that was to be crowned by a copper bell shipped from Norway. The bell would

chime over land that nobody named Grimstad or Torvik had ever before tried to call home, where meals of lefse and lutefisk would break
the routine of beef and barley. Alas, the new church bell went down
with the Titanic. Oslo was doomed by lack of rain and no rail line. A
drought in 1913 broke the colony, and Mordt declared bankruptcy in a
summer when not a drop of rain fell and temperatures reached 112 degrees. Oslo disappeared, though the Lutheran church still remains on
the grounds of the old colony.

The Germans stayed with the land because their nearly two centuries in Russia had taught them how to live in a treeless place. George
Ehrlich's first job in Oklahoma was as a ranch hand. To learn English,
he carried a notebook in his back pocket, and asked the other cowboys for help, pointing out animals.

"There's cow." *Spell it, please.* And George would write c-o-w in
his book.

"There's a prairie chicken." And George would scribble p. c-h-i-c-
k-e-n.

"And you're a Kraut."

George burrowed into a side of the hill, building a dugout, the first
home. He married a fellow Volga German, Hanna Weis, put in rows of
wheat and corn on 160 acres, raised a few cows for milk. He also
started breeding horses. The Ehrlichs had a girl, then another baby
girl, then a third girl, and a fourth girl — each of them barely one year
apart — before they moved out of the dugout. George built a frame
house. They had yet two more girls. The seventh child was a boy —
William George Ehrlich, who was called Willie. Then came two other
girls, and a second boy, George Ehrlich, Jr. Now there were ten children. During World War I, the Ehrlichs were nearly run out of Shattuck. George used to invite the schoolteacher to his home on weekends. Early in the war, the teacher saw a picture of the Kaiser in
Ehrlich's house, next to a portrait of Catherine the Great. She reported it to authorities. Two days later, police surrounded the Ehrlich
homestead. The house was searched, turned inside out.

You are spy, they told him.

Spell it, please. S-P-Y.

Ehrlich and eleven other German immigrants were taken to Arnett, the county seat. Word was, they would be hanged as traitors. Around midnight, the police came to the jail and herded Ehrlich and his neighbors out, headed for Woodward, a bigger town just to the east, to appear before a federal judge. It was January, the night air cold, and Ehrlich nearly froze from hypothermia on the long ride, handcuffed in the back of a truck. About 2 A.M., Judge T. R. Alexander appeared, bleary-eyed. The police explained that they had rounded up a pro-German cabal. One of the Germans, who was retarded, started sobbing, blubbering in his native language. A guard told him to shut up — if he heard another Kraut word out of any of them, he would cut their hearts out. He flashed his knife.

"George Ehrlich," the judge said, repeating the name several times. "What are you doing here?"

The judge remembered Ehrlich from an earlier appearance, when he came to Woodward for citizenship proceedings.

"What are you doing here?" the judge asked again.

"I cannot talk," Ehrlich answered, in his hybrid English-German. "This guard will stab my heart out."

"You talk to me," Judge Alexander told him. "Now what are you people here for? It's the middle of the night."

"Pit-schur."

"What's that? A picture?"

"Yah."

An officer produced the picture that Ehrlich kept in his house — Kaiser Wilhelm and his family in formal pose.

"That's a beautiful picture," the judge said, then turned to the police. "Is that all you got against these people?"

"They're pro-German. They're hurting the war effort. Spies, for all we know."

The judge turned to the Germans from the Volga. "How many of you are supporting America in the war?"

All hands went up. Ehrlich reached into his pocket and produced two hundred dollars' worth of government stamps issued to support the war effort. A friend produced war bonds. The judge looked at the sheriff and asked him how many of *his* officers had war bonds or stamps. None.

"Take these people home," the judge said. "If anything happens to them, I'll hold you responsible." They drove back in the freezing pre-dawn darkness and released the men to their families at sunrise. A daylong party followed.

The youngest of the Ehrlich ten became everyone's favorite. Georgie, they called him, a kid full of energy. He was changing by the hour, but so was the land. People were buying cars and tractors, adding rooms to houses, using fine material for clothes. On a summer evening, August 14, 1924, Georgie wandered out to the road as the wind carried sand from the tractors. A cattle truck came along. The driver never saw Georgie and ran him over. He died on the spot. After George and Hannah lost their little boy, the life seemed to go out of them. For years thereafter, Hannah said she had no desire to live. George would admonish her, reminding her of all the hardships the Germans had gone through. But his wound had not healed either. At times during the day, when he was alone in the fields, he cried so hard his body shook.

Another toast — the last of the schnapps, more dessert of stewed apples. Ehrlich finished his story of the trip to America and a neighbor, Gustav Borth, raised a glass. Gustav's story was similar: he had dodged a draft notice from the czar and sailed to America, but he was held at Ellis Island, quarantined. He almost went to South America. The stories that George Ehrlich and Gustav Borth told the children were almost forty years old; it seemed as if they were describing another world, a time of unfathomable hardship. Life in America in September 1929 was almost too sweet, too bountiful, too full of riches the Germans in Volga could not have imagined.

Even with wheat prices falling now, George Ehrlich saw only good years ahead. Having escaped the czar's army, Atlantic seas that pummeled the immigrant ship, fires that had burned Oklahoma, the anti-German sweep during the Great War, and the loss of little Georgie, he thought he could live through anything. But in the next five years, he would find himself in the middle of something meaner than old Russia, crueler than the storm-tossed ship, longer than any grass fire — an epic of pain.

5

Last of the Great Plowup

THE STOCK MARKET CRASHED on October 29, 1929, a Tuesday, the most disastrous session on Wall Street to date in a month of turmoil. Investors were relieved at the end of the trading day.

"RALLY AT CLOSE CHEERS BROKERS; BANKERS OPTIMISTIC" was part of the three-stack headline in the next day's *New York Times*. The show business paper, *Variety,* was more direct: "WALL ST. LAYS AN EGG."

It was nothing, brokers said, a correction at the end of a dizzying decade, the most prosperous in the story of the republic. It got worse, quickly. Over the next three weeks, the market lost 40 percent of its value, more than thirty-five billion dollars in shareholder equity — money enough to float a hemisphere of nations. The entire American federal budget was barely three billion dollars. For someone who had followed the advice of the day and taken their savings out of the bank and put it all into General Electric, say, shares had grown by 500 percent from 1925 to 1929. In a month, they lost it all. More likely, they had bought more shares on margin, borrowing on the bet that stocks were going only skyward. To pay the margin loan after the crash — sometimes as high as 18 percent — they had to sell at a time when many stocks did not get any bids at all. Banks had gone on their own speculative binges, reaching into people's savings accounts to make millions in interest-free loans available to bank officers and other insiders for stock purchases. When stocks tanked, banks were hollowed out until the money was gone. One company, Union Cigar, went from $113 a share to $4 — in a single day. The company's owner jumped to his death from a building on Wall Street.

But plunging investor suicides were rare, an urban myth. Most Americans did not own stock: at no time in the 1920s did more than 1.5 million people purchase shares of the stock market. At the most, 4 million people owned some stock — through gifts, inheritance, or purchase — in a nation of 120 million. What Americans still did was work the land. In 1929, the jobs of nearly one in four people were on a farm. The country had one foot in the fields, one foot in a bathtub of gin in the city.

On the High Plains, the Wall Street gyrations were a distant noise. The crash hurt rich people, city slickers, all those swells and dandies. It could not reach the last frontier of American farming. The newspaper in Boise City boasted that the ripple of the crash never touched the Panhandle in 1929. Instead, with record harvests, a new railroad, and even dreams of a skyscraper in town, the paper said, "Our ship is coming in."

But while prairie families may not have owned stock, they did own wheat, and it was starting to follow the course of the equities market. On Wall Street, people put 10 percent down to borrow against the future growth of a stock; in Kansas a dryland wheat farmer did the same thing — gambling on grain. The 1928 crop had come in okay, the price holding at about $1 a bushel at the end of the year. Most people had anticipated $1.50 wheat; some even talked of the $2 yield they had been getting at the start of the decade. There was a drought elsewhere, covering Maryland and the Carolinas all the way to Arkansas, that should have pushed prices up.

Outside of Boise City, the Lucas family was getting ready to start the first harvest of their winter wheat, a June cutting, when the sky darkened and rumbled. Carlie Lucas had died, suddenly, leaving the farm to his widow, Dee, and her five children. She had help from her late husband's brother, C.C., and two young sons, now stout. Her daughter, Hazel Lucas, had married Charlie Shaw and headed off for Cincinnati. With the prices down and loans to repay for all the new farm machinery, the Lucases needed this crop. Maybe, if the wheat came in right, Dee Lucas could get shoes for the kids and bring something special into the house that Carlie had built next to the old dugout. Electricity was not an option. In town, there was a picture show with a piano player accompanying the screen narrative, and diners were lit up, as were some houses. But in the rest of No Man's Land, the juice had yet to arrive. Nobody had washing machines, vacuum cleaners, or incandescent light bulbs. But the farmers did have their miracle machines. In fifteen years, the Lucas family had gone from a walking plow pulled along behind a mule, to a riding plow, in which horses carried the blade through the soil, to a fine-tuned internal combustion plow.

"Machinery is the new Messiah," said Henry Ford, and though that sounded blasphemous to a devout sodbuster, there was something to it. Every ten seconds a new car came off Ford's factory line, and some of them were now parked next to dugouts in No Man's Land.

A few miles from the Lucas homestead, Fred Folkers had his new threshing machine oiled and cleaned, and his crew in place, when the sky filled with ink. He leaned against the side of his new house, the eaves just long enough to cast a shadow over the windows, the new Dodge sitting out front. His daughter Faye was becoming a decent musician, taking regular lessons on the piano they had just bought on credit in Boise City. His tractor, his new car, his new house, his piano — it all came from this little half-section of No Man's Land. He needed wheat to hit somewhere in the dollar a bushel range to cover his costs. The debt was piling up. Whiskey, the one-hundred-proof Cimarron County hooch, made him forget. A couple times a week now, Fred Folkers needed more than a sniff of that broomcorn whiskey. He was more attached than ever to his orchard. People throughout the High Plains had been told to plant trees as soon as they got their dugouts in shape. It was said that trees would increase precipitation, diverting moisture upward. Nebraska gave tax breaks to anyone who planted trees. Folkers just wanted to grow fruit, his way of defying those who said apples and peaches couldn't come from No Man's Land.

A June storm is always troublesome, carrying the currents of systems confused by the cold of late spring and the heat of early summer. The most severe hailstorms on the High Plains are in May and June. When two systems struggled — humid east, dry west — it usually meant friction, strong wind, and clattering. A glance at the sky and here it was, the roll of the squall line. Dee Lucas ordered her children to the root cellar. The hail fell fast, pounding hard, the big ice stones bouncing when they hit, though some exploded on impact. It got louder. The hail balls were as big as grapefruits. They smashed north-facing windows. It sounded like a stampede of horses over the field. When Dee Lucas emerged from the cellar, she saw that the wheat field was flattened, covered with ice balls. Hail sometimes fell bigger; in Kansas a storm dropped ice that measured six inches in diameter, big enough to knock a person cold or cause a concussion. Anything above a marble in size could be ruinous, breaking windows, cracking or denting cars and houses. C.C. Lucas looked out: the damage stretched all the way to his eighty acres of wheat as well. Nothing was spared; all the grain lay squashed on the ground. Nearby, on land that was supposed to get Fred Folkers through next year, the hail hit just as hard — a thrashing that covered the fields in white. His fruit trees still stood, but the buds were stripped. The grain crop was lost — a year's work gone in five minutes. Dee Lucas tried to hold back tears; her eyes clouded and they came quick, in a torrent. C.C. Lucas started to cry as well. Sure they were next year people — you had to be to make your peace with the Panhandle — but that didn't make it easier. Anybody who lived in No Man's Land for long knew about nature's capricious power. It was abusive, a beater, a snarling son of a bitch, and then it would forgive and give something back. When the two adults fell to their knees in a field of hail and wept in front of the children, it was something the young ones had never seen, and it scared them.

The hailstorm crushed much of the wheat crop in Cimarron County, but elsewhere on the High Plains, the grain came in on time. The Germans from Russia brought so much wheat into Shattuck they were told it would soon be burned if they brought any more. Already, in

Iowa and Nebraska, people were burning grain for heat; one court-house kept its furnaces going all winter on surplus corn. In southwest Kansas, the harvest was up 50 percent in a year. In the county around Dalhart, it was up 100 percent. The wheat sat in elevators, in piles; some of it moldered on the ground or blew away. At the start of 1930, wheat sold for one-eighth of the high price from ten years earlier. At forty cents a bushel, the price could barely cover costs, let alone service a bank note. Across the plains, there was only one way out, a last gasp: plant more wheat. Farmers tore up what grass was left, furiously ripping out sod on the hopes they could hit a crop when the price came back.

While the widow Lucas was wondering how to make it through the next year with the crop ruined, her daughter Hazel was trying to start fresh in Cimarron County after her return. The bride had picked up white gloves in the city and felt regal in the clothes from Cincinnati. On the train ride home, she had anticipated getting a job as a teacher, while waiting for her husband's return. They would try to find a house in Boise City and make it nice, like some of the homes she had seen in Cincinnati. When Charles arrived at Christmas, he told his wife that everything had changed. The country was sick. You could see it in people's faces, hear it in the cafés and on the train ride back to No Man's Land. Confidence was shot. Money was tight. People were closing bank accounts, panicked. By the end of 1932, one fourth of all banks would be closed and nine million people would lose their savings. In New York, men in suits were selling apples on the streets, a nickel a pop. They were at every street corner. Even millionaires were scared.

"I'm afraid I'm going to end up with nine kids, three homes, and no dough," Joseph Kennedy, the patriarch of America's best-known Irish-American family, told a friend.

The stock market's loss was up to fifty billion dollars. In three months' time, two million Americans lost their jobs — a tripling of what unemployment had been at the end of summer. Charles saw something in the city he had never seen in No Man's Land: young people, dressed well, heads toward the ground, waiting on line to get something to eat. And he saw some of those same types of people sleeping under bridges.

"No one has yet starved," said President Hoover, trying to calm people at year's end. He spoke too soon. A few months later people rioted in Arkansas, demanding food for their children. Then it happened closer to home. A mob stormed a grocery store in Oklahoma City, after the mayor had rejected their petition for food. Rioting over food: how could this be? Here was all this grain, food enough to feed half the world, sitting in piles at the train station, going to waste. Something was out of balance. Productivity surged, while wages fell and jobs disappeared. That left too much of everything — food, clothes, cars — and too few people to buy it. At one point, the going rate for corn was listed at minus three cents a bushel.

Hazel heard about a job opening the next year, 1930, at the New Hope School outside Boise City.

"What salary would you like?" the clerk asked her.

Hazel had been thinking about this for some time and was ready with her answer: "One hundred per month."

The clerk frowned.

"Is something wrong?" Hazel said. "If you can't pay a hundred, I would accept ninety."

"We can't pay you anything," said the clerk.

"Nothing?"

"But we still want to hire you. We need another teacher."

"You can't pay anything?"

The New Hope School was broke. Farmers were drowning in debt and had stopped paying taxes. Without taxes, the school could not pay teacher salaries. But they still wanted Hazel. They offered to pay her a warrant, a paper that could be cashed in later for ten dollars.

She accepted the job and the warrants. But when Hazel took the first of her paper promises to the bank she was turned away. John Johnson's bank refused to cash them. There was simply no way to expect that tax receipts would ever make the schools solvent. As each month of the school year passed, Hazel realized that the New Hope

School would not be paying a teacher for some time. She worked that
year without pay.

In the fields, more sorrow. Oh, the grain was fine. Again, in 1930, just
enough rain came in the spring and the wheat turned green and upright, fattened under the sun, and the harvest was a flurry of fiber. At
the start of the early wheat harvest, in June, the price had rebounded
some, up near eighty cents a bushel. But by the time Fred Folkers got
the grain threshed and loaded onto a truck and delivered forty miles
to the market in Texhoma, the price was down to twenty-four cents a
bushel. He was stunned. Folkers continued to drift back to his old
whiskey habit, and as the summer progressed, he needed more of Dan
Eiland's joy juice than ever before. Twenty-four cents a bushel! He
could not live on that. Nor could widowed Dee Lucas. On eighty
acres planted in wheat, twenty-four cents a bushel meant that an average harvest would bring a family four hundred dollars. That had to
cover an entire year, and provide enough for equipment, seed, gas,
paying hired hands, and interest on loans, not to mention food, shelter, and clothes. Four hundred dollars. For a year. In 1921, that same
amount of wheat had brought over four *thousand* dollars. Nobody
with fields to plow and tractors to tend and loans to service could live
on four hundred dollars a year.

Farmers begged the banks to give them one last chance. Foreclosure sales in Boise City, held in front of the new Cimarron County
Courthouse, became a regular event. John Johnson, the banker who
had been so friendly throughout the Roaring Twenties, stood next to
sheriff Hi Barrick and asked for bids to take somebody's property, always a neighbor, somebody who had walked out with a bank loan
from Johnson just a few years earlier. If no one offered a minimum
bid, John Johnson's bank was going to get another piece of property.
Farmers drove by and shouted at the sheriff, standing there next to
Johnson with his rifle, foreclosing on a nester in No Man's Land.

After a while, farmers got wise to the sales and devised a scheme.
Before each foreclosure event, they agreed to bid a dime for a horse or
combine, and no more. Anyone who bid higher would be taken care

of later. The bank knew what was up, and so did Sheriff Barrick, but they couldn't stop it. It was a legal bidding process. For a time, these ten-cent sales kept a few bankrupt nesters in the game.

In the fall of 1930, farmers took their tractors to the buffalo grass again, this time in desperation. They plowed up more land than had ever been plowed before for wheat. But as the Lucas family and the Folkers and the others put in next year's crop in the fall of 1930, they noticed some fields that had been cut and opened just twelve months earlier went bare now. The suitcase farmers who had rushed into Boise City to hit a crop had disappeared with the price collapse. They had no sooner plowed up several million acres than they walked away, leaving the land stripped, not even planted in wheat. Just naked, exposed to the wind.

Up north across the state line, in Baca County, farmers had taken seriously their boast of making this weather-beaten corner of Colorado the dry farming capital of the state. Baca was the last big section of the southern plains to be torn up and planted. In ten years' time, horse freighters had disappeared, cattle were run off the land, and the grass overturned. Some of the last of Baca's cowboys had worked on the XIT and they didn't like being chased away by nesters here in Colorado any more than they liked it down in Texas. As a last-ditch effort, a handful of ranchers formed a committee to go around and visit with sodbusters, warning that if they continued to break up the grass in such a fury the land would be no good to anyone, cowboy or nester — it would blow away. But the cowboy's day had come and gone in Baca, same as it had in Texas. They had their free grass boom at century's end, when the land was stuffed with cattle. The nesters didn't trust the cowboys of Baca anymore than they trusted the ranch hands of the XIT.

The wagon ruts left by immigrants going west over the Santa Fe Trail shortcut were fresh on the land, as if they had passed through last Thursday. Baca County was trying to shed the woolly coat it had worn since the late eighteenth century, a cowboy's home. Just as people were pulling out of eastern Montana and the Dakotas, it was city building time in Baca County. The Santa Fe put a branch line in from

Satanta, Kansas, to Baca County, which was completed in 1927. The counties along the rail line grew nearly 200 percent in a few years. In Springfield, Baca's county seat, new streets were going in, electricity bringing lights on after dark. One town dared to call itself Boston and said it would match that big city in New England someday, you watch. Another town, Richards, grew out of the prairie grass. Before even a single tree took hold, Richards got itself a school and a teacher, two general stores, and a post office.

Ike Osteen, the old man on the steep roof of his home in modern-day Springfield, was a boy of twelve when he first realized there was money to be made for his widowed mother and siblings bunched in the dugout. The family got their first tractor in 1929, and Osteen and his brother Oscar went around the county, asking people if they wanted their grass turned. It wasn't much of a machine: with steel wheels, instead of rubber ones, you bounced in the seat so hard it blistered your butt. But with the tractor, the Osteens could cut three rows at a time. A decade earlier they would have been cussed at or ridiculed — the thought of pulverizing Baca's grass being the stupidest idea a person could come up with. Ike and his brother charged one dollar an acre to plow up somebody's field. It took longer than he thought to rip the skin from Baca County, which was tougher than that of the Llano Estacado, even. Ike was easily distracted, too. He liked to play in the remains of the old Penitents ghost church, the rock foundation sitting roofless in the grass, in the shape of a cross. The Penitents used to whip themselves; they were self-flagellants living in Baca before anybody tried to plant a stalk of broomcorn. Even Don Juan Oñate, the last conquistador, had his back scarred and bleeding in the time he moved through Baca County in 1608, for he too was a Penitent. Ike nearly got himself shot another time, tearing up a half-section near a whiskey still. He and his brother hid in the rocks and watched the mule trains come in, the pack animals bringing in sugar and rye and that good Baca County broomcorn, then hauling barrels of whiskey — two hundred gallons a day, he was told.

It wasn't hard to make a batch of hooch. A person needed a vat big enough to hold water, sugar, rye or corn, and something such as yeast to help with fermentation. You'd get the water boiling on a coal-fired burner, get it going enough so the alcohol rises to the top and begins to condense. It goes through a tube of copper and then cools, turning back into liquid. When ready to sell, it was strong enough to fire a tractor. "A great social and economic experiment," President Hoover had called the eighteenth amendment, implementing Prohibition, which started in 1920. A moneymaker and job-creator was what it was. Cimarron, Dallam, and Baca Counties boomed with the black-market whiskey trade. It was impossible for a hypocrite to blush. In Texas, a still turning out 130 gallons of whiskey a day was found operating on the farm of Senator Morris Sheppard, a Lone Star state political heavyweight who happened to be one of Prohibition's biggest backers — an author of the eighteenth amendment.

Ike kept out of the bootleggers' way and made himself good money with the tractor plowing up the fields in 1929. His days were long: up well before the sun, hitting the dirt floor of the dugout, out to get cow chips for the stove. In the winter he had to make sure there was hay enough in the barn for the animals. It made him sad, sometimes, to go inside the barn and remember his daddy and the freighters who overnighted there and the music they played on Saturday night, fiddles and French harps, singing and telling stories that no woman was supposed to hear. Now it was all about getting the grass turned and crop in the ground, and ever more land for wheat. Farmers needed three times the biggest homestead allowed just to make enough in 1929 to cover costs. People bought, rented, or shared any land that was lying about doing nothing, and by the start of the new decade there was very little left of Baca County as the Comanche or the cowboys had known it.

"Hoss-steen," the farmers called out to Ike. "You get that tractor over here fast as you can, boy."

By 1930, Baca was the largest wheat-producing county in Colorado. It could not last, the cowboys told the nesters. Look at the averages: Baca usually gets barely sixteen inches of rain a year. The wet years in the late 1920s were not normal.

Ike gave his earnings to his mom, who was trying to raise eight kids in a dugout. Sure she wanted a floor that was not dirt, and a roof that did not leak, but she wanted more than anything for Ike to stay in that

Richards School and make it all the way like no Osteen had ever done — to get off this scab of the earth. She had lived in her Baca County dugout long enough to know the sky held more betrayal than love.

What the stock market collapse and tight money meant for a forward-looking man in Dalhart was opportunity. Uncle Dick Coon saw it, and he took it. Prices were coming down on property in the Texas Panhandle, a perfect time to buy. Uncle Dick picked up more real estate in downtown Dalhart and did not express a grunt of doubt that the value of his newfound property would soar. Uncle Dick continued at his regular poker games at the DeSoto, the hundred-dollar bill always in his pocket, playing out his hands with other men who believed in Dalhart, City on the High Plains. There was talk of putting in a college. John McCarty certainly thought Dalhart would not stumble in the troubles of late 1929. The newspaper editor exhorted citizens on. Some days folks in Dalhart actually felt sorry for people in New York or Philadelphia who had tied up all their money in worthless paper. In Dalhart, wealth was bound to the "one inexhaustible," the most permanent thing on the planet — land.

And so Doc Dawson felt, though he was getting a little concerned about the money he had invested in dirt outside of town with still not much to show in return. Dalhart finally got a real medical facility in 1929, after Catholic sisters opened the Loretto Hospital. For McCarty and Uncle Dick, it was evidence of the town moving forward, as it must, as the two men kept saying. Never look back, never slow. But for the Doc and his Willie, it meant he was finally unbound of duty to the little building with the Bull Durham tattoo on its side, free for the first time since 1912. At last, the Doc could become a full-time farmer.

One prospect was off the table: no longer did people talk about striking a vein of crude oil on the old XIT lands. The price of oil crashed not long after the stock market fell. It went from $1.30 a barrel to twenty cents. The world economy was a mess. In Germany, where reparation payments for the Great War sapped the treasury, people carted their near-worthless currency to the market in wheelbarrows. A stiff American tariff on imports — a demand of industry in a time when the government rolled over for every whim of big business —

sent the European economy further into a tailspin. On the giddy ride up, there had been no cop, no regulator to enforce basic rules of an American economy that had become the world's biggest casino. Real estate in Florida, oil in Texas, wheat in Kansas, and stocks on Wall Street — they all had their time when gravity was willed into oblivion. And the rules put in place on the way down, the tariffs and tighter money, only made the problem worse. The consumer stopped consuming all but basics. The depression was now global.

The bank in Dalhart was a trouble spot. Rumors were flying that it was not as flush as people let on, that the officers had looted people's savings to buy stocks for themselves. The Dawsons had not received a statement for October or November 1929, and when they got one at the end of the year, it showed their savings drained and no income from the thousands of acres outside of town that were supposed to be their liberation after seventeen years at the sanitarium with its pickled organs and smell of ether. It snowed early that fall, and what grain they did have was lying under a fourteen-inch blanket.

Willie kept on with the literary society, the country club, dinner parties of wild duck and venison. As 1930 dawned, the Doc used the last of his savings to buy property in town. He was losing sleep again, fretting about his nonproducing fields. Strange things were happening on the old grasslands. He had tried again to plant cotton on a couple of his sections, but just as it started to mature, the cold back hand of a blue norther came down and killed it, with the temperatures down around zero. What did grow on Doc Dawson's land was Russian thistle — tumbleweed, which nobody ever planted on purpose. When his land was still in buffalo grass, the seeds lay dormant. But once he'd ripped it up for a commercial crop, it freed the thistle to take over. By the fall, Dawson had raised several thousand acres of tumbleweed. He hired a field hand to get rid of the damn thistle, tear out the dead cotton plants, and get the field disked and planted in winter wheat.

In 1930, Bam White and his family still lived in a little rental house, a place they could never seem to warm. The price was right, though: three dollars a month. At times, he told his boys, he still wanted to roam. It could have been the Indian blood stirring again. It was the great Kiowa leader, Satanta, who expressed the native love of mobility, a people who lived best on this land when they moved with the seasons. "I don't want to settle down in the house you build for us," Satanta said when the government ordered him off the grasslands. "I love to roam over the wild prairie."

The wanderer's urge would not help a family now. There were no animals to follow — cattle or bison. Wasn't much grass, either. Bam decided to find a house of his own, a place to get established, to give the family some certainty, some place to prove that when the horse died in Dalhart it meant God was telling them to settle here 'cause good things had to come. Bam got by with odd jobs in the field, selling his turnips and skunk hides. He did not always feel welcome in Dalhart, with his hands creased and stained, and here were all these folks wearing new clothes and dining fine and drinking the best hooch from the county stills. It could have been worse. He heard that a black man had come into town, got out at the railroad station, and tried to get a drink at Dinwiddie's, apparently ignoring the sign warning blacks not to let the sun go down on them in Dalhart. Next day, the man had disappeared, and people in town said he was killed and no one was less for it. It made Bam shudder.

Saving money from skunk skins, field labor, and turnips, Bam finally put together enough of a nest egg to get his own place. It was a half-dugout, not as deep as the typical hole in the ground; it measured fourteen feet by thirty-six feet, just over five hundred square feet of High Plains habitat for Bam, Lizzie, and the three kids. The roof was tarpaper, which shrieked like a hag in the spring winds. The walls were fingernail thin, and Lizzie said she could not live in a place so cold. Bam and the boys tried to insulate it, tacking pasteboard to the walls. They put in six layers, and now the place was sealed against the more severe exhalations of the High Plains. The dugout was divided into two sides: in one half was a cook stove and table, the eating and cleaning area; in the other half were beds for Bam and Lizzie, a cot that the two boys shared, and a bed for their sister. The house had no water. No toilet. No electric power. It was young Melt's job to haul in buckets of water for cleaning and cooking and to collect cow chips for the stove. This place ain't much, Bam White would say, twisting the edges of his handlebar mustache, but it's ours, and dammit we finally got something here in Texas.

The wheat came fast off the fields outside of Dalhart and over to the elevators by the train station, where it was stacked next to last year's wheat, which had not moved. In Boise City, Fred Folkers cut more grain than anytime since he had come to No Man's Land, and it too went to piles by the train depot, next to piles that had been there through the year, going nowhere. And in Shattuck, Oklahoma, George Ehrlich and Gustav Borth took their harvest to town and were met by men with arms crossed and faces stern, warning them off. Wasn't room for any more grain. The elevators were stuffed. If the Germans from Russia insisted on trying to get their grain to market, there was another man they could see, standing nearby with a rifle. The farmers had done everything right: planting in the fall, spreading mulch over the ground for cover, watching the wheat through spring rains, and praying that hail would not kill it in the summer. The reward at the end of a year? Wheat at thirty cents a bushel, far below what it cost to grow and harvest it. Other farmers got no bid. Nothing. They could give their year's work away for free if they wanted. Or they could throw their arms up and walk away. That's what the suitcase farmers were doing. Salesmen, druggists, barkeeps, docs, mechanics, teachers — the range of day-jobbers who thought they wanted to be wheat farmers, ripping up a half-section here and there, trying to hit a crop — they were getting out before they got in any deeper.

How could this be: the drought had persisted through 1930 in much of the country, while the High Plains got enough moisture to produce a bumper crop, and yet . . . and yet . . . nobody would buy it? In New York City, Gold Medal Flour put up large billboards that exhorted people to "EAT MORE WHEAT — THREE TIMES A DAY." Were people going hungry in the world? Yes, plenty of them. And in America, as well, in the Mississippi Delta and in Arkansas, where the skies had been so stingy. Food followed the roller coaster of the free market. In the throngs of a technological revolution, a nation of farmers produced way too much wheat, corn, beef, pork, and milk, even when a half dozen or more states were crippled by drought. What they got for their labors could not cover costs. Why not have the government buy the surplus wheat to feed the hungry? Farmers demanded as much. President Hoover rejected the idea out of hand. In anger, farmers burned railroad trestles to keep their grain from going to market or hijacked milk trucks on the road and forced them to spill their insides. In furtive meetings inside barns and small granges, farmers planned a general strike — withholding all their remaining wheat and corn as a way to make people notice that they were dying on the Great Plains. But if Shattuck's farmers agreed to keep their grain off the market, folks up in Baca County were more than willing to dump theirs. They would take *anything*.

In Baca, it had been a record harvest. Same in the Oklahoma Panhandle. Ditto Texas and most of Kansas, parts of Nebraska, in the dryland belt that drains into the Republican River. The government men shrugged; it was a free market, just like stocks, and you boys got stung by speculation. The volume of shares sold on the New York Stock Exchange had doubled in a year's time in the late twenties, and wheat production did the same thing. President Hoover wasn't going to step in and muddle the dynamics of agrarian capitalism. But congratulations, the government men said. You grew seven times as much wheat as you did a dozen years ago. A new national record. Keep this up and next year you'll do something no nation has yet done: produce more than 250 million bushels. In all the history of the world no country had ever tried to grow so much grain.

Walking off this land was out of the question for George Ehrlich; he didn't flee the czar's army, survive a hurricane at sea, and live through the homegrown hatred caused by the Great War just to abandon 160 acres of Oklahoma that belonged to him and his ten American-born children. And Bam White, having been tied to Dalhart by the wagon that would not move, finally had a home of his own; he wasn't going to retreat, either. Same with Hazel Lucas. She and Charles were trying to start something at the worst time in the history of buying and selling. She had seen the city life, sampled St. Louis, danced late at night in Cincinnati. The city was just too crowded.

How could people live like that? Home was the flat frontier. Ike Osteen felt the same way, though he had never been outside of Baca County, never seen a moving picture, never walked the streets of a town bigger than Boise City, Dalhart, or Springfield. He knew what it was like to hunt deer in the fall, to ride his horse over the golden-sheened fields in October, to hide in a wallow where Comanche had crouched. This land was pure magic. You simply had to learn to see it right, to develop proper vision. Ike lived in a hole in the ground, hired out his tractor to earn money, but eventually he could own a home-stead — or part of one, in the half-section where his daddy decided to start the Osteen family.

They were bound, each in their way, to the High Plains, because it was home and because a new decade was dawning, and it had to be better than the last year of the old one, and because they knew this was the only roll of the dice left.

On September 14, 1930, a windstorm kicked up dust out of southwest Kansas and tumbled toward Oklahoma. By the time the storm cut a swath through the Texas Panhandle, it looked unlike anything ever seen before on the High Plains. People called the government to find out what was up with this dirty swirling thing in the sky. The weather bureau people in Lubbock didn't know what to make of it or how to define it. Wasn't a sandstorm. Sandstorms were beige, off-white, and not thick like this thing. And it wasn't a hailstorm, though it certainly brought with it a dark, threatening sky, the kind of formation you would get just before a roof-buster. The strange thing about it, the weather bureau observers said, was that it rolled, like a mobile hill of crud, and it was black. When it tumbled through, it carried static electricity, enough to short out a car. And it hurt, like a swipe of coarse-grained sandpaper on the face. The first black duster was a curiosity, nothing else. The weather bureau observers wrote it up and put it in a drawer.

II

BETRAYAL

1931–1933

6

First Wave

THE FIRST NATIONAL BANK of Dalhart did not open for business on June 27, 1931. The doors were locked, the shades down. People banged on the windows and demanded answers — this was their money, not the bank's. *Open the door!* A sign said the bank was insolvent. *Thieves!* The same day, the temperature reached 112 degrees, the hottest in the short history of Dalhart. The villainous sun and the starved bank did not seem related — yet. People slumped against the side of the building, in the oppressive shade, wondering, *What now?* Nearly two years into the Depression, the town was taking on a meaner edge, more desperate, like the rest of the country. What started on Wall Street twenty months earlier now hit the High Plains, a domino of distrust. The more things unraveled, the more it seemed like the entire boom of the previous decade had been helium.

Doc Dawson had money in the failed bank. He was approaching sixty and was worried about his future. Social Security did not yet exist. He had no pension. People owed him money from way back. Patients had offered him chickens, venison, old cars. Usually, he waved it off. The Doc looked strong, usually, but it had been a struggle to overcome his own infirmities. Bright's disease. Tuberculosis. Asthma. He didn't need much sleep, running from operation to operation, the spittoon by his side, the black Stetson atop his head. He trained himself to relax at intervals, nearly shutting his body down, and through this method he said he could go days without a normal man's sleep. It was easier to do when his labors were not so physical. Since giving up the sanitarium, he had become a full-time farmer. The work caught up with him. He felt sharp pains running up his arm, and then the lightheadedness and trouble getting his breath — a heart attack. During a month of recuperation, he took stock of his life. It boiled down to the land; he had to make the dirt work for him. But on the day the First National failed, with the temperature at 112 degrees, his fields looked dry as chalkboard.

A crowd formed outside the office of the new sheriff, Harvey Foust. They wanted him to force the bank to open. Use your power to get our money back, they said. Denrock was full of angry people, blocking the street. The fear spread with fresh rumors. Late in the day, the crowd's mood turned ugly; they went from citizens to a mob, and the heat made it like the worst kind of sweat-soaked nightmare: *Knock the bank door down! It's our money! Where did it go?* Bank accounts were not backed by anything but the good name of the people who ran the bank. And too many of them saw the personal savings of High Plains nesters as just another source of cash for the stock market or an ill-conceived business loan. No matter the exact cause: the First National was broke.

Sheriff Foust tried to calm the mob. There wasn't much he could do; it was a federal matter. But the national government could not do anything either. Deposits were uninsured. In one month alone — November 1930 — 256 banks failed. The question grew louder, a demand now: *where did our money go?* The mob turned on Foust: was he afraid to do his job? They'd been robbed by the First National. *Do something!*

Foust did not seem himself of late. People saw him drinking, his words slurring, even at midday. He talked to himself, withdrew quickly, didn't look people in the eyes. Just a year earlier, Foust — then a deputy — was a hero. He was serving a warrant along with Sheriff Lon Alexander on a pair of low-level bootleggers, Spud and Ron Dellinger. At the Dellinger house, Spud fired at the sheriff, killing him with a single bullet to the brain. Foust had waited outside. When he heard gunshots, he stormed into the shack, his revolver drawn. Spud's brother lunged for the deputy. As the deputy and the bootlegger struggled, Ron's wife entered the shack with a shotgun. Foust broke away and fired at the wife, then at Ron Dellinger. He turned to a corner and got off a third shot, this one at Spud. Three shots: one killed Spud, the other killed his brother Ron, and the third wounded the wife. A week later, Foust was made sheriff. But he was a haunted man, second-guessing himself.

One block from the bank, at the DeSoto Hotel, Uncle Dick Coon tried to keep spirits up, telling the same jokes, saying failure was not going to drag Dalhart down. People thought Uncle Dick kept his dough in a mattress or a ditch out back. Big shots and paupers did the same thing. Senator "Cotton Ed" Smith of South Carolina hauled all his money around in a belt that never left his waist. Dick had his poker face on and not just for the card game. He was in trouble. The properties he had picked up after the crash were not paying rent. He knew the tenants and sympathized with their plight. Business was dead. People had stopped buying cars, clothes, hats, bicycles, even basics. Once the fear started and the wave of collapse started to spread, it was hard to let a buck go, because there might not be one to replace it. Usually, a few wildcatters could be counted on to throw money around when everyone else had closed their wallets. But oil had fallen from $1.43 a barrel to a dime. A dime! Nothing was moving. The economy was a pool of glue. The wildcatters fled as quickly as they had arrived. Dick had his hundred-dollar bill, of course. To his friends, though, he seemed worried. They could see through his poker face. The man had survived the Galveston hurricane, for Christ's sake. At Galveston, he ran a casino, and he lost it all — money, the building, all washed away. More than six thousand had died, so Uncle Dick did not mourn the paper money buried by rampaging sea and eighty-mile-an-hour winds. He knew poverty and he knew death in their worst forms. But like everyone in the summer of 1931, he had the jitters. Dalhart was sick, acting like a dog with rabies, and that mob outside the bank: what would they turn on next? Uncle Dick's namesake, the Coon Building, was empty, sitting like a hobo on the street right across the way from the DeSoto. And the hotel business had slowed to a crawl, people no longer pouring into Dalhart looking to strike oil or hit a crop.

In Dalhart's grim decline, the Number 126 house flourished. The girls were not afraid of showing it, either. The house had more girls than they could use and a fiddler, Jess Morris, who played with his band on Saturday nights until dawn. The Number 126 kept some commerce in Dalhart going: the girls getting their hair tinted and coiffed, buying new clothes, the mustard-colored house always in need of fresh blinds, new sheets, furniture. The owner, Lil Walker, drove a pink Cadillac — the nicest car in three counties. She would pile her new girls in the car, dressed to the nines, their hair up like Mae West, and cruise past the crumbling empire of Uncle Dick. The girls waved and shouted yoo-hoo, leaving a trail of perfume.

It steamed John L. McCarty, sitting in his editor's office at the *Texan,* working to keep alive the Dalhart vision. The town had nearly eight thousand people now, almost double what it was ten years ago. In McCarty's mind, it would double again by the end of the 1930s. But Dalhart needed to be slapped to its senses time and again, and it was the job of the loudest voice in the Panhandle to do just that. McCarty could not stand that the one business still thriving in Dalhart was the whorehouse. It was time to drive Mrs. Walker and her pink Cadillac out of Dallam County, out of the Panhandle, out of Texas. McCarty prepared the front page of the *Texan* with a searing exposé, a write-up on the doings at the Number 126, and how it was a moral abomination to have these hookers parading around in a pink Caddy when Dalhart limped along, the Coon Building empty and people no longer showing up with suitcases and ambition to spare.

"SO THE PEOPLE MAY KNOW" was his headline for the next day's *Texan.* When he took the page dummy to the shop, his printer shook his head. He refused to print it. The printer had lived in Dalhart since its creation and he knew the Number 126 like people knew Rita Blanca Canyon south of town. McCarty was indignant. This whorehouse was a sore on the face of Dalhart; it had to go. It was one thing to be invisible at the edge of town but another to flash and parade painted women and their dresses and the pink Caddy. Sorry, Mr. McCarty, the printer said. Can't do it. Won't do it. We need them girls. McCarty pulled his story.

As the ranks of the jobless grew, they took to the rails, going from town to town, dodging Rock Island bulls in the south, Burlington

Northern bulls in the other direction, swapping stories about places where the sun shined and a man might still get paid for a day's work. Two million Americans were living as nomads. They were not long-time drifters, most of them, according to reporters who had spent some time on the trains. They were family men, farmers and factory hands, merchants, some professionals among them, writers and bank clerks and storeowners — all broke, people who could not stand to see their kids in rags, hungry. When they arrived in Dalhart — sometimes as many as eighty people a day — at the railroad crossroads that could lead a man north to Denver, west to Santa Fe, or east to Kansas City, Sheriff Foust was supposed to put them back on the train. And if they were black, they weren't even supposed to step off the tracks, or he could arrest them for vagrancy. The penalty for "vag" was stiff: four months on a chain gang, doing hard labor. In September 1929, just over 1.5 million people were out of work; by February of the following year, the number had tripled. The economy was not fatally ill, President Hoover said; Americans had simply lost their confidence.

"All the evidences indicate that the worst effects of the crash on unemployment will have passed during the next sixty days," Hoover said on March 3, 1930.

By the end of that year, eight million people were out of work. The banking system was in chaos. The big financial institutions had once looked invincible, with the stone fronts, the copper lights, the marbled floors, run by the best people in town. Now bankers were seen as crooks, fraud artists who took people's homes, their farms, and their savings. In 1930, 1,350 banks failed, going under with $853 million in deposits. The next year, 2,294 banks went bust. At the end of 1931 came the biggest failure of all — the collapse of the Bank of the United States in New York. When the Bank of the United States folded, it had deposits of two hundred million dollars. Fittingly, the bank's biggest office was next to Union Cigar, the company whose president had committed suicide after the stock fell from $103 to $4 in a day. When the bank failed, twelve million people were without jobs — 25 percent of the work force. Never before had so many people been thrown off payrolls so quickly, with no prospects and no safety net.

Never before had so many people been without purpose, direction, or money.

In Dalhart, with the First National shuttered and downtown merchants unable to pay city taxes, John McCarty now worried about the survival of his paper. The *Texan* had been his before his thirtieth birthday. He had taken it from a weekly to a daily, and circulation growth had been robust. The paper would grow into a great daily only if Dalhart kept reaching for legroom. McCarty begged his advertisers to stick with him. He presented a new strategy for survival: he would emphasize good news. Good news? In the worst depression in history. Good news? When stacks of grain rotted near the railroad. Good news? When the land was starting to dry and crack with a spell of drought that had become more than a curiosity. It sounded preposterous. But from here on out, McCarty would only see the omelet in the broken eggs. A bank collapse was an opportunity. A store closing was a competitive advantage. A death was not nearly as important as a birth. As for the heat wave: it's the golden sun at its best. Other states would kill for it. He got the Mission Theater, the grocery store, a couple of lawyers, and Uncle Dick to keep advertising. And he leaned on Herzstein's, the clothing store that gave people in Dalhart something to dream about.

Some people said Jews were to blame for the bad times — that they did not belong in this country, a place where the *Texan* had boasted that its citizens were "of the highest type of Anglo-Saxon ancestry." In Nebraska, four thousand people gathered on the capitol steps, blaming the "Jewish system of banking" for the implosion of the economy. They held banners with rattlesnakes, labeled as Jews, coiled around the American farmer. Father Charles E. Coughlin, the mellow-voiced radio priest from Detroit, also blamed Jews for America's stumbles as he spoke to a weekly audience of more than a million listeners. Often, he would read the names of Hollywood movie stars and then "out" them, revealing their original Jewish names as if detailing a sinister plot.

Herzstein's filled a need in Dalhart, Boise City, and across the line at their headquarters of Clayton, New Mexico, and the fact that they were Jews in the Anglo prairie was secondary. Their customers let them be. Their sign read: "HERZSTEIN READY TO WEAR." The idea of buying a complete outfit — or even a shirt or pair of pants — that came fully stitched to size was novel. Most people bought bolts of material and sewed their own clothes. In the early years of the Depression, people made clothes from burlap potato sacks, the labels still printed on them, or tore out the seat covers from junked cars and refashioned them as something to wear. Herzstein's slashed prices below their break-even point. McCarty convinced the family to run a small ad, once a week: "new shirts, two for three dollars." But they were bleeding money like everybody else, falling further behind, looking at a growing mountain of unpaid bills. In 1931, over 28,000 businesses failed; it did not matter if they were family run institutions or big corporations, they were sucked under by the same force. Money did not circulate. Those who had jobs saw their wages collapse by a third or more. The average factory worker, lucky to be still drawing a paycheck, went from earning twenty-four dollars a week just before the collapse to sixteen dollars a week in the early thirties.

Relatives from Philadelphia would visit the Herzsteins and wonder why they held on in land so foreign, so full of cowboy twang, wildcatter bluster, and two-fisted Christianity. But the family had been in the High Plains longer than anyone in Dalhart or Boise City, and they were here to stay. As the first Jewish family in the High Plains, they had spilled blood in this land. Their struggle, their despairs and triumphs, were as tied to the hard brown flatland as anybody's. The Herzsteins had come west over the Santa Fe Trail with the first group of Jews in New Mexico — Spiegelbergs, Zeckendorfs, Floersheims, and Bibos among them — beginning in the late 1840s. In New Mexico, they found an open world: cultures of old Spain, Indians from the pueblos, and Yankee traders. The light was different. The landscape was unreal. And socially, it was unlike the layered, segregated world of the East or old Europe. One of the Jews, Solomon Bibo, married into an Indian family in Acoma, a pueblo on a high mesa that is the oldest continuously inhabited town in the United States. Bibo even became governor of Acoma, known as the Sky City, a thousand-year-old community. The Herzsteins drifted north and east of Santa Fe to the high desert and a wind-tugged piece of New Mexico Territory. They were counting on a railroad line putting down tracks and a depot in Liberty, the town they had selected as their stake. The railroad never came. But one day in 1896, a gang led by Black Jack Ketchum rode into Herzstein's general merchandise store. Black Jack was thirty-two, at the height of a reign of terror across the High Plains. He had killed more than a dozen men, according to the wanted posters, robbing trains, banks, stores, and homes throughout Oklahoma, Texas, and New Mexico.

What do you want? Levi Herzstein asked Black Jack.

Everything you got.

Black Jack robbed the store of all its cash and much of its merchandise. His gang knocked off the post office next door as well. Levi Herzstein organized a posse and they chased Black Jack's gang up among the dormant volcanoes north of the Llano Estacado, and then in the draws near No Man's Land. When the posse caught up with them, Black Jack offered to surrender. As Levi Herzstein moved forward to disarm him, Black Jack pulled his pistol from his side and shot Herzstein and two Mexicans in his posse. Herzstein fell to the ground, his guts ripped open. He bled to death, as did the two other men.

It took four years for the law to catch up with Black Jack. While robbing a train, Ketchum took a shotgun blast from close range fired by a conductor. It shattered his arm, which was later amputated. He was tried for multiple crimes and sentenced to death. By popular consent, it was agreed to hang Black Jack in Clayton, New Mexico, which soon was said to have more guns per capita than any place in the West — a safety precaution against any attempt by Black Jack's old gang to free him. It was also where Morris Herzstein — the surviving brother — had set up a new store and decided to settle down. Black Jack was scheduled to be hanged on April 26, 1901. That week, another Herzstein arrived in town, Simon, aged nineteen. He had been summoned by his uncle to come west from Philadelphia and help him build a chain of stores. Simon brought along his bride, Maude Edwards, a woman of gentile breeding and European manners who had grown up in London and Philadelphia. She was blond, very pretty, small, and well-dressed. She spoke the crispest English heard in New Mexico Territory. When she got off the train in Clayton after crossing the empty plains and the wind-harried Llano Estacado, she found saloons doing business in the streets, the hotels full, and posters everywhere advertising the festive, upcoming execution of Black Jack Ketchum. Maude Edwards was horrified, but Simon found it fascinating. Life on the High Plains had an urgency that it did not have back in Philadelphia.

People came from hundreds of miles to see the one-armed killer hang. Newspapers from as far away as Denver, Los Angeles, and St. Louis sent correspondents. The execution was set for 1:00 P.M. Crowds jammed around the execution site, a scaffolding built next to the jail. The sheriff gave a solemn intonation and a prayer was read. Black Jack stepped to the gallows. He was a young man still, not quite thirty-seven, with a shock of black hair, his face somewhat puffy and bloated. He looked fat, having gained more than fifty pounds in jail. The crowd quieted. A noose was put around his neck.

Any last words?

"Let her rip," Black Jack said.

The trapdoor sprang open and Ketchum fell through. But the hanging went wrong. Instead of snapping his spine behind the ear, the tightened rope caused Black Jack's head to pop off. Some said the sheriff had greased the noose so it would slide quickly and snap the neck. Others said it was the way the noose was tied. But decapitation by hanging was extremely rare, and Black Jack's case is one of only a few recorded in American execution. His hooded head broke clean and rolled around at the feet of the crowd.

Welcome to the High Plains, Morris Herzstein told Maude Edwards, late of London and Philadelphia.

Simon Herzstein never tired of telling the story about Black Jack's decapitation. It became part of the lore of the store as Simon traveled the High Plains selling fine clothes to nesters, cowpunchers, and their wives. When people would ask him what a Jew was doing peddling stiff collars in No Man's Land, he said he was doing the same as anybody else, only taking a different route. He let people buy on credit and never kept a ledger. It was all in his head. He knew they would

pay. He loved baseball, poker, and bridge. He loved throwing big dinner parties, giving Maude something to take her mind off the wind
and the empty skies. And he loved the West, the freshness of it all, the
Indians who came into town to trade from Navajo lands, the sons and
daughters of Comancheros, who could match Simon story for story.

When the banks closed and people scrounged for food, Simon
Herzstein kept up with the well-told jokes and the optimism, never
letting on that he had his own troubles. As businesses folded in
Dalhart, Clayton, and Boise City, the triangle of towns at the center of
the High Plains, the Herzsteins fell further behind. The town of
Dalhart went after Simon Herzstein, claiming in foreclosure papers
that he had not paid his taxes in more than a year. Dick Coon owned
the property, and he now consulted his lawyer about what to do about

Failed bank, Kansas, 1936

the only man on the High Plains trying to keep people dressed to match their lost dignity.

As Dalhart collapsed, people in other parts of the Panhandle kept their faith, looking to the upcoming harvest of 1931 to rescue them. Sure, the First National was gone, all that money vaporized in the prairie heat, but these folks had something more lasting: they had land, and from this land came food. People *were* starving now in parts of the United States, despite what Hoover had said and despite the song that played in the background, Rudy Vallee's "Life Is Just a Bowl of Cherries." American families were reduced to eating dandelions and foraging for blackberries in Arkansas, where the drought was going on two years. And over in the mountains of the Carolinas and West Virginia, a boy told the papers his family members took turns eating, each kid getting a shot at dinner every fourth night. In New York, nearly half a million people were on city relief, getting up to eight dollars a month to live on.

But here on the High Plains — look at this wheat in the early summer of 1931: it was pouring out of threshers, piling high once again, gold and fat, and so much of it that it formed hillocks bigger than any tuft of land in Dallam County, Texas. On the Texas Panhandle, two million acres of sod had been turned now — a 300 percent increase over ten years ago. Up in Baca County, two hundred thousand acres. In Cimarron County, Oklahoma, another quarter million acres. The wheat came in just as the government had predicted — a record, in excess of 250 million bushels nationwide. The greatest agricultural accomplishment in the history of tilling the land, some called it. The tractors had done what no hailstorm, no blizzard, no tornado, no drought, no epic siege of frost, no prairie fire, nothing in the natural history of the southern plains had ever done. They had removed the native prairie grass, a web of perennial species evolved over twenty thousand years or more, so completely that by the end of 1931 it was a different land — thirty-three million acres stripped bare in the southern plains.

And what came from that transformed land — the biggest crop of all time — was shunned, met with the lowest price ever. The market held at nearly 50 percent below the amount it cost farmers to grow the grain. By the measure of money — which was how most people viewed success or failure on the land — the whole experiment of trying to trick a part of the country into being something it was never meant to be was a colossal failure. Every five bushels of wheat brought in from the fields was another dollar taken out of a farmer's pocket.

The grain toasted under the hot sun. With the winds, the heat gathered strength; it chased people into their cellars all day, and it made them mean. Their throats hurt. Their skin cracked. Their eyes itched. The blast furnace was a fact of summer life, as the Great Plains historian Walter Prescott Webb said, causing rail lines to expand and warp. "A more common effect is that these hot winds render people irritable and incite nervousness," he wrote. The land hardened. Rivers that had been full in spring trickled down to a string line of water and then disappeared. That September was the warmest yet in the still-young century. Bam White scanned the sky for a "sun dog," his term for a halo that foretold of rain; he saw nothing through the heat of July, August, and September. He noticed how the horses were lethargic, trying to conserve energy. Usually, when the animals bucked or stirred, it meant a storm on the way. They had been passive for some time now, in a summer when the rains left and did not come back for nearly eight years.

7

A Darkening

WINTER CAME WITH a fly-by snowstorm, here and gone, and the northern winds finding the cracks of every dugout and aboveground shack holding to the hard top of No Man's Land. It came without snow up north, two years into a drought so severe that less rain fell in eastern Montana than normally fell in the desert of southern Arizona. Farmers needed the snow for insulation, the blanket that covered nubs of wheat during their dormancy in the dark months. They needed it for the first moisture of spring, a taste of water to get the wheat started again. But they got nothing from the sky. The soil turned to fine particles and started to roll, stir, and take flight. The wheat from the last two harvests on the High Plains rotted. In elevators, field mice and jackrabbits gorged themselves on it. Life was gray, flat, rudderless. There was no work in the cities. And the harder people worked in the country, the poorer they got. Wheat hit nineteen cents a bushel in some markets — an all-time low. It perplexed farmers in No Man's Land as much as it baffled the policymakers in Washington.

"Tens of thousands of farm families have had their savings swept away and even their subsistence endangered," the Agriculture Secretary, Arthur M. Hyde, wrote the president on November 14, 1931. "Usually when weather conditions reduce production, prices rise. No such partial compensation came to the drought-stricken areas because demand and prices declined under the impact of world depression." Again, farmers begged Washington for relief. Herbert Hoover knew about toying with the market; as the U.S. Food Administrator during the Great War, he had helped establish the first price guarantee for wheat, at two dollars a bushel, setting off a stampede of planting that would transform the grasslands. But now that all this surplus grain was rotting, he was not about to interfere with the market. Let the system cull out the losers.

Many farmers refused to surrender. The National Farmers Holiday Association urged its members to "stay at home — buy nothing and sell nothing," as a way to force Hoover to set a minimum price for grain. But people were already buying and selling nothing, farmers and city folk alike. It was as if all of American capitalism were held by ice in a deep winter freeze. "I feel the capitalistic system is doomed," said the head of one farmers' group.

By 1932, nearly a third of all farmers on the plains faced foreclosure for back taxes or debt; nationwide, one in twenty were losing their land. And since more Americans still worked on a farm than any other place, it meant every state was swimming in the same drowning pool. Farmers charged a courtroom in Le Mars, Iowa, demanding that a judge not sign any more foreclosure notices. He was dragged from the courthouse and taken to the empty county fairgrounds. There, a rope was strung around his neck and tied to a tree. The judge's life was spared by cooler heads. The farmers were rounded up by the Iowa National Guard and detained behind a makeshift, barbed-wire outdoor prison.

"Unless something is done for the American farmer we will have revolution in the countryside in less than twelve months," Edward O'Neal of the American Farm Bureau told Congress at the beginning of 1932. It wasn't just wheat that had sunk below the cost of producing it; milk, cattle, and hogs were all in the same depressed situation. Farmers continued to block and spill milk on the streets. If the American farmer went down, they warned in angry protests, they would take the rest of the country with them.

"The greatest emergency that ever faced this country in time of peace is confronting it now," said Congressman Wilburn Cartwright of Oklahoma.

In No Man's Land, the Folkers family learned to use their wheat for something in every meal. They ground it for harsh breakfast cereal, sifted it to make flour for bread, blended it in a porridge with rabbit meat at dinner. Fred Folkers's life's work had become worthless, and the despair drove him to his jars of corn whiskey. He could not control the weather. And he could no longer plow any additional land; every bushel of wheat harvested led him deeper into poverty. His homestead was a quicksand of debt. The new house he had built by hand, the Model-T, the new kerosene cook stove, the piano that he and Katherine had purchased for their daughter Faye — he might lose it all. He would need two years, maybe three, of prices back up in the high range, a dollar or more a bushel, just to pay his debts, just to get even. Katherine was homesick and wanted to go back to Missouri again. She cried at night, dreaming of green valleys and land with trees. But Folkers said it wasn't any better in the Midwest. They had to hold on and hope that next year would be better. During the boom years, Folkers had been wise enough to put some money away. But now his savings were gone, wiped out in the banking collapse. He withdrew into a paralysis, blank-faced, skulking around the homestead and talking to his fruit orchard, the one thing that still gave him hope. At night, he sat in a chair, his fingers tapping away, going over the figures in his head. Faye never saw her father so broken.

Outside, the wind blew with a callous edge. It would come in hard from the southwest, and then shift, pick up in intensity, and barrel in from the north. The wind was always there in No Man's Land, even when it was just lying low, between breaths. It seemed different now, in the early stages of a dry spell, hotter and harsher, as if it sucked the life out of anything it touched. The spring of 1932 was too dry to plant and with no ground cover, some of Folkers's land began to peel away. It takes a wind of thirty miles an hour to move dirt; at forty or fifty, it's a dust storm. Folkers tried to keep his orchard alive through the spring and summer of that first dry year. In the evenings, he hauled water by milk pail from the tank to the orchard. But the heat bore down on the trees, pests swarmed on the leaves, and what little fruit came after the bud quickly browned and shriveled like raisins. One thing that did grow was the Russian thistle, as Doc Dawson found on his land just to the south in Dalhart. The tumbleweeds blew against

Folkers's barbed-wire fences, forming a barrier that trapped blowing dust. The children hauled the tumbleweeds away from the fence and stacked them in the cow lot for winter feed. We might need it, he said. Feeding tumbleweeds to cattle — it was a frontier in American agriculture, but not the one prophesied by the government.

Folkers complained about stomachache. Deep in his gut, something cried for relief, like an ulcer, growing sharper as the winter wore on. He did not think much of doctors, and it was always trouble to find one. Like most prairie nesters, the Folkers had their own remedies. When a tooth hurt, they sucked on a clove. When the heat of summer became unbearable, they drank sassafras tea to thin the blood. For a severe cold or cough, there was a chest plaster of turpentine and kerosene. And so now when Fred Folkers's gut started to whine, he drank more corn whiskey. Katherine begged him to see a doctor. There was somebody new in town, a woman doc who had just shown up in Boise City. When Folkers went to see her, she diagnosed him with stomach cancer. Cancer? That meant death, surely. No, the doc assured Folkers. She had developed a cure for cancer, salve and bandage, the special ointment drawing out the disease. Folkers would have to spend several weeks in the woman's small hospital, while she applied fresh salve every day. But how? He was broke. Sell something, she suggested. Folkers had some cattle, a few dairy cows, and he could give up the Model-T. But he needed both of them to stay alive. If he sold his cattle and his car, he would have only the fallow ground. At home was one small stash, the money he never put in a bank. He gave it to the cancer doctor in Boise City and agreed to her treatment. After a few weeks, he returned home with a scar on his stomach where the salve had been applied. It worked, Folkers told his family. He was cured. But not long after he finished his treatment, the cancer doctor left town, never to be seen again, and Folkers's gut burst. Turned out, he never had cancer; it was appendicitis. A doctor in Texhoma saved his life.

Folkers's neighbor, the fat man Will Crawford, who had met his wife, Sadie, after finding a note in his bib overalls, had taken another mortgage out on his half-section as a way to stay alive at the start of the Depression. The money dwindled; their old car up and died. Will was ashamed to look at other people now, hiding in his hole, and neighbors said it was because he could not be the "real man" that Sadie had been seeking when she left her note in his overalls. They did not go to church and seldom went to town. Will looked like he had stopped caring about life, his clothes tattered, his hair mashed, his eyes hollow. Sadie was in rags as well. She planted a garden, using a row of tin cans lined end to end, the openings cut out and half-buried as a primitive irrigation system. To keep the wind from knocking down her plants, she put up a fence of sticks and canvas. From this little patch of ground next to their dugout, Will and Sadie grew enough to stay alive: cabbage and potatoes, onions and corn. But as a winter without rain dragged on, the blue northers wore them down and left them hungry, shivering in their dugout.

Cash was scarce in Boise City. It was a hard-shelled, stiff little town that clung to a sense of destiny despite all evidence to the contrary. A visitor from Denver, getting off the train, said rusted cans scattered over the dusty plain would be an improvement. People swapped a hen — live and clucking — for a year's subscription to the *Boise City News*. They bartered a bushel of wheat for an oven stove wick. They brought in fifteen dozen eggs and got back a pair of overalls. They traded turnips for two cans of Franco-American spaghetti. Or they took the quarter they had been staring at for five days and went down to the little café run by Mrs. Skaggs, where two bits could buy a hamburger, a piece of pie, and a glass of milk. The Palace Theater closed, cutting off the one source of reliable fantasy, and then reopened after considerable pleadings, with ten-cent picture shows. The joy had gone out of living. Subsistence was a trial. But even though people were hurting, the town refused to slouch or cower. Boise City did not need help from anybody. The town was too proud to take anyone's charity. Pain was submerged until it screamed to the surface, as with one local businessman who had lost his life savings. He shot his wife first, then put the gun to his head and blew his own brains out.

The Cimarron County sheriff, Hi Barrick, was a former doughboy who had come back from the Great War intending to get rich like everyone else in the wheat bonanza, but he never got a big enough crop. One day then farmer Barrick saw the sheriff drunk on duty, and he reported it. Hell, then why don't you run for sheriff? He did. Sheriff Barrick moved to Boise City and took up residence in the courthouse, next to the jail. Barrick chased a regular cast of bootleggers around No Man's Land, brought them in for jail time, released them after a few days, then chased them again. Both sides of the law laughed about it. It was a game that kept everybody in business. Sheriff Barrick knew his moonshiners better than he knew some members of his family. And busting up a still was a good way to spread a commodity around town. Stills required a lot of sugar. After a bust, Barrick would bring the sugar into town and give it away in front of the courthouse. There was always a line, waiting on the sheriff. It was better than taking someone's property at the weekly foreclosure auction held by John Johnson's bank. The banker had caught on to the conspiracy of low bidding among farmers — the ten-cent sales, with people offering no more than a dime for a tractor or car — and he brought in his own bidders. But then a hangman's noose appeared outside the auction site. The implication was clear to anybody thinking of picking up a neighbor's homestead in a bankruptcy sale.

The new governor of Oklahoma gave people hope, but he also tried to get them to hate. William Henry David Murray had been elected in 1930 after scandal drove the last two governors from office, both of them impeached. With a campaign slogan that railed against what he called "The Three C's — Corporations, Carpetbaggers, and Coons," Murray won by a huge margin, 301,921 votes to 208,575. He was known as "Alfalfa Bill" for his ceaseless advocacy of agriculture as the cornerstone of society. Alfalfa Bill said anything could grow in Oklahoma. His daddy, David, had made wine not long after grabbing a piece of dirt in the 1889 Sooner land rush; his Murray Mosel was so well-known that President Teddy Roosevelt had declared it "the bulliest wine of the land." Alfalfa Bill was himself a bully, but these times needed such a man, he said. Born in Toadsuck, Texas, in 1869, Murray ran away from home at the age of twelve, worked on a series of farms, and then got involved in populist politics. He bought a newspaper, educated himself so well he passed the bar, and made a name as president of the Oklahoma statehood convention in 1906. Oklahoma, he said at the time, could be a great state only if blacks were separated from whites and kept in the proper jobs — in the fields or factories. Next door, in Texas, lawmakers had institutionalized that sentiment forty years earlier with Reconstruction laws that said blacks could work only as field hands. Blacks were inferior to whites in all ways, Murray said, and must be fenced from society like quarantined hogs. At the start of the twentieth century, many people felt otherwise, but Alfalfa Bill tried to set his view into the proposed constitution. At the same time, he welcomed even black support, if done properly.

"I appreciate the old darkie who comes to me talking softly in that humble spirit which should characterize their actions and dealings with the white man," he said to wide applause at the constitutional convention. Murray hated Jews as well. Blacks had some virtues, but Jews had none, in his view. Nor did he like the handful of Italians who had come to the High Plains. The "low grade races" of southern Europe, he said, were a threat to civilization. Oklahoma became the forty-sixth state only after President Theodore Roosevelt forced Murray to remove the segregationist planks of the constitution. Murray was furious; he never let go of his grudge against the Roosevelt family.

At the start of the Depression, Alfalfa Bill was a mustachioed, haunt-eyed, big-eared man of sixty who could talk for hours without interruption, fueled by caffeine and nicotine. He drank two pots of black coffee a day and was never without a cigar — his method of ingesting "the great civilizer," as he called tobacco. Storming around Oklahoma in 1931, he said he could not make the sun less oppressive, but he promised to use muscle to fix the broken land. His muscle was the National Guard. As governor, Murray ruled by martial law, calling out the guard twenty-seven times in his first two years in office. When oil prices fell to a new low in 1931, the governor sent his troops to the oil fields to force a shutdown of three thousand wells as a way to drive up prices. When Texas backed a toll bridge across the Red River on the border with Oklahoma, Murray sent the guard to the bridge, nearly provoking a shooting war between the two states. In the midst of the standoff he showed up with an antique revolver, waving it in the faces of Texas Rangers. And when blacks tried to hold an Emancipation Day parade in a park in Oklahoma City, the governor imposed martial law on the city and ordered his guard troops to shut them down. Blacks were supposed to be invisible in his state, quietly working the land or manning a factory station. All told, the governor issued thirty-four declarations of martial law during his four years in office.

The land dried up in the spring of 1932. Month after month, going into the height of the growing season, there was no rain. The sky was white and hot, and it took until well after midnight for the heat to dissipate. Alfalfa Bill urged people to fight nature with force. The unemployment rate in his state was 29 percent. To show them what could be done, he plowed up the grass on the grounds of the capitol and let people plant vegetable gardens. And to demonstrate how water could be taken from the ground, Murray went on a building binge, trying to create lakes and ponds in places that had neither. The ground could be mined at the deepest levels for water, using new and powerful centrifugal pumps, to create the garden state of Oklahoma. They could grab onto that underground lake, the Ogallala Aquifer, like the Sooners had grabbed the old Cherokee lands, and so what if the water was nearly seven hundred feet deep and had taken at least a hundred centuries to build up — it was there to be grubstaked.

In Boise City, Alfalfa Bill's plans sounded like a tonic. God knows they needed water. It wasn't trickling out of the distant Rockies. The Cimarron, once a roaring river, was now a tear trail. And it wasn't coming from overhead. It rained barely ten inches in all of 1932. The sun glared down at nesters in No Man's Land, every dawn a new punishment. It was time for man to stand up to the puckered face of the elements.

"Human progress has now reached the stage where it can master these mighty forces of nature," wrote the *Boise City News*, in support of a proposed dam in No Man's Land.

In the spring of 1932, Alfalfa Bill decided to run for president. He would follow the model that got him elected governor. In running for the statehouse, he had campaigned on the Three C's. Now he ran on a platform of promising people the "Four B's: Bread, Butter, Bacon, and Beans." That a governor could run for the highest office of the land with a campaign that offered people calories said something about 1932.

By late winter, the suitcase farmers who had flooded into the southern plains during the biggest wheat-growing boom in the nation's history had completely disappeared. They had scalped the sod in the pan- handles of Texas and Oklahoma, had followed the new rail lines into day-old towns in Nebraska, southwestern Kansas, and Baca County, Colorado. For a few years, they hit the crop just as anticipated, but if they hit a crop in the early 1930s, it was worthless. When they walked away, they left behind torn-up land, abandoned like a played-out strip mine. Other people, some with homesteads or mortgages, started to leave as well, just disappearing, not even locking the door behind them. But most drylanders had no plans to go anywhere. They saw the newsreels in the Mission Theater in Dalhart and the Palace in Boise City, showing those breadlines in the big cities, the apple ven- dors on every street corner, the millions crying for relief. At least here, in a cashless economy, people could squeeze a dozen eggs every day from a house of hens, or get a pail of milk from an old cow, or spread water from the windmill onto the ground to grow vegetables, or fatten up a pig, then smoke a winter's supply of bacon. They also thought, in the first year of the epic drought, that things had to change because they always did. Wet years followed dry years. You hung on, as Hazel Lucas Shaw did, even though she worked for nothing at the one-room schoolhouse. They hung on because this was still the only place they could call theirs. Going to the city, or to California, was a journey to the unknown.

Subsistence farming may have kept people alive, but it did nothing for the land, which was going fallow section by section. At the end of 1931, the Agriculture College of Oklahoma did a survey of all the land that had been torn up in their state during the wheat bonanza. They were astonished by what they found: of sixteen million acres in culti- vation in the state, thirteen million were seriously eroded. And this was before the drought had calcified most of the ground. The erosion was due to a pair of perennial weather conditions on the plains: wind and brief, powerful rain or hailstorms. But it was a third element — something new to the prairie ecosystem — that was really to blame, the college agriculture experts reported: neglect. Farmers had taken their machines to the fields and produced the biggest wheat crops in history, transforming the great grasslands into a vast medium for turning out a global commodity. And then they ditched it.

"The area seems doomed to become in dreary reality the Great American Desert shown on early maps," wrote Lawrence Svobida, a Kansas wheat farmer who kept a journal of his slow decline. Svobida had started to see the wheat game as an elaborate fraud if not a tragic mistake. He had come to the plains in 1929, a young man whose motto was "Never defeated." He pronounced his first crop "breathtaking." He never made money afterward. When the land started to blow, he was not even sure if he would live to tell his cautionary tale. The sky, choked with topsoil, frightened him. And the heat — nobody alive had ever seen the sky like this, day after day, the white bowl overhead.

"This was something new and different from anything I had ever experienced before — a destroying force beyond my wildest imagination," he wrote.

When the native sod of the Great Plains was in place, it did not matter if people looked twice at a piece of ground. Wind blew twenty, thirty, forty miles an hour, as always. Droughts came and went. Prairie fires, many of them started deliberately by Indians or cowboys trying to scare nesters off, took a great gulp of grass in a few days. Hailstorms pounded the land. Blue northers froze it so hard it was like broken glass to walk on. Through all of the seasonal tempests, man was inconsequential. As long as the weave of grass was stitched to the land, the prairie would flourish in dry years and wet. The grass could look brown and dead, but beneath the surface, the roots held the soil in place; it was alive and dormant. The short grass, buffalo and blue grama, had evolved as the perfect fit for the sandy loam of the arid zone. It could hold moisture a foot or more below ground level even during summer droughts, when hot winds robbed the surface of all water-bearing life. In turn, the grass nurtured pin-tailed grouse, prairie chickens, cranes, jackrabbits, snakes, and other creatures that got their water from foraging on the native turf. Through the driest years, the web of life held. When a farmer tore out the sod and then walked away, leaving the land naked, however, that barren patch posed a threat to neighbors. It could not revert to grass, because the roots were gone. It was empty, dead, and transient. But this was not something farmers argued about in meetings where they clamored for price support from the government. Nor was it the topic of scientists or government specialists, at least not early on. People were frantically trying to find a way out of the hole of an economy without light. They were struggling to stay alive, to find enough money to buy shoes, fuel, goods that could not be made by hand at home. What was happening to the land in the early 1930s was nearly unnoticed at first. Still, it was a different world, off balance, and ill. So when the winds blew in the winter of 1932, they picked up the soil with little resistance and sent it skyward.

Around noon on January 21, 1932, a cloud ten thousand feet high from ground to top appeared just outside Amarillo. The winds had been fierce all day, clocked at sixty miles an hour when the curtain dropped over the Panhandle. The sky lost its customary white, and it turned brownish then gray as the thing lumbered around the edge of Amarillo, a city of 43,000 people. Nobody knew what to call it. It was not a rain cloud. Nor was it a cloud holding ice pellets. It was not a twister. It was thick like coarse animal hair; it was alive. People close to it described a feeling of being in a blizzard — a black blizzard, they called it — with an edge like steel wool. The weather bureau people in Amarillo were fascinated by the cloud precisely because it defied explanation. They wrote in their logs that it was "most spectacular." As sunlight came through the lighter edge of the big cloud, it appeared greenish. After hovering near Amarillo, the cloud moved north up the Texas Panhandle, toward Oklahoma, Colorado, and Kansas.

Bam White saw this black monstrosity approaching from the south, and he thought at first he was looking at a range of mountains on the move, nearly two miles high. But the Llano Estacado was one of the flattest places on earth, and there was no mountain of ten thousand feet, moving or stationary, anywhere on the horizon. He told his boys to run for protection and hide deep under their little house. The cloud passed over Dalhart quickly, briefly blocking the sun so that it looked like dusk outside. It dumped its load and disappeared, its departure as swift as its arrival, the sun's rays lighting the dust.

Some sandstorm, they said down at the DeSoto.

No, sir, that was no sandstorm, others said.

Did you see the color of that monster? Black as the inside of a dog.

The storm left the streets full of coal-colored dust and covered the tops of cars and the sidewalks on Denrock. The dust found the insides, too, coating the dining table and wood floor of Doc Dawson's place, and the fine furniture inside the DeSoto lobby, and the pool tables at Dinwiddie's, and the baseball stands at the edge of town. Folks had it in their hair, their eyes, down their throat. You blew your nose and there it was — black snot. You hacked up the same thing. It burned in the eyes and made people cough. It was the damnedest thing, and a mystery.

What is it? Melt White asked his daddy.

It's the earth itself, Bam said. The earth is on the move.

Why?

Look what they done to the grass, he said. Look at the land: wrong side up.

8

In a Dry Land

LIFE WITHOUT WATER did strange things to the land. It was typical in the spring to find a tarantula in the bathtub, centipedes on the ceiling, or spiders freshly hatched from winter nests. But as the drought on the southern plains entered its second year, a profusion of bugs appeared. Insects bred and hatched through months that normally would have killed a generation in colder, wetter years. They emerged in huge numbers. Grasshoppers swarmed over wheat fields, chewing down the tender shoots left in the abandoned grounds, and massed over gardens, consuming in a few minutes food that could provide a nester with a winter's worth of canned goods. Centipedes crawled up drapes, over floors — buckets of them. They had to be swept outside with the dust. In Dalhart, Willie Dawson awoke one morning to a black tarantula with two-inch-long legs and a body the size of an apple prowling around her kitchen. She shrieked for the Doc. Later in the week, two more tarantulas appeared. It was the big dust cloud of January that had carried them to Dalhart, people in town said. In No Man's Land, black widows crawled out of woodsheds and corn stacks, over dugout floors and up the walls of frame houses. An elderly man died of a bite. A boy screamed for half a day from the pain of a similar bite. He passed out and was rushed south to the new hospital run by the Catholic nuns. The child in Boise City was lucky to live; a boy in Rolla, Kansas, died from his black widow bite.

Rabbits had the run of the land, crowding fields, yards, streets. They were an easy source of food, but they also took away food, gnawing en masse in places where some farmers still hoped to raise a crop. People saw the rabbits as a scourge, a perpetual motion of mastication, indifferent to the human alterations that were blowing away.

"BIG RABBIT DRIVE SUNDAY — BRING CLUBS"

In the pages of the *Texan,* John McCarty thought it was time to get rid of the big-eared menaces. People gathered in a fenced field at the edge of Dalhart, about two thousand folks armed with baseball bats and clubs. The atmosphere was festive, many people drinking corn whiskey from jugs. At last, they were about to do *something,* striking a blow against this run of freakish nature. They spread to the edge of the fenced section, forming a perimeter, then moved toward the center, herding rabbits inward to a staked enclosure. As the human noose tightened, rabbits hopped around madly, sniffing the air, stumbling over each other. The clubs smashed heads. The bats crushed rib cages. Blood splattered, teeth were knocked out, hair was matted and reddened. The rabbits panicked, screamed. It took most of an afternoon to crush several thousand rabbits. Their bodies were left in a bloodied heap at the center of the field. Somebody strung up a few hundred of them and took a picture.

Melt White had disobeyed his daddy and gone to the rabbit drive. He did not take part, but he watched at the edge of the slaughter. As citizens of Dalhart closed in, the boy cringed at the sounds: swinging clubs, whoops and hollers, and the anguished howls — he told his mama he heard the rabbits cry — as they died. He ran to his house with the tarpaper roof and carried with him nightmares that never left.

The rabbit drives caught on and became a weekly event in some places. In a single square mile section, people could kill up to six thousand rabbits in an afternoon. It seemed a shame to let all those dead rabbits go to waste when so many people were hungry in the cities. After one drive, in Hooker, Oklahoma, people shipped off two thousand rabbits as surplus meat. But it was hard to keep the meat from spoiling, and the logistics of butchering them proved too much.

The rabbits were left to buzzards and insects or shoveled into pits and buried.

The heat of that year broke all records. One day it hit 115 degrees up in Baca County, and the Osteen dugout was unbearable. The children wanted to sleep outside, but their mother considered it dangerous, with the fields starting to fly. She had an idea: why not cool the dugout with water from the well? Using buckets, Ike and his brother got water from the windmill's holding tank and poured it over the roof. Their little home steamed like a sauna. They had just one window on either side of the dugout, which measured twenty feet by sixteen feet. And when the earth started to move, the dust covered their portholes to the outside world, making it black inside the Osteen home even at midday. One of Ike's jobs was to shovel the dust that drifted up against the dugout. He did his chores, but then he often skipped school. In 1932, Ike was fifteen, and the classroom felt like prison to him. There was no longer any money to be made plowing up people's fields at a dollar an acre. Nobody was turning over fresh ground now. Baca County was spent.

At a time when bankers were seen as thieves behind a till and government was a cold brother who would not help a family in need, an old outlaw of the High Plains came in for a second look. Black Jack Ketchum had been in the ground for more than thirty years, buried with his severed head in a little patch of dirt across the Texas line in Clayton, New Mexico. But now some people were saying maybe Black Jack wasn't such a cur after all. In these days of dust and despair, Black Jack took on new qualities. He had robbed trains, and everybody knew what bastards the railroads were. He had robbed banks, and good for him. And it was a shame, folks said, that he never got a proper resting place. Here he was, perhaps the most famous outlaw of this withered prairie, having ridden with Butch Cassidy and the Hole in the Wall Gang in between his deeds in No Man's Land. His legend expanded as Hollywood scoured the West for stories of thugs on horseback. A group of prominent citizens decided to dig up

Black Jack and move him to the new Clayton Cemetery. There Black Jack would be given his proper due. They put out a call to newspapers, hoping the outlaw's notoriety could bring a few visitor dollars to a place getting a reputation for nothing but dust and failure. And while a civic moralist like John McCarty did not approve of the disinterment, he too thought Black Jack looked better when judged by modern standards.

"There is, however, one good point in reviving his history. It shows that Black Jack did his robbing in a more or less manly manner," McCarty wrote. "He was a train robber and six-gun killer and he made no bones about it. He wasn't a dirty, rotten, sniveling, stinking polecat of a gangster . . . Black Jack had his good points when you compare him with the rats modern civilization is having to deal with . . ."

Such words did not sit well with the Herzstein family. This manly man had robbed Levi Herzstein's store and then shot him dead after pretending to surrender. He was never charged with killing Levi. Instead, he went to the gallows on a capital robbery crime — after the railroads lobbied to set the death penalty as a punishment for certain kinds of train heists. Simon and Maude Herzstein had tried to live through these dark days by holding on to a few special things. The store in Dalhart had gone under, lost in foreclosure because the Herzsteins couldn't pay the city taxes. About once a month, though, they would host a big Friday dinner party, cooking up duck or venison with a few bottles of wine left over from buying trips in the more prosperous days. It was a way to forget about the ragged wind outside.

On Sunday afternoon, September 11, 1933, nearly three thousand people gathered around a rocky scab of land at the edge of Clayton. The grave was opened, a pine box was lifted up out of the ground, and the top removed. An ex-sheriff, brought in from Tom Green County, Texas, where Black Jack had done some robbing, was called forth to take a good look.

"Yup. That's him."

And by God, Black Jack's head did not look too bad. He'd been remarkably well-preserved, thanks to the limestone layer that covered his casket. His black suit was in mint condition. His ink-black hair and his mustache were still dark and bushy. He was taken to the new cemetery and buried at some distance from the others. Although people thought Black Jack deserved a better final resting ground, they did not want him too close to the finest corpses of Clayton. They put him deep in the ground and left the grave without a tombstone. They had done right by the Ketchum boy, it was said in the papers. But to the Herzsteins, giving Uncle Levi's killer another chance to face the sky was appalling.

In the fall of 1932, many farmers did not plant a crop of next year's wheat. What was the point? They could hope for the drought to end and bring in a good harvest next year, but if the price was anywhere close to what it had been for the last two years, it meant only another shove toward bankruptcy. The challenge was to keep a smidge of self-respect while living on what you could kill or grow in a garden. Life was on hold, suspended until the rains returned. To see land that you had brought to life turn to nothing was as sad as watching a friend die of a long illness. And then to fallow that land, because hope itself was gone, was harder still.

For the Lucas clan and the Folkers and other farmers in the High Plains, it was a daily struggle not to think that more bad times were on the way. From dawn that brought yet another cloudless day, to an evening supper of wheat porridge or rabbit hind again, there was no escape from the thorns of failure. This year fulfilled the long ago warnings of Stephen Long and John Wesley Powell — that this arid land was not fit for normal agriculture. For the land had not just failed them, it had turned against them. In all of 1932, only twelve inches of rain fell in No Man's Land — barely half of what was needed, as a rough minimum, to produce a crop. The Lucas clan had kept food from the 1931 harvest, corn, maize, and wheat, as insurance. By the fall of 1932, it was gone. Most families had a few row crops, but they were shriveled by the drought. The corrosive dust drifted thick enough to bury what little natural sod was left. With the grass under sand, there was no pasturage for animals. They had nothing to feed their animals but tumbleweed, which the Folkers were already using. If you ground up the tumbleweed and salted it, Fred Folkers told his neighbors, the animals would eat it.

Hazel Lucas Shaw was living in town, still teaching at a school that could not pay anything but scrip, and her husband was trying to start a funeral home in the rental house they had moved into. When she visited her uncle C.C. Lucas on his homestead south of Boise City, she found a man struggling to survive. Hazel clung to the beauty of years past. She remembered how the country would open to so much color, the fields of coreopsis, the purple verbena, the patches of green buffalo grass.

It had all disappeared in a wash of brown. Uncle C.C. could not get the milk he normally drew from his dairy cows, and it wasn't just because the animals were hungry, living on a ration of last year's grain and this year's tumbleweeds. He examined their udders and found they were sore and reddened from the dust. The cows would not even let their calves suckle. His remedy was one that he heard from another farmer in No Man's Land — rub a little axle grease on the cows' udders, just enough to take away the chafing from the dust. By using grease, he got some milk, even if it came with nondairy drippings.

C.C. Lucas had no prospect of making money from the land. The family would have to get by on salt pork, dried beans, and a dwindling supply of canned vegetables and fruits. The children were bothered by the bugs, so many crawling, biting critters, and insects they had never seen before. Green worms, for example, on the fence, inside the house, over the porch, in the kitchen. Where did they come from? The kids would not get into bed without scanning for black widows or tarantulas. Hazel tried to get her cousins to see beyond 1932. Hazel believed in tomorrow perhaps more than any member of her extended family. She had seen hailstorms that collapsed a dugout; she had seen lightning scatter a horse team, and prairie fire come right up to the house. This arid, tortured stretch of slow time — it was just another trial, and then the purple verbena would bloom again, and the labors of No Man's Land could mean something, surely. Look at all they had accomplished in half a generation's time: going from dirt-dwellers with nothing to making a decent living. To return to subsistence was something a Lucas could put up with.

The best way around the ubiquity of despair was to think of new life. Hazel wanted to start a family, but who could bring a baby into a world without hope? That's why you had to banish the negative thoughts, she said. She could *will* a positive day. The color would come back to life when the water returned. This drought could not last to 1933.

The dust storm that blew up from Amarillo at the start of 1932 was treated as a freak of nature, a High Plains anomaly. The weather bureau studied pictures of the duster and was fascinated by its enormity, its dark color, the way it moved unlike any other phenomena of weather. It was not a normal sandstorm and not a tornado. They still had no technical term for it.

In March the wind was often at its most fierce, and when it blew in the late winter of 1932, it picked up the earth in No Man's Land and scattered it all over the High Plains. These storms were shorter and smaller than the big duster of January, but they were similar in other ways: black, rolling, sharp and cutting on the skin. The cows bawled when a duster rolled in and hit like a swipe from the edge of a big file. The dirt got in their eyes and blinded them, got in their noses and mouths, matted up their hide, and caused skin rashes and infections. The weather bureau counted half a dozen black blizzards on the Oklahoma Panhandle in late winter of 1932. At the end of March, the sky brightened, no wind for a day. Fred Folkers walked among his fruit trees, one of the few things still alive on his dead land. Little buds had started to form. But the next day, a chill, blue norther came through; it was so cold it killed the fruit crop for a second year in a row.

April came with the winds nonstop, the fields swirling up high and rolling north. A farmer could see but barely farther than the length of his section on most days. The weather bureau started to classify dusters by visibility. A bad one, a storm in which a person could see no more than a quarter mile, was the worst. In 1932, there were fourteen of these blinding storms. The biggest one, in April, scared children at Hazel's school in No Man's Land. The sky darkened, as if the sun was blocked by an eclipse, and then — *bang! bang!* — like gunshot, the school windows were blown out, shattered, and the dust poured in, covering desks, the floor, faces. It was gone in a minute, leaving glass shards on the floor and the hard, tiny particles of fields that had been plowed for wheat just a few years earlier. Some of the children could not stop crying. They went home with tears turned muddy and told their parents the school had exploded that day. Afterward, some parents kept their children home. School was too dangerous.

Now the dust was no longer a curiosity but a threat; the land had become an active, malevolent force. If windblown dirt could break windows in school and make cattle go blind, what was next? Children were coughing, unable to sleep at night, hacking until their guts hurt. Something was seriously wrong with this land, but nobody had any experience with it. The county agriculture man in Boise City, Bill Baker, was a history buff, and living at the far edge of No Man's Land he was in a place that presented a host of discoveries to a curious mind. Baker found a cave in a corner of Cimarron County. After considerable excavation, a mummy was discovered inside the cave: a child, perfectly preserved. The mummy was thirty-eight inches long with a broad face and forehead, and a head of shoulder-length hair. Cornhusks, a bag stuffed with pumpkin seeds, and a small cord made of yucca plant fibers were buried with the child. The college archaeologists who finished the dig said the boy was from the Basket Maker period more than two thousand years ago. To Bill Baker, this meant people had farmed No Man's Land well before it was thought anyone had ever put a shoot in the ground. Baker took possession of the mummy and put it on display under glass in the courthouse in Boise City. The tiny boy with the tuft of hair who appeared to be sucking his thumb became a big draw in the town built on railroad fraud. To Baker, trying to make sense of a land that was a danger to people, this mummy held some secrets. No Man's Land was not an empty plain after all. There *had* been people living on this accursed ground, dating to the time of Christ or earlier. And yet here they were in Boise City, barely a full generation into the life of the town, and everything was going to hell, the place collapsing from within, the land lethal. The mummy's people had figured out some way to live in this place. It baffled Baker — the small cornhusks, the tools. He also knew he would not be able to find anybody who could provide answers, oral history, or a link between this mummified past and the desperation of the twentieth century. The Indians knew something, but they were gone, pushed from the plains before they could hand off a guide to living.

Sitting Bull had predicted the land would get its revenge on whites who forced the Indians off the grasslands. He saw doom from the sky. During this drought, his nephew, One Bull, tried to reverse Sitting Bull's prophecy. One Bull sent a letter from the reservation in South Dakota to a professor at the University of Oklahoma, Stanley Campbell, asking him to return the Sioux *wotawe*, a medicine bag with human hair, stones, dried food, and other artifacts. The rightful owners of the *wotawe* could influence the weather, One Bull explained.

There was another band of people who might have some answers. The Mexicans, like the Indians, were largely invisible. They had some history with the place, at least more than anyone in Boise City. Juan Cruz Lujan and his brother, Francisco, had a sheep ranch up north in Carrumpa Valley — the oldest home in Cimarron County. Lujan was born in Mexico in 1858, and as a little boy he ran away and worked as an ox team driver, traveling the Santa Fe Trail and Cimarron Cutoff, right through the heart of the Oklahoma Panhandle. Lujan remembered the Comanche, the Kiowa, the boundless prairie chickens and pronghorn antelopes, the big bison herds and the sea of grass — the whole intact, full-dimensional original High Plains. He had lived it, gloried in it, bound up his future and family in it, thanked God for it. He and his brother ran sheep in No Man's Land and set up a ranch even before the cattlemen came. They built a rock house next to a spring-fed creek. His animals were fat and woolly and didn't fuss or need much, but then, it was the best sheep country in the world. Don Juan fell in love with a rich man's girl, Señorita Virginia Valdez, daughter of the Baca family, who ran sheep all over New Mexico. They were married by a Jesuit priest who encouraged them to build a chapel on the ranch in No Man's Land. The ranch became the center for Catholics and Mexicans in Cimarron County. Children were homeschooled there, learning the ways of sheep trailing and how to read the sky. Virginia Lujan had nine children, though five of them died in childbirth or shortly thereafter. The families of ranch hands had their own families, and by the start of the Depression, the Lujan ranch was a community unto itself, with three generations. One of the ranch hands, José Garza, was born on the banks of Carrumpa Creek in a tiny shed and grew up loving horses and running sheep, bucking broncs, and praying like everyone else that Señora Lujan would have a boy to go with her family of girls. The Lujans treated Garza like a son.

When Boise City's ag man, Bill Baker, saw Don Juan Lujan and his cowboy Joe Garza in town, he asked them about the early days. Was there ever a time when it had been this dry? Had the air ever been so hot, for so long, or had the climate itself changed? Did the dust blow like this before? Had the skies ever been so agitated? Was the grass ever so diminished? Had the Cimarron River ever run so dry? Had the Rockies ever had so little snow? And . . . how did people live in those days? Lujan was a storyteller, but his brow wrinkled as his face turned sad the more he talked about what had happened to the best sheep-grazing country of all. It was hard to conceal his rage. He hated what the sodbusters had done to the grasslands. He remembered the sound of a thousand bison hooves pounding over ground where Boise City now stood paralyzed and lost. He remembered buffalo grass covering every section that now lay tired and broken. Damn sure there were dry times before. He rattled off the years — 1889–1890, 1893–1894, and then 1895, when only seven inches of rain fell, and 1910–1912. Droughts were a way of life in this country. But the grass was still around, and stayed put, through those dry years. Now it was gone, ripped out and thrown to the wind. The Lujan sheep could not find pasturage. The ocean of grass was down to a few islands of brown. As for this dust, it was killing the love of Lujan's life, his wife, Virginia. She was afflicted with the same kind of cough that rattled through every dugout, every tarpaper shack, every mud-walled hacienda. Same with Joe Garza's dad, Pablo. They both had bronchial fits, spitting up the residue of No Man's Land.

And though Lujan had lived in the far Oklahoma Panhandle longer than any Anglo, he and his ranch hands feared deportation. Lujan was American, but there were people in Boise City who suspected that the Lujan ranch was a refuge for Mexicans who took jobs away from Anglos. By 1930, there were about 1.5 million Latinos, mostly of Mexican ancestry, living in the United States. Sugar beet farms in southeastern Colorado and Kansas and cotton farms in Texas had attracted them to the southern plains. In the early years of the Depression, cities were shipping Hispanics out of the country. Los Angeles spent $77,000 to send 6,024 deportees to Mexico. Lujan knew everyone on his ranch, and he treated them like family. Nobody was going to be forced out, he assured them. Most of them had been born on this land. Joe Garza's dad was from San Antonio, Texas — "old Mexico," he always called it. A bigger question for Lujan was whether he could keep the ranch alive with the grass gone.

While the first dusters of 1932 were a mystery to farmers and meteorologists, a man who had spent his life studying cultivation of the earth thought he had some answers. Hugh Hammond Bennett toured the High Plains just as the ground started to blow, and he, too, had never seen anything like the black blizzards. But to Bennett, a flap-armed, big-eared, well-spoken doctor of dirt, the diagnosis seemed obvious. It was not the fault of the weather, although this persistent drought certainly didn't help. The great unraveling seemed to be caused by man, Bennett believed. How could it be that people had farmed the same ground for centuries in other countries and not lost the soil, while Americans had been on the land barely a generation and had stripped it of its life-giving layers?

"Of all the countries in the world, we Americans have been the greatest destroyers of land of any race of people barbaric or civilized," Bennett said in a speech at the start of the dust storms. What was happening, he said, was "sinister," a symptom of "our stupendous ignorance."

Hugh Bennett was a son of the soil, growing up on a 1,200-acre plantation in North Carolina that had been planted in cotton since before the Civil War. There were nine kids in the Bennett family, which was mixed Scots-Irish and English stock. As a boy, Hugh rode a mule to school using a fertilizer sack for a saddle. He spent part of every day on the family land east of the Blue Ridge Mountains, helping his father on steep terrain. He learned early on that the land would not wash away as long as they kept it terraced. His father also taught him that the soil of their farm was not simply a medium through which passed a fibrous commodity but also a living thing. His interest in the complexities of soil led him to the University of North Carolina and graduate school, where he studied and wrote about how different societies treated land. Out of school, he was part of a team hired by the government to do the first comprehensive soil survey of the United States. Big Hugh, as he was called since his teens, took to the road, camping out next to his car, taking soil surveys in every state. He knew more about the crust of the United States — from close personal inspection — than perhaps any person alive in the early twentieth century. His work also took him abroad, where he learned how old societies had grown things in the same ground for thousands of years without wasting the soil.

In the last years of the wheat boom, Bennett had become increasingly frustrated at how the government seemed to be encouraging an exploitive farming binge. He went directly after his old employer, the Department of Agriculture, for misleading people. Farmers on the Great Plains were working against nature, he thundered in speeches across the country; they were asking for trouble. Even in the late 1920s, before anyone else sounded an alarm, Bennett said people had sown the seeds of an epic disaster. The government continued to insist, through official bulletins, that soil was the one "resource that cannot be exhausted." To Bennett, it was arrogance on a grand scale.

"I didn't know so much costly misinformation could be put into a single brief sentence," he said.

He cited the land college report, which stated that Oklahoma had lost 440 million tons of topsoil, and another survey out of Texas, which said 16.5 million acres had been eroded to a thin veneer. And now that people were leaving the land to blow, it looked to Bennett as if they were walking away from an accident without accepting any responsibility. What people were doing was not just a crime against nature, he said, but would ultimately starve the nation. The land would become barren; the country would not be able to feed itself.

Americans had become a force of awful geology, changing the face of the earth more than "the combined activities of volcanoes, earthquakes, tidal waves, tornadoes and all the excavations of mankind since the beginning of history."

9

New Leader, New Deal

A SEARCH FOR SKUNK HIDES sent Bam White wandering around the High Plains in the year that Americans threw out their president. On the road, the cowboy found that a lot of his countrymen were living like him, close to the bone, looking twice at another man's garbage, swapping half a day's labor for a meal. He hoisted his bindle and moved from camp to camp, hearing about low-grade opportunities to stay alive. A man could pick citrus in deep Texas for a nickel a bushel, or collect bottles for bootleggers at a dime a bucket load, or cut asparagus in the spring for twelve cents an hour. Cashing in a skunk hide, at $2.50 apiece, seemed more dignified and less hard on the back of a man in his late fifties. What Bam White saw on the road made him shudder. There was a big "Hooverville" in Oklahoma City, thousands of people living out of orange-crate shacks or inside the mildewed, rusted-out hulks of junk cars. Entire towns were broke, shutting down city services. In the string of communities that had sprouted up along the new rail lines, schoolhouses closed, unable to pay teachers or heat classrooms. Texhoma, just up the road from Dalhart, disconnected its streetlights. Couldn't afford to bring light to darkness. The land was baked, brown, and blowing, and there wasn't much feed left for cattle, and still in the cafés of Clayton or Boise City was Rudy Vallee singing that life is just a bowl of cherries. Bam returned home to kids sick and coughing in the two-room house that leaked wind. He rubbed a mixture of skunk oil, turpentine, and kerosene on Melt's chest, a family remedy, and Melt said he felt better. But at school, the kids said the boy smelled like road kill.

When you're hungry, you listen when a politician talks about food, and in the election of 1932, growling stomachs drove many people to develop a sudden interest in democracy. Alfalfa Bill Murray said if he were president nobody would go without bread, butter, bacon, or beans. The man from Toadsuck said the problem was that America had gone soft. Look at those college people at Oklahoma A&M, asking for public money to build a swimming pool. "As far as I am concerned they can go to the creek to swim," he said. Murray thought everyone should get a piece of land, get out of the crowded and unworkable cities, and turn back the clock. With his wrinkled suits and cigar that seemed to be an extension of his mouth, Murray took to the hustings in the 1932 Democratic primary season, planting Four B's clubs. Hoover was sinking fast. Most Americans paid no federal income tax in 1932. But Hoover wanted to tax the untaxed to pay for a sizeable deficit. He scoffed at the pictures of fruit vendors on city streets; they were selling apples at five cents apiece, he said, because it was more profitable than working a regular job. The Republicans had been routed in the 1930 midterm elections, losing seventeen seats in the Senate and control of the House. The presidential election year of 1932 looked to be even worse for Hoover's party. In the capital, a whiff of genuine class warfare was in the air. Congress voted to raise taxes across the board on the wealthy to cries of "Soak the rich!" Others pushed for an estate tax, taking nearly half the worth of anything over ten million dollars.

Hoover was an engineer and entrepreneur who was worth four million by the start of the First World War. As president, his past statements haunted him like a bill collector. It was not just his inaugural prediction that the United States was close to eliminating poverty forever, nor his prosperity-around-the-corner forecasts. One statement, defining character by how much money somebody had, followed Hoover everywhere. "If a man has not made a million dollars by the time he is forty, he is not worth much," Hoover had said in the giddy days, when America was a crapshoot with good odds.

The national unemployment rate remained at 25 percent. It seemed as if the country had been sick forever. The economist John Maynard Keynes was asked if there was ever a worse time. "It was called the Dark Ages," Keynes said. "And it lasted four hundred years."

To Murray, anybody who could stand up straight and string four sentences together had a shot at being president. One wing of the Democratic Party favored the 1928 nominee, Al Smith, but you know about Catholics, Murray said. And then at the other end of the spectrum were the Reds; Murray had shown he would deal with socialists when he sent the National Guard to Henryetta, Oklahoma, to break up a May Day parade last year.

Out of New York came a governor from the moneyed class, Franklin Delano Roosevelt, and he drove Murray to fits — being from that hated family. (FDR's cousin, Teddy, had forced Murray to remove a white supremacist plank from the Oklahoma constitution before he would allow it to join the union.) At first, Franklin Roosevelt was dismissed as a man without heft, a dilettante running on one of the nation's great names. Then he took up the cause of the "forgotten man" — the broken farmer on the plains, the apple vendor in the city, the factory hand now hitting the rails. And though he spoke with an accent that sounded funny to anyone outside the mid-Atlantic states, and he seemed a bit jaunty with that cigarette holder, Roosevelt roused people with a blend of hope and outrage. He knew hardship and the kind of emotional panic that comes when your world collapses. He had been felled by double pneumonia in 1918, which nearly killed him, and polio in 1921, which left him partially paralyzed. He had been told time and again in the prime of his young adulthood that he had no future, that he would not walk again, that he might not live much longer.

"If you spent two years in bed trying to wiggle your toe, after that anything would seem easy," he said.

Hoover believed the cure for the Depression was to prime the pump at the producer end, helping factories and business owners get up and running again. Goods would roll off the lines, prosperity would follow. Roosevelt said it made no sense to gin up the machines of production if people could not afford to buy what came out the factory door.

"These unhappy times call for the building of plans that rest upon the forgotten, the unorganized, the indispensable units of economic powers," FDR said on April 7, 1932, in a radio speech that defined the central theme of his campaign. He called for faith "in the forgotten man at the bottom of the economic pyramid." That forgotten man was likely to be a person with prairie dirt under the fingernails.

"How much do the shallow thinkers realize that approximately one half of our population, fifty or sixty million people, earn their living by farming or in small towns where existence immediately depends on farms? They have today lost their purchasing power. Why? They are receiving less than the cost to them of growing these farm products."

As the campaign wore on, prices fell further. In No Man's Land, a farmer could get only six cents for a dozen eggs, four cents a pound for a hog or chicken.

At the Democratic convention in Chicago, Murray roared one last time, joining the forces trying to stop Roosevelt. But FDR won the nomination on the third ballot. Alfalfa Bill was crushed; he finished with twenty-three delegates, a curious presence, the Four B's clubs gone, unbending even as "Happy Days Are Here Again" started to play and people sang:

> *"Your cares and troubles are gone*
> *There'll be no more from now on."*

Murray glowered. "Object of many an urban stare was the rustic figure of Governor William Henry (Alfalfa Bill) Murray of Oklahoma sipping gallons of black coffee, chewing soggy cigar butts," wrote *Time* magazine. Oklahoma, Murray insisted, would vote for Roosevelt only " 'after frost — and frost our way don't come until after the election.' "

In November, Roosevelt carried Oklahoma and every other state but six, mostly in New England. Hoover said the Democrats under Roosevelt had become "the party of the mob." The mob voted. FDR's take in Oklahoma was 73 percent; in Texas it was 88 percent. Alfalfa

Bill Murray later said that Franklin Roosevelt — son of Hudson River Valley Protestant aristocracy, cousin to a president, product of Groton and Harvard — was a Jew, who kept his ancestry secret.

In March 1933, the new president was sworn in on a snowy day that seemed to match the winter mood of the country. Hoover, his tank of ideas empty, handed Roosevelt a shell of a country, its confidence shot. "We have done all that we can do," Hoover said on his last day in office. "There is nothing more to be done."

Roosevelt did not waste an hour. The gates of possibility sprang open, and Roosevelt went on a hundred-day dash. For American capitalism, it had been a truly frightening time, full of "dark realities," as Roosevelt said. Money was not circulating, even in the capital. James A. Farley, the postmaster general, said he could not cash a check in Washington. The president blamed "unscrupulous money lenders" and "a generation of self-seekers." Some in his government urged him to nationalize the banks. After all, they had robbed a nation of savers, the argument went, disregarding the laws of nature in a binge of speculative excess. Roosevelt immediately called a bank holiday, four days to stabilize a system in which nine thousand banks had failed in three years. And then he took to the airwaves.

"I want to talk for a few minutes about banking."

It was his first radio chat with the country, just days after his inaugural. Roosevelt tried to reassure people that when the banks reopened, the system would stay afloat. But privately, he told reporters later in what he thought was an off-the-record session, he was afraid that there was not enough money to prevent another run. "On Friday afternoon last we undoubtedly didn't have adequate currency," he said to the informal press gathering. "No question about it: there wasn't enough circulating money to go around." He called Congress into session and signed the Emergency Banking Bill into law — eight hours after it had been introduced. It worked. By the end of Roosevelt's first week in office, deposits exceeded withdrawals. A few months later, more provisions were added to the new law, insuring individual deposits up to ten thousand dollars. He told people they could take their savings out of mattresses and from beneath the floor. The government would back their dollars.

Next up: try to save the farm. Free-market agricultural economics was over, for good. Look what it had done, Roosevelt said: America had produced more food than any country in history, and farmers were being run off the land, penniless, while the cities couldn't feed themselves. The average farmer was earning three hundred dollars a year — an 80 percent drop in income from a decade earlier. From now on, government would try to shape the price and flow of food. To force prices up enough for farmers to make a living, Roosevelt had the government buy surplus corn, beans, and flour, and distribute it to the needy. Over six million pigs were slaughtered, and the meat given to relief organizations. Crops were plowed into the ground — like slitting your wrist, to some farmers. In the South, when horses were first directed to the fields to rip out cotton, they balked. Next year, the government would ask cattlemen and wheat growers to reduce supply in return for cash. Hoover had been leery of meddling with the mechanics of the free market. Under Roosevelt, the government *was* the market. The Agricultural Adjustment Act created the framework, and the Civilian Conservation Corps drummed up the foot soldiers. They would try to stitch the land back together. Build dams, bridges. Restore forests. Keep water from running away. Build trails in the mountains, roads on the prairie, lakes and ponds. In May, Roosevelt signed a bill giving two hundred million dollars to help farmers facing foreclosure. Now, before some nester's land could be taken to satisfy a bank loan, there was a place of last resort.

The Volstead Act was amended to permit the sale of 3.2 percent beer, and by December, the rest of federal prohibition was gone. Signs went up in Boise City: "BEER IS HERE!" But some counties in the southern plains kept prohibition. Dalhart was still dry, meaning the whiskey stills would stay in business and prescriptions for spirits would continue at the drugstore.

That son of a Carolina cotton farmer, Big Hugh Bennett, continued to rage against the killing of the land by his countrymen. What was happening in Oklahoma, in particular, appalled him.

"It seems not so long ago since hundreds of homesteaders, at the crack of muskets fired by United States troops, were rushing into the

Cherokee Strip of Oklahoma for the purpose of locating free farm-steads," he said. "What has happened in this region since is tragic beyond belief."

Bennett could make these kinds of statements and not seem like a scientific nag or an urban elite, because he had an earthy populism. He milked cows and fed slop to hogs on his own farm. He chopped cordwood for winter fuel. He knew soil, but he also knew every farmer's daughter joke. He could talk cotton in the South, wheat in Kansas, oranges in California. He loved nothing more than digging with his big hands in earth that was the greatest of American endowments. And at the end of the day, he poured himself a few tumblers of bourbon and swapped tall tales.

Most scientists did not take Bennett seriously. Some called him a crank. They blamed the withering of the Great Plains on weather, not on farming methods. Basic soil science was one thing but talking about the fragile web of life and slapping the face of nature — this kind of early ecology had yet to find a wide audience. Sure, Teddy Roosevelt and John Muir had made conservation an American value at the dawn of the new century, but it was usually applied to brawny, scenic wonders: mountains, rivers, megaflora. And in 1933, a game biologist in Wisconsin, Aldo Leopold, had published an essay that said man was part of the big organic whole and should treat his place with special care. But that essay, "The Conservation Ethic," had yet to influence public policy. Raging dirt on a flat, ugly surface was not the focus of a poet's praise or a politician's call for restoration.

But one of the first things Franklin Roosevelt did was summon Bennett to the White House. Bennett said Americans in the nation's midsection had farmed too much, too fast. The land could not take that kind of assault. The greatest grassland in the world had been hammered and left without cover. The dusters that were just starting to make national news were not a work of God. And they would get worse. Well then, the president asked: was it possible to undo what man had done?

Bennett made no promises. He was forceful, he had charisma that Roosevelt liked, and he took to the task — as director of a new agency within the Interior Department set up to stabilize the soil — with relish. He had little money or staff. But Big Hugh was a showman and a scientist who knew his subject. If Roosevelt believed, as he said in his forgotten man speech, that the core problem of the Depression was that farmers and the small towns dependent on them had fallen completely out of the economy, Bennett was his intellectual soul mate as he looked at what caused the Great Plains to break down. He knew in his heart that something profound had occurred, that man had changed nature. The balance would have to be restored from the ground up. Bennett must get people to see the crisis in a different way, to accept some of the blame. It called for a period of shock therapy. By some estimates, more than eighty million acres in the southern plains were stripped of topsoil. A rich cover that had taken several thousand years to develop was disappearing day by day.

Big Hugh was only a few weeks into the job when he started with speeches that attributed the failed farm system to "a pattern of land use that was basically unsound." Millions of years of runoff from the Rocky Mountains had deposited a rich loam over the plains, held in place by grass. For that land to be restored, Bennett suggested, people should look back to the days before the plow broke the prairie. The answer was there in the land, in what had been obvious to XIT cowhands and Comanche Indians all along: it was the best place in the world for grass and for animals that ate grass. But could the native sod ever be put back in place, the balance restored? Or had they killed it forever?

The drought did not take a holiday. Weather forecasts took on a dreary similarity: dry, with dusters. The wind rumbled through and tore off great sheets of prairie soil. As storms darkened the skies, people started to believe they were being punished for something awful. When Roosevelt took a trip to the plains, a farmer in North Dakota held up a hand-painted sign: "YOU GAVE US BEER. NOW GIVE US RAIN."

The president was not optimistic. "Beer was the easy part," he said.

10

Big Blows

T HE LAND WOULD NOT DIE an easy death. Fields were bare, scraped to hardpan in places, heaving in others. The skies carried soil from state to state. With no appreciable rain for two years, even deep wells were gasping to draw from the natural underground reservoir. One late winter day in 1933, a battalion of heavy clouds massed over No Man's Land. At midday, the sun disappeared. Lights were turned on in town in order to see. The clouds dumped layers of dust, one wave after the other, an aerial assault that covered streets in Boise City, buried brown pockets of grass, and rolled over big Will Crawford's dugout and the patch of ground where Sadie had tried to establish her garden with a tin-can irrigation system. They had to shovel furiously to avoid being swallowed by the enraged prairie.

Hazel Lucas Shaw watched the dust seep through the thinnest cracks in the walls of their rental house, spread over the china, into the bedroom, onto the sheets. When she woke in the morning, the only clean part of her pillow was the outline of her head. She taped all the windows and around the outer edge of doors, but the dust always found a way in. She learned never to set a dinner plate out until ready to eat, to cook with the pots covered, to leave no standing water out for long or it would turn to mud. She had decided to give up the teaching job that paid worthless scrip and to try and start a family. Her husband, Charles, had at last opened his business, a funeral home in the rental house. Town was supposed to be an easier place to live than a dead homestead to the south. But Boise City faced the same tormenter — the skies that brought no rain, only dirt. Some days Hazel put on her white gloves and sat at the table — a small act of defiance that seemed both silly and brave.

The temperature fell more than seventy degrees in less than twenty-four hours one February day in 1933. It reached fourteen below zero in Boise City and still the dust blew in with the arctic chill. Hazel tried everything to stay warm and keep the house clean. Dust dominated life. Driving from Boise City to Dalhart, a journey of barely fifty miles, was like a trip out on the open seas in a small boat. The road was fine in parts, rutted and hard, but a few miles later it disappeared under waves of drifting dust. Unable to see more than a car length ahead, the Shaws followed telephone poles to get from one town to the next.

At the Panhandle A&M weather station, they recorded seventy days of severe dust storms in 1933. Weather forecasting was still a rough skill in that year, a hit and miss game. The basic instruments for measuring air movement, temperature, and all that fell from the sky were little changed over the previous 350 years. The government predicted the weather by rounding up readings from more than two hundred reporting stations across the country and from air balloons, planes, and kite stations. The information was sent by Teletype to Washington twice a day. There, a map was drawn up and a forecast went out from the weather bureau for different regions of the nation. It was based on the movement and struggle between high and low barometric pressure — an ancient way of predicting weather. The forecast always originated in the capital, which is one reason why older, more skeptical nesters still referred to weather prediction by its nineteenth-century term — the "probability." A hardy homily such as "Clear moon, frost soon" or "Red sky at night, sheep herder's delight, red sky in the morning, sheep herder take warning" was more trusted, and not just by those who worked the land. During his days as an airmail carrier, Charles Lindbergh said he ignored the official weather bureau forecast; it was useless. Throughout the 1920s, as one technological marvel after the other changed American life, the tools of weather forecasting remained items that would have been familiar to

Benjamin Franklin. And there was a dire need for some sense of what tomorrow would bring, especially with the dawn of widespread air travel. When weather turned lethal without notice, it killed people — sometimes in large numbers. For tornadoes, there were no warnings at all. A big twister roared through the Midwest in 1925, killing 957 people. The weather bureau's only great achievement was taking accurate measurements: atmospheric pressure, days without rain, total precipitation, swings in temperature, and wind speed.

March and April 1933 were the worst months of the year — a two-month block of steady wind throwing fine-grained dirt at the High Plains. The cold snap had killed what little wheat had been planted last fall. There was now an expanse of fallow, overturned land nearly half the size of England, no pasture for cattle, and no feed for other animals.

Fred Folkers spent most of his days shoveling dust. The shovel was his rescue tool; he never went anywhere without it. In a long day's blow, the drifts could pile four feet or more against fences clogged with tumbleweeds, which created dunes, which then sent dust off in other directions. He tried to modify the fences so dunes would move along, below the rails. Some mornings, Folkers did not recognize his land as the shifting dunes produced dust mounds with ripples holding the imprint of winds from overnight. Other mornings, his car was completely covered. And after he wiped his car clean, it was hell to start it, the dust clogging the carburetor.

He knew now he was probably going to lose the orchard, the last living thing on the Folkers farm. All the pails of water he'd hauled from the tank to the little grove of trees seemed for naught. His living memory patch of the old Missouri home, the peach and cherry trees, plum and apple, the gooseberry, currants, and huckleberry — they could not live through the howling dirt of 1933.

At the end of April, with no green on the land and no rain from overhead, came a duster that lasted twenty hours. For most of the storm, the winds blew at better than forty miles an hour. The dust was strong and abrasive enough to scrape the paint off the Folkers house, to get into the digestive system of cattle.

"Here comes another roller!" was the shout in Boise City, a warning to take cover. People watched the horizon darken with the approach of the duster. There was no escape. They could not stay outside for fear of getting lost or of choking on a blast of gritty air. And while indoors offered protection from the wind, it was no respite from the fine granules.

Lindbergh, the greatest aviator of his day, flew into this corrosive air space on May 6 while trying to cross the Texas Panhandle. His plane choked, the engine sputtering, and bucked wildly in the turbulent currents. Six years earlier, Lindbergh had crossed the Atlantic, flying just barely above the ocean on his way to Paris. Now, he could not cross the flattest part of the United States. He made a forced landing in the part of Texas where a promoter had tried to plant a part of Norway. He was greeted by children as a god sent down from the heavens, with front-page headlines throughout the southern plains. Lindbergh wanted no part of it. He seemed spooked by the dusters. He slept in his plane, then flew out after a two-day delay.

One day in late May, just as the high wind season started to ebb, the dust disappeared, and out came the blue empty skies that had so enticed nesters in years past. But by midmorning, dark clouds were back. They looked like rain clouds — an answer to everyone's prayers. Bigger, darker, heavier clouds were on top of them — dusters piggybacked on a system that would normally bring only rain. In the early evening, the skies broke, delivering hard brown globs of moisture — rain and hail, which had picked up dust on the way down, falling as mud pellets. The dirty torrent smashed rooftops, buckled car hoods, made cows bawl in agony. More was on the way. A funnel cloud appeared.

"Twister!"

People raced for shelter, praying for deliverance. The tornado touched down in Liberal, Kansas, near the Oklahoma border, in the heart of tornado alley. It lifted roofs from barns, knocked down warehouse walls, pushed houses from their foundations. An old broomcorn factory was completely destroyed. Stores were pulverized into piles of sticks. Windows shattered. Downtown was reduced to a heap of timber and bricks. Four people were killed; nearly eight hundred were left without homes. And then not long after the tornado swept through, destroying the heart of one of the bigger towns on the High Plains, the mud pellets came again, tossed from the sky, a final insult.

In the summer, winds knocked down telephone poles on the Texas Panhandle and shoved aside grain silos holding the wheat that nobody wanted. At the end of summer, another twister, this one at the southern edge of No Man's Land, hit the area. This furious funnel was strong enough to carry off the roof of a hotel. For the record, there had never been a drier summer.

The High Plains lay in ruins. From Kansas, through No Man's Land, up into Colorado, over in Union County, New Mexico, and south into the Llano Estacado of Texas, the soil blew up from the ground or rained down from above. There was no color to the land, no crops, in what was the worst growing season anyone had seen. Some farmers had grown spindles of dwarfed wheat and corn, but it was not worth

An Oklahoma farmhouse, 1930s

the effort to harvest it. The same Texas Panhandle that had produced six million bushels of wheat just two years ago now gave up just a few truckloads of grain. In one county, 90 percent of the chickens died; the dust had got into their systems, choking them or clogging their digestive tracts. Milk cows went dry. Cattle starved or dropped dead from what veterinarians called "dust fever." A reporter toured Cimarron County and found not one blade of grass or wheat.

People from four states gathered in Guymon, Oklahoma, east of Boise City, to share stories and plead for help. The Red Cross was overwhelmed, with far more people begging for assistance than the agency could respond to. Some relief was on the way from one of the new agencies of the federal government: it would provide enough money to pay men to shovel dust from the streets of Guymon, Liberal, Texhoma, Shattuck, Dalhart, and Boise City. The wage was one dollar a day, and a man could not work more than three days a week in order to give others a chance.

A distress telegram was sent to Congress from the sodbusters of the High Plains. It was something these nesters never thought they would do — beg. In Dalhart, the editor of the *Texan,* John L. McCarty, was against asking for help. It was humiliating, his town with its head down and hand out. He preferred defiance, scoffing at people who complained of the dust — "the softies, the tenderfeet, the cry babies," he called them. Still, people on the dust-sweeper rolls and those who had broken the prairie grass, only to have it break them, took up a collection and sent out the urgent request, a telegram signed by 1,500 people:

WE ARE FIGHTING DESPERATELY TO MAINTAIN OUR HOMES, SCHOOLS, CHURCHES, AND VARIOUS ENTERPRISES TO MEET LOCAL NEEDS. WE DON'T WANT DOLE OR DIRECT RELIEF. WE WANT WORK.

Other farmers were leaving, joining the exodus of tenants from the drought-crushed eastern half of Oklahoma and from Arkansas and Missouri, where cotton farming had crashed. But most people decided to hunker down and see it through. After all, there was a new president. The drought was longer and harsher than anyone could remember, but this had to be the bottom of the pit. The law of averages said so.

One night just before dinner, after clearing the floor, the dining table, the lampshades, and the kitchen counter of their daily dust at her home in Boise City, Hazel Shaw put on her white gloves and smiled. She had an announcement for her husband.

"I'm pregnant."

III

BLOWUP

1934–1939

11

Triage

THE GOVERNMENT MEN came to the High Plains in the second year of the new president's term with a plan to kill as many farm animals as possible. There was not a buyer in the hemisphere for the wretched-looking cattle stumbling over the prairie, many of them blind, their ribs outlined through the skin, scabby with sores, and their insides all bound up with dust. And nobody was going to get much grain out of this anemic, flyaway ground, not with the drought in its third year, and less than five inches of rain so far by mid-1934. Every day presented another bleak task for a farmer who had raised a calf to maturity only to see it break a leg in a blinding dust cloud or choke trying to get a breath. It made silent men cry to see herbivores on what had been the greatest grassland under the heavens dying cruel deaths from this lifeless, cursed turf. A cow could live only so long chewing salted tumbleweeds and swallowing mud. The job of the government men was to set things right by drying up the market of surplus beef, hogs, and grain. They gathered a crowd of gaunt-faced nesters into the Palace Theater in Boise City. In between takes of Mae West's *I'm No Angel*, they put an offer on the table:

Tell you what: bring those tired animals to us and we'll give you cash dollar, up to sixteen bucks a head. The ones that can still walk, the cows with a pinch of flesh left between their bones and saggy skin, we'll send down to a butchering plant in Amarillo, and the meat will go to hungry people. The others will probably fetch no more than a

145

dollar — the minimum buyout — and we are going to kill them here. Could use a cowboy or two to help us along. That's our deal.

Okay, fine by me, said Fred Folkers. He was down to a few head of cattle, and they were having trouble standing. He had a dairy cow still and milked her, but what came into the pail looked like chocolate milk, and he had to put a dishrag into the bucket to draw out the dust.

And Hazel Lucas's uncle, C.C., agreed it was probably the only way to get a dollar to keep the homestead going. He did not like the idea of shooting your cow in the head and shoving her into a ditch after raising her from infancy. But it was either that or watching her die, gagging like the others, or fevered and blind. It was wrong keeping an animal alive in the No Man's Land of 1934. Lucas's old milking cow was already gone, and he had just a small herd of cattle and two horses left. Some people asked the government men what would replace the cattle after they had been shot. What were they supposed to do now? The year before, the government had bought up more than five million hogs for slaughter, focusing on "piggy sows," or pregnant pigs. The plan was to get farm animals off the land. Period. Shrink the expansion. The government men had set a goal of killing eight million cattle over the next year to bring prices up enough for farmers to get a fair return on their labor. As they worked the new towns of the southern plains, they found the worst stragglers they had seen. Nearly one out of every three cattle bought were judged too sickly to be butchered. The Lucas animals were typical. Uncle C.C.'s cattle were condemned; not a one was healthy enough to get shipped to Amarillo. The government men told Lucas he could do the shooting, or they could let the cowboy they had hired execute the Lucas animals. He chose the cowboy.

On the day the Lucas farm animals were rounded up for killing, the children went down to the cellar, closed the door, and covered their ears. Gunshots rang out, a bullet to the head for each animal, and the children started to cry. Now only a few horses remained to show for C.C.'s time on this Oklahoma dirt. Everything else was gone. One of his daughters tried to scrounge up enough feed to keep the horses alive, but the animals could not hold down tumbleweed like the cattle. One horse chewed on the fence. The dust had piled so high that the fence line was a shifting dune, which made it hard for the horse to stand. Later, the mare was found on her side, nibbling at the edge of a fence, gums bloodied and eyes clogged with dirt. She died shortly thereafter. Hazel Lucas tried to soothe the children, her nieces and nephews. *Think about tomorrow. Think about green fields and new life. Think about water. Think about clear skies and spring the way it used to be . . .*

Hazel took the children up to the Kohler ranch north of town, by the trickled remains of the Cimarron River. It had become a Sunday drive destination for people in Boise City — a place to see something green. Julius Kohler was one of the first Anglo settlers in No Man's Land; he came to the edge of the territory in 1902, when the grass was free from the Texas line to Kansas. Using horses, Kohler built eight miles of canals from the Cimarron River to his ranch. Just a crawl of water made it out of the river now, the worst drought the Kohlers had ever seen. All but one of their springs were dry. By diverting just enough liquid from the Cimarron, they were able to keep a small oasis going while everything else in No Man's Land looked like the surface of Mars. Hazel walked the children over the grass, had them touch the original prairie. This is what it all used to look like when our family came here, Hazel told the children. New life amid the death — think of that, the story of No Man's Land. Renewal. One of the reasons Hazel was going to bring a baby into this blast furnace of coarse air was because she believed the land could look like the little patch at Kohler ranch. Someday. But the Sunday drive back to Boise City would grind up hope, as they passed one blowing, sandblasted homestead after the other. The town itself was cloaked in a haze; you could not tell you were close to Boise City until the car rumbled over the railroad tracks into town. Used to be, Boise City looked like toy buildings on a Monopoly board; it was an oasis as well. But now it was dirt-wrapped and camouflaged, without any distinct lines, a half-existence amid the runaway prairie.

People who traveled through predicted it would all soon be gone — houses, towns, even railroad tracks. "The tracks will soon be mere streaks of rust through a howling desert, which separate by 1,500 miles the two inhabitable coastal regions," wrote a reporter for *New*

Outlook magazine in May 1934. There was an exodus, small but steady, of people who folded their lives in No Man's Land and headed for some place where the sky was not so enraged.

South in Dalhart, the government men bought four thousand cattle for killing. Those animals did not look any better than the cattle of No Man's Land. Some were dying of thirst and starving. Roaming over the tattered remains of the XIT, they looked for water until they dropped, their tongues coated with sand. Bam White took a short-term job, getting two dollars a day shooting cattle, work for a cowboy. The government hired cowboys because they would not go soft when it came time to look a hungry, wet-nosed calf in the eye and shoot her dead. The old XIT hands took the emaciated cattle out to a ditch near town and gunned them down. People in town were welcome to come pick over the carcasses, looking for salvageable meat, before the burial. Sometimes the animals didn't die right away; they lingered in pain and moaned, and their cries were carried by the wind at night, people in town said. It was hard for Bam to explain to the children what they were doing, killing animals that had been brought here for people to make a living. Nothing was right in the world anymore. And these animals were gonna die anyway, might as well get a buck or two for killing them.

Fifty years earlier the government had cleared this land of the finest grass-eating creature on four legs, had cleared away every bison to make room for cattle. Barely one year after Quanah Parker's Comanche had surrendered and were pushed off the treaty land that had been promised to the Lords of the Prairie for eternity, Charles Goodnight moved his cattle onto the grass, pronouncing it the richest sod on earth. That was yesterday — an eye blink in time. And now the cattle brought to replace the bison were being mowed down because they were starving: they could not stand, could not drink, could not live another day, and even if they could people were unable to make a living off them. The government killings were supposed to restore market balance, not right nature's wrong. It was a sick thing, harder still to comprehend, to cowboys like Bam White. The XIT was so exhausted that barely a blade of grass was seen in the summer of 1934; a ranch that had been bigger than some Eastern states was a drifting wasteland, and probably all the better that most days the wind blew dust so hard a man could not see far enough to get a sense of how awful it was. That prairie writer, the Kansas newspaperman William Allen White, said he knew what was to blame, and it was time for people in the Great Plains to look inside themselves and acknowledge what they had done. He blamed the wheat farmer who broke ground at a gluttonous pace.

"His good times had ruined him," White wrote.

The Fourth of July was so hot nobody wanted to stir. Same as the day before, and the day before that. Winds were down a bit, but dust was in the air. People wore scarves or one of the surgical masks distributed by the Red Cross. It was a rare person who did not have the dust hack — a gut-turning cough. If you smoked, and most people rolled their own cigarettes, it made it all the tougher to get through a night without the lungs trying to shake out prairie topsoil coated with nicotine. Thanks to the government cattle-culling operation, there was a little money coursing through town. John McCarty tried to get people out of their smothered dugouts and houses. There was a baseball game at the Dalhart diamond, fifteen cents a head to watch the cellar-dwelling Texans take on the Clayton nine, composed mostly of cousins of Don Juan Lujan. The rabbit drives were on hold because it was too hot to club animals. And while nobody felt like going out into sun-scorched fields and corralling big-eared pests, the campaign against rabbits continued nonetheless. It was us or them, many people felt. The Chamber of Commerce passed the hat for money to hire a man who claimed a good knowledge of how to mix a large batch of poison, and he was contracted to find a biological solution to the rabbit problem.

McCarty kept his pledge to stress the good news in his paper.

"Conditions are going to be much brighter and better," McCarty wrote in his column, "and when they are we will hardly realize what has happened."

He tried to dissuade every person who considered leaving Dalhart.

Move out of the Texas Panhandle for California? He argued that Dalhart had more sunny days than California, that its people were hardier, its soil better, and that the long drought was in its last gasp.

"The law of averages are working in our favor now," he wrote. "We are overdue for rain, prosperity and lots of good things, and it is coming as sure as two plus two makes four."

It would take a powerful dose of amnesia to block out what had happened on the High Plains, but McCarty gave it his best.

"Aside from wind and sandstorms," he wrote, "there is really no disagreeable weather in the north Panhandle."

Beer was back in Dalhart, after a sixteen-year absence. The Busy Bee Café sold cold pints for a nickel a pop. But liquor was still against the law. The Number 126 house, having survived McCarty's stillborn campaign, went about its business of selling sex out of sight in the mustard-colored house, though the girls tried to be a little less conspicuous. For people who did not like baseball, whores, or cold beer for their diversions, the Reverend Joe Hankins held a revival on the Fourth of July, at the First Baptist Church, titled, "What's Wrong with Card-Playing and Dancing." He swept the dust off the pews and welcomed a hundred young people. Following the sermon, the kids crowded to the front of the church and pledged never to dance and never to play cards.

On May 9, 1934, a flock of whirlwinds started up in the northern prairie, in the Dakotas and eastern Montana, where people had fled the homesteads two decades earlier. The sun at midmorning turned orange and looked swollen. The sky seemed as if it were matted by a window screen. The next day, a mass of dust-filled clouds marched east, picking up strength as they found the jet stream winds, moving toward the population centers. By the time this black front hit Illinois and Ohio, the formations had merged into what looked to pilots like a solid block of airborne dirt. Planes had to fly fifteen thousand feet to get above it, and when they finally topped out at their ceiling, the pilots described the storm in apocalyptic terms. Carrying three tons of dust for every American alive, the formation moved over the Midwest. It covered Chicago at night, dumping an estimated six thousand tons, the dust slinking down walls as if every home and every office had sprung a leak. By morning, the dust fell like snow over Boston and Scranton, and then New York slipped under partial darkness. Now the storm was measured at 1,800 miles wide, a great rectangle of dust from the Great Plains to the Atlantic, weighing 350 million tons. In Manhattan, the streetlights came on at midday and cars used their headlights to drive. A sunny day, which had dawned cloudless, fell under a haze like that of a partial eclipse. From the observatory at the top of the Empire State Building, people looked into a soup unlike anything ever seen in midtown. They could not see the city below or Central Park just to the north. An off-white film covered the ledge. People coughed, rushed into hospitals and doctors' offices asking for emergency help to clear their eyes. The harbor turned gray, the dust floating on the surface. The grass of the parks and the tulips rising to break the Depression fog were coated in fine sand. From Governors Island, visibility was so bad a person could not see the boats just beyond the shore. Baseball players said they had trouble tracking fly balls.

Reporters rushed out to query the experts. "I spent my youth in the south, where such occurrences are more common, but I didn't remember one in which the dust was carried so high," said a New York meteorologist, Dr. James H. Scarr. "I can't say I like this air. It cuts off all my free-breathing."

The pyrheliometer, an odd-looking instrument that resembled something vaguely futuristic with an art deco touch, measured sunlight at 50 percent — that is, only half the ultraviolet rays of a normal sunny spring day made it to the city.

New York was a dirty city in 1934, the air clogged with auto exhaust and the effluents of thousands of small shops, factories, bakeries, and apartments. The air could be so hazardous that people with respiratory problems were advised to move out to the Western desert for life. On a typical day, the dust measured 227 particles per square millimeter — not a good reading for someone with health problems. But on May 11, the dust measured 619 particles per square millimeter. It got inside as well. In the NBC radio studios, air filters were changed hourly. A professor from New York University, Dr. E. E. Free, calculated that on the seventeenth floor of the Flatiron Building on Fifth

Avenue, the thickness of the dust was about forty tons per cubic mile, which meant all of New York City was under the weight of 1,320 tons.

New Yorkers did not like this monstrous visitor from the heartland. They had heard reports about blowing homesteads and had seen a few newsreels, but it was a world away, far beyond the Hudson River. On May 11, the orphaned land of the Great Plains came to the doorstep of the nation's premier city. For five hours, the cloud dumped dirt over New York. Commerce came to a standstill. The captain of a cargo ship, the *Deutschland,* delayed coming into anchor because he was not sure what had happened. The outline of the Statue of Liberty was barely visible, and it wore a coat of light gray topsoil. The *Deutschland*'s skipper said it reminded him of the Cape Verde Islands, where the sands of the Sahara blew out to sea.

"HUGE DUST CLOUD,
BLOWS 1,500 MILES,
DIMS CITY 5 HOURS"

That was the *New York Times* headline the next day. The paper called it "the greatest dust storm in United States history."

The storm moved out to sea, covering ships that were more than two hundred miles from shore. Its rear guard also spread south, leaving a taste of prairie soil in the mouths of members of Congress. Dust fell on the National Mall and seeped into the White House, where President Roosevelt was discussing plans for drought relief. Dust in Chicago, Boston, Manhattan, Philadelphia, and Washington gave the great cities of America a dose of what the people in the little communities of the High Plains had been living with for nearly two years. People in the cities wondered why the plains folks could not do something to hold their soil down. One man suggested laying asphalt over the prairie. Another idea was to ship junked cars to the southern plains, where they would be used as weights to hold the ground in place.

At least on the Eastern seaboard, the dust came and went like a snowstorm, and then the normal seasonal fluctuations resumed. But in No Man's Land or the Texas Panhandle or Kansas the seasons varied only by temperature or the ferocity of the wind. Dust blew every season. It had become life itself. Even snow brought little change from the choking gray and black. A snowstorm in March dumped twenty-one inches in No Man's Land, but it fell as dark flakes. They called it a "snuster," snow mixed with dust. St. Patrick's Day had beer but no sunlight — a duster hung over the land for sixteen hours. Late in the month, the sun was obscured for six days in a row. In January 1934, there were four dust storms in the southern plains, followed by seven in February, seven in March, fourteen in April — including one that lasted twelve hours — four in May, two in June and July, one in August, six in September, two in October, three in November, and four in December. That year was not even the worst. For most of these storms, daylight was still visible; the sky never went completely black. But visibility was reduced to a quarter mile or less.

The dust blew all over the Great Plains, but the worst and most persistent storms were in parts of five states — southern Colorado, southwestern Kansas, the Texas and Oklahoma Panhandles, and northeastern New Mexico. The government placed the geographic heart of the dust-lashed land in Cimarron County, in the middle of No Man's Land. In places where the cover of the land had not been completely stripped, the drifts swooshed in, leaving a fresh source of dust.

Even with Vaseline in their noses and respiratory masks over their faces, people could not keep from inhaling grit. Dust particles are extremely fine, sixty-three microns or smaller. By contrast, a period at the end of a typewritten sentence is three hundred microns. It could take less than an hour outside to darken one of the masks distributed by the Red Cross. The windows of houses were covered with wet sheets and blankets, the doors taped, the wall cracks stuffed with rags and newspapers. Men avoided shaking hands with each other because the static electricity was so great it could knock a person down. They also put cloth on their doorknobs and metal oven handles to inhibit the electric jolt. Car owners used chains, dragging them along the street as a ground for the electricity in the air. Hospitals postponed operations because they could not keep their surgical wards clean. And flour mills in Kansas had to curtail work because the dust mingled with grain.

"Rarely a day appears when at some time the dust clouds do not roll over," wrote Caroline Henderson, a Mount Holyoke College graduate and a farmer's wife who lived in No Man's Land just north of Boise City. Out of college, she had fallen for a farmer, and they made a go of it during the wheat boom. Their well gave them enough water to grow a big garden, slake the thirst of hogs, chickens, and cows, and even bring a few flowers to blossom. The wheat shined in the good years, and Caroline had a telephone installed and got a daily newspaper delivered, bringing the world to their homestead. The bust left the Hendersons living a subsistence life in a place where people seemed to age rather quickly. A forty-five-year-old woman looked sixty, it was said, and a man of the same age without a deeply creased face was a rarity. They lost the phone, the newspaper, the garden, the farm animals, and all their crops. By 1934, they had gone three years without income from the land. Caroline's daily tasks began to seem ever more meaningless and hopeless. She clung to small things — a houseplant in the windowsill, pictures of the farm when it was full of grain, a belief in tomorrow. And through the first three years of the dust, she never lost her faith in the land. She felt "a primitive feeling of kinship with the earth — our common mother," Caroline said, writing in a letter to a friend. She made hand towels out of cement sacks and used cheap lye for washing clothes, though it left her hands so rough it frightened her. By 1934, they did not even bother to plant a crop. The Hendersons had some chickens, a few animals, and a garden, enough to keep them alive. Caroline gathered cow chips for fuel, but as the pasture disappeared, and the animals starved, the supply of "prairie coal" dried up as well.

Like her neighbors, Henderson's thirst for the base elements of life grew with every arid, dust-filled day.

"We dream of the faint gurgling sound of dry soil sucking in the grateful moisture," she wrote to a friend in the East, "but we wake to another day of wind and dust and hopes deferred."

12

The Long Darkness

T HE DUST PRESSED HARD on the High Plains when Hazel
Shaw traveled over the state line to Clayton to have her baby in
the spring. Expectant mothers were told to stay in the hospital
or a rest home for a month before their delivery date, and Hazel did
not want to take chances. Boise City had no hospital. In New Mexico
the air was supposed to be cleaner at the higher ground a mile above
sea level. From Clayton, the horizon was not all flat: mesas and ancient volcanoes broke the skyline, and on those days when the light
was just right in the evening it was as enchanting as the best parts of
New Mexico. The light was one of the reasons the Herzsteins loved
Clayton. In town, Charles got his wife settled into a boarding house
near the hospital, the doors and windows sealed three times over with
sheets and tape to keep pregnant women from breathing particles.

Charles returned to Boise City. After one week, a message came: it
was time. He fired up the Model-T and headed down the dirt road to
New Mexico. The distance was barely sixty miles, but with the drifts
it could take half a day to make the drive. Even though the road was
mostly straight, and he was driving on a cloudless day in April,
Charles could not see more than a few car lengths ahead of him. Every
driver in No Man's Land knew this kind of blizzard well by now. He
paced the Model-T, afraid of crashing head-on with another car coming out of the dust the other way. At times, it was like vertigo, or driving in space. He hung his head out the window to keep track of the
roadside ditch, and in that way he was able to follow a line toward

Clayton. The message had been urgent — Hazel was starting her contractions, the baby was on its way. Sand heaved up and over the front of the car, swirling, creeping across the hood and into his lap. On sections of the road where the wind had scraped everything down to hardpan, the traction was good, and Charles sped up, doing nearly thirty-five miles an hour. But just as he started to make good time, the car plowed into a drift. He was stuck, the Model-T held by dust that had glommed onto the width of the road. He jumped out and tried to scoop away sand with the shovel he always carried. But the drift was too deep, and even as he shoveled, more dust blew onto the dune. The Model-T was trapped in nearly three feet of sand.

Unable to free the car, he took off on foot. There was nothing to see in any direction, just the predatory beige sand in his eyes, his hair, blowing against his face. The authorities had warned people not to travel alone and particularly not to walk when a duster was on. In Kansas, one farmer's car broke down and he set out on foot for help. He suffocated to death. But Shaw had no choice. His wife was giving birth. If he stayed in the car and waited for help, he could be buried by the time somebody came along. It would be dark in a few hours.

He followed the ditch line of the road until it came to a narrow lane that angled away to a small farmhouse. He figured he had walked, at a brisk pace, two miles. Shaw banged on the door of the shack and explained to the farmer what had happened. The farmer started his tractor and the two men rode back to the car. After tugging, digging, and a push from the tractor, they were able to free the Model-T.

Shaw continued toward Clayton. Anxious, thinking about the baby, worried about more drifts, he kept the speed up, pushing the car to its limit. When he came to a sudden swerve in the road, he was going too fast to correct his speed. The Model-T teetered on two wheels and tipped on its side. For an instant, Shaw thought he was pinned. He was bruised and bleeding but otherwise all right. As he crawled out the window, he saw two wheels still spinning in the dust. He was able to pry the car out of the dust and tip it back, right-side up. The engine started. He finished the drive and made it to St. Joseph's Hospital. Just as Hazel went into her high contractions, in walked a bruised, bleeding, dusty man, his eyelids clogged with mud, his fingers oiled and dirty.

Hazel gave birth to a girl late that day, April 7, 1934. They named her Ruth Nell. She was plump and seemed healthy, but the doctor was concerned about taking her outside. The air was not safe for a baby. He ordered Hazel to stay in the hospital for at least ten more days and remarked that the young family might want to consider moving out of No Man's Land. Others were buttoning up their homes and getting out before the dust ruined them. But the Lucas family had planted themselves in this far edge of the Oklahoma Panhandle at a time when there wasn't even a land office for nesters. They were among the first homesteaders. What would it mean for the pioneers to leave? And if they moved, it was not just the uncertainty of where to go and what to do but also the feeling that they would never again own something. It was a big step down from working on your own quarter-section to being adrift, with strangers staring at you like just another piece of Okie trash, saying you should be deported. Deported! Where? Uprooted, nesters were tumbleweeds. At least here, a hungry man had pride of place and ownership. The family optimism ran through Hazel. She and Charles had opened a business in Boise City and were not going anywhere. It was settled: no matter how ugly the air, no matter how dead the ground, how cashless the economy, new life in No Man's Land — Ruth Nell — was something that did not come around very often. The baby had to be savored and given a proper start in the place called home.

For others, 1934 was the worst year. In early May, the temperature reached one hundred degrees in North Dakota. Parts of Nebraska, spared some of the earlier storms, were starting to blow. Fields that had yielded twenty bushels of wheat per acre were lucky to get a single bushel. On eight million acres, crops were so withered that there was no harvest. Another two million acres were fallowed — not planted at all. With ten million acres bare, farmers in Nebraska fell into the same desperate straits as their neighbors to the south.

Not only was 1934 the driest year to date in the arid siege — just under ten inches of rain fell on the Oklahoma Panhandle — but the pockets of original buffalo grass that had kept sheep and some cattle alive were vanishing as well, smothered by dusters. About a third of Cimarron County was blowing, by the estimate of the ag man, Bill Baker. Some grass was under ten feet of sand. Other parts, stripped and buffed by the wind, were as hard as a basement floor. Even the Kohler ranch was losing the last of its grass, and they had irrigation water from the Cimarron River, a lifeblood that most people had lost. The Kohlers could spread water on the sod but could not keep it free of the galloping sheets of dust. They tried fences and windbreaks, but the rampaging soil skipped over the barriers and drifted anew. Nearly three dozen sheep choked to death in the Kohler corral, gagging on the dust.

Later that year, the government men offered contracts to wheat farmers if they agreed not to plant next year. This idea seemed immoral and not the least a bit odd to people when they first heard about it. Like the cattle slaughters, it was a part of a Roosevelt initiative to bring farm prices up by reducing supply — forced scarcity. In the end, many farmers were not going to plant anyway — what was the use, with no water? — so the idea that they could get money by agreeing to grow nothing was not a hard sell. More than twelve hundred wheat farmers in No Man's Land signed up for contracts and in turn got a total of $642,637 — an average of $498 a farmer. Thus was born a subsidy system that grew into one of the untouchable pillars of the federal budget. It was designed for poor grain growers, one foot in foreclosure, near starvation, pounded by dirt. And plenty of farmers were starving.

"I fell short on my crop this time," a farmer from Texas wrote President Roosevelt in late 1934. "I haven't got even one nickel out of it to feed myself and now winter is here and I have a wife and three little children, haven't got clothes enough to hardly keep them from freezing. My house got burned up three years ago and I'm living in just a hole of a house and we are in a suffering condition."

For people who had been without income since 1930, a check of $498 was a sufficient enough windfall to keep them on the land, though not enough to run a farm for another year. It allowed them, though, to exist. They paid just enough of their overdue taxes, and just enough of the outstanding interest on their bank loans, and just enough to get seed, to keep them from closing the door and walking away. Without the government, all of Cimarron County might have dissipated in the dust in 1934. For that year, the government bought 12,499 cattle, 1,050 sheep, and gave out loans to 300 farmers. The government estimated that 4,000 of the 5,500 families in six counties of the Oklahoma Panhandle were getting some form of relief, from a few dollars a week to work on road crews to forced scarcity payments. All told, nearly a million dollars came from Washington to the distant corner of No Man's Land.

Hugh Bennett thought if he could rest the land in some of these blowing prairie states, nature might have a shot at a comeback. Bennett was trying to change agricultural history. One idea was to put new growth on the bald grasslands, a restoration project that had never been tried before on such a scale. His other idea was to get individual farmers to break down their barriers of property and think beyond their fence lines. It wasn't enough for one farmer to practice soil conservation if his neighbor's land was blowing. Bennett wanted people to see the whole of the living plains, not the squares of ownership.

Bennett put one of Roosevelt's alphabet agencies, the Civilian Conservation Corps, to work on some of his early demonstration projects, and tried to inspire them with a sense of urgency about their mission.

"We are not merely crusaders," he said at a rally of CCC workers, "but soldiers on the firing line of defending the vital substance of our homeland."

Oklahoma's governor, Alfalfa Bill Murray, was furious as the first benevolent acts of the New Deal began to arrive on the southern plains. It was making the Sooner state into a bunch of "leaners," as he called them. Of course, Murray had run for president by promising every American an entitlement to the four B's — bread, butter, bacon, and beans. Patronage flowed from Alfalfa Bill outward. Now his old rival, the dandy with the tilted cigarette holder and the funny accent, was bypassing him; FDR was the face of salvation. Nearly one in five people were still unemployed, but government jobs had given four

million people a paycheck. Because there were far more willing workers than jobs, the government set a quota for each county based on
population. Fueled by his customary two pots of black coffee a day,
the titan from Toadsuck railed against Roosevelt and his public works
projects, calling him a communist. He quit the Democratic Party in
protest of the New Deal. But his power was ebbing away. He could
not use the National Guard to halt government help for farmers or to
keep people from building roads and bridges. The people in his state
loved the new president, and the papers were full of praise for the
New Deal. Murray became increasingly irritable. In one speech late in
the year, while puffing on a cigar, Murray lit into the president as
usual. Just then, a schoolboy raised a voice. Murray exploded, snapping at the child.

"You little screw worm!" the governor shouted at the boy. "Get out
of here!" Alfalfa Bill's political career never recovered.

One proposal that Murray had championed was a plan to dam the
Beaver River near Guymon, the first sizable town east of Boise City.
As envisioned by promoters in No Man's Land, the dam would hold
enough water to allow people to irrigate, and then they would no
longer have to rely on rain. And if the Beaver ran dry, as it often did,
they could mine the big aquifer that underlay the southern plains, the
Ogallala, for water. So long as they put water in a pen, it didn't matter
how it got there. Hydrologists were just starting to grasp the magnitude of the Ogallala: it was nearly the size of Lake Huron, nestled several hundred feet below the surface. With steam engines and windmills, nesters were barely able to reach the upper part of the aquifer.
But what if big natural gas engines were put to work, sucking the water up to make the arid land green? The technology was not there yet,
FDR was told. In the meantime, the plan to build a dam in No Man's
Land landed with a thud in Washington. Harold Ickes, the Interior
Secretary, was having second thoughts about encouraging people to
stay on the land. Ickes believed it was better to give people incentive
to leave. The land had been settled on the slogan of "a quarter-section
and independence," and now that quarter-section could kill you and
people were becoming dependent on the government. Ickes wanted

to get the land back into the public domain and move upward of half a million people out of the area. His idea was heresy to some — by peeling back manifest destiny, it was an admission that American settlement in the southern plains had been a colossal failure. By Ickes's reasoning, the High Plains could never be productive farmland again. Why delay the inevitable?

The president had his doubts about reverse homesteading. He did not want an uninhabited expanse of sifting sand in the middle of the country. Why not try and change the land itself? Roosevelt, like his fifth cousin Teddy, was an authentic conservationist from the start. As a child, he learned to love nature and was fascinated by the variety of plant life in the Hudson River Valley. When Roosevelt suggested planting a great wall of trees from the Canadian border to Texas, people derided the plan as a Soviet-style joke. If God wanted trees to grow on the Great Plains, he would have put them there himself. The wind blew too hard for saplings to take root; there was too little rain. But Roosevelt persisted: why not plant rows, and in between would be farmland protected from the wind, a "shelterbelt"?

"The forests are the lungs of our land," he said, "purifying our air and giving fresh strength to our people." The president asked the Forest Service to draw up a plan, to span the globe and see if there were tree species that could survive the hot breath of the plains in summer and the deep freezes of winter. At the same time, he asked Hugh Bennett and others to examine the larger question that Ickes had raised: whether to encourage any future farming at all, or to empty the plains before it was too late and the nation's midsection became a sandbox.

With the Kohler ranch losing the last of its green, the Cimarron River down to a feeble presence, and the other river in No Man's Land, the Beaver, dried up, the desire for water was all-consuming. Shallow wells, those of about eighty feet or less, were coming up dry, forcing nesters to carry water from neighbors' wells to their homes, or from town. The *Boise City News* ran a front-page picture of a pond the owner had created by pumping water into a basin, using a windmill for power.

"CIMARRON COUNTY OASIS" was the cut-line under the picture. In 1934, a simple pond in No Man's Land looked like heaven.

Fred Folkers lost his orchard, the last living thing on his ranch. It had been a struggle to keep the fruit trees alive through the previous two years, but 1934 delivered the knockout blow. In the spring, he had still carried buckets of water to the apples, peaches, and mulberries, but the garish orange sun bore down and the wind lashed away, and the drifts rose uncontrolled and buried the trees up to their necks until they gave up. Folkers was left with bare sticks poking out of the dunes.

Just to the north, the life-draining drought also killed the trees that Caroline Henderson, the college-educated farmer's wife, had nurtured.

"Our little locust grove which we cherished for so many years has become a small pile of fence posts," Caroline wrote to a friend.

The last of the grain left over from the big harvest of three years earlier was gone. Even the tumbleweeds that had kept farm animals alive were in short supply. Folkers had been one of the first nesters to salt his thistle, making it edible for cattle. Now some of his neighbors wondered: why couldn't people eat tumbleweeds as well? Ezra and Goldie Lowery, homesteaders in No Man's Land since 1906, came up with an idea to can thistles in brine. Friends asked them how they could eat such a thing, the nuisance weed of the prairie. It was as dry as cotton, as flavorless as cardboard, as prickly as cactus. Well, sure. Indeed they tasted like twigs, no debate there. But the Lowerys said these rolling thistles that the Germans had brought to the High Plains from the Russian steppe were good for you. High in iron and chlorophyll. Cimarron County declared a Russian Thistle Week, with county officials urging people who were on relief to get out to fields and help folks harvest tumbleweeds.

The Lowerys also started using a native plant for feed, the flowering yucca that clung to unplowed parts of No Man's Land. They dug up the roots, cut off the spines, and ground the tubes into food for cows. When mixed with a little cake meal, the pulverized yucca roots kept the animals alive, which in turn kept the milk and cream coming at a time when there was no money to buy groceries. But it also meant that yuccas, one of the last plants holding down the powdered prairie gumbo, were now being yanked from the ground. With these two innovations — canned tumbleweeds and ground yucca roots — the Lowerys, a family of five, were able to feed themselves.

It had been a long fall for them. During the wheat boom, the Lowerys traded in their horse and buggy for a Model-T, added two rooms to the house, doubling the size, put up wallpaper to cover the newspaper on the inside walls, got linoleum floors, replaced the scrub board with a hand-cranked washing machine, and bought a generator, powered by the wind, which allowed the family to listen to the radio. Now their cattle were gone, shot and buried in a ditch. The orchard had died. The fields were bare, and the family was digging roots and canning tumbleweed. Why not leave?

"I'm not gonna put my family in a soup line," said Ezra Lowery. "Not me. We have food here and a roof over our heads."

The experiences of families that had fled served as cautionary tales. A neighbor, Clarence Snapp, and his wife, Ethel, had moved out of Boise City that year to Arkansas, where it was supposed to be wetter, with more opportunity. Clarence had been so poor when he married Ethel that he borrowed his mama's wedding ring; it was meant to

Boise City, Oklahoma, April 1936

be temporary, he said. In Arkansas, Clarence worked in the fields, digging turnips and sweet potatoes. But he never made a dime. He was paid in his diggings, as he told his neighbors when he returned to No Man's Land.

The Ehrlichs tried grinding up thistle for cattle feed, but it did not seem to work as it did for the Lowerys; their stock herd was thinning, unable to sustain itself. Newborns came out sickly and small. For Willie Ehrlich, the only surviving boy from a family of ten, who was trying to build a life by following in his father's footsteps, the calves were his future. But he could see at birth that the animals would not live, that they looked half-formed, sickly, not ready for life. Sometimes, it made him cry to kill his calves at birth, using the blunt end of an axe to crush their heads. He was married, with two children of his own, still living with his parents on the homestead the Ehrlichs had acquired in 1900 after getting off the immigrant train. The travails of his father, George, fleeing the czar's army in Russia, surviving that typhoon at sea, and living through the cold hatred of people who thought all German Americans were suspect, gave Willie and his father enough faith they could crawl through this long hole of dirt and depression. The Ehrlichs had established themselves with a typical homestead — 160 acres, a quarter-section big enough for cows, a garden, hogs, a few rows of oats, and some wheat. Nearly all of it was gone, reduced to a barren patch in the dun-colored air around the Texas-Oklahoma border. They lived on what they could make and store. After killing a hog, they would trim off the fat and use it for canning gel or mix it with lye to make soap. The meat was salted and rubbed with a solution of brown sugar and brine. They would let it dry for weeks, hanging from the windmill, then rub it again in salt and sugar, injecting the solution near the bones with a syringe. It would go into a bag and hang in the basement for months. They ate everything but the squeal.

Ehrlich's neighbor, Gustav Borth, did not have even a hog to slaughter for his winter sausage, or cow chips for fuel. He borrowed twenty-five dollars from a bank — pledging part of his homestead and his combine to buy coal for his stove. A proud man, descendant of a line of Germans who prospered after Catherine the Great opened

Russia to them, Borth was crushed by the America of 1934. Deeply homesick and disillusioned, Borth would go behind the shed of his farm, trying to hide from his family, and there he would cry. His daughter, Rosa, saw him several times as he wept; he was hunched over, the tears pouring out of him. It broke her heart. He sold the last of his cattle to the government for seven dollars a head. With this money, the children wanted shoes. Rosa Borth, age fourteen, had only a single pair, and she had outgrown them. She painted them black for church, white for school. When the weather was warm, she went barefoot. Next year, Rosa's mother told her — shoes will come next year, with the rains. Rosa was frightened after seeing her father, the brave bull who broke the Oklahoma crust by hand, crying behind the shed. She could go a while longer without shoes. Her father was afraid of losing his combine — his last possession of any worth. Borth owed four hundred dollars on the machine that helped deliver wheat in the boom years. Four hundred dollars — it looked like a Mount Everest of debt. He had no money for his little girl's shoes, let alone for payments on a debt like that. His sobs behind the shed were carried by the wind.

Some Germans gave up. They could not go back to the Russian steppe. In Stalin's grip, the old homes were no longer safe. Germans who stayed behind in the villages on the Volga River had been routed, their houses confiscated. In America, the ones who now joined the exodus of tenant farmers from Arkansas, Missouri, and eastern Oklahoma moved to the orchard country of Washington State, or north to Minnesota, or to Saskatchewan.

For people in No Man's Land without a cow or a hog of their own, there were three ways to get food. They could wait on the soup line that had opened a few blocks from the courthouse in Boise City. They could wait on another sort of food line, this one courtesy of Sheriff Hi Barrick. If it wasn't sugar from the bootleggers, which the sheriff gave out free, it was roadkill, which he had his deputies bring in for distribution. There were always takers for the critters smashed by a car or a train on a dust-clogged highway or track. Their third option: they could steal food.

Crimes were no longer petty in the sheriff's jurisdiction. One man took a car by force in broad daylight, sticking a gun to the head of the driver.

The sheriff lived in the courthouse, next to the jail; Hi Barrick and his wife, Inez, raised their three boys there. The kids roller skated and played marbles and catch in the hallways, weaving among the legal proceedings and jailings. Inez ran a business on the side sewing suits for lawyers — $3.50 for a three-piece job, tailor-made. Living next to the jail was better than their last home, a dugout. Peering out the window of his home and office, Barrick learned to judge when a heavy duster had moved along by the First State Bank sign across the street. When he could see the sign, it was clear enough to drive.

The handsome mugs of Bonnie Parker and Clyde Barrow, in their mid-twenties, were posted in Barrick's office. Joyriding, robbing banks, and killing their way through Texas, Oklahoma, Arkansas, and Missouri, the Barrow gang was declared Public Enemy Number One by a law enforcement posse headed by a former Texas Ranger. Bonnie and Clyde made fools of cops in dozens of counties, once kidnapping a lawman and having him steal a car battery to replace one in their stolen roadster. Bonnie wrote a poem for her mama, which the newspapers published. She sensed their imminent death and said that she and Clyde were friends to all but snitches and stoolies. It contributed to their heroic stature among some people in No Man's Land. They robbed banks, just as the banks had robbed people. But they were killers as well, as Barrick reminded people. With that pair on the loose, hungry people floating through town, and bootleggers still selling the hard fuel that was illegal in this part of Oklahoma, the sheriff had no time for politics. Though he was a Republican in a county where eight out of ten people gave their vote to Democrats, Barrick was respected. It was no secret how much he despised working at the foreclosure auctions for John Johnson's bank every Monday on the steps of the courthouse; he had even tried to get out of them until he was told by the court that it was his legal duty to stand by as some nester's land was sold for pennies on the dollar. These forced sales were just about the only real estate business left in No Man's Land. Plenty of farms were for sale on the open markets, but there were no buyers. When asked by a reporter about his plans, Barrick said, "I haven't anything new to say. Just tell 'em I'm running again."

Barrick at least could expect to keep his salary — $125 a month. Some teachers had gone nearly two years without pay, living on the room and board of a student's parents and nothing else. Hazel Shaw thought she could use her "salary," the scrip, to buy groceries. But the bank stopped honoring the school scrip when it became clear the system was bankrupt. The county's coffers were empty. By 1934, more than 60 percent of property owners were delinquent in their taxes in Cimarron County. They stopped paying because they had nothing. For the schools, heated by stoves burning cow chips, with dust drifts covering windows, it meant they could no longer afford books. The children would have to continue with broken-spined, ragged old texts perforated by the abrasive air of No Man's Land. Cimarron County High School fell into further disrepair; it was one of the most forlorn sites in a town of dirty-faced buildings, just two clapboard shacks attached at the shoulder. Before the dust, parents had been able to clean the windows and keep the roof in shape. Now the exterior was worn, as if it had been chipped by vandals, the gutters had fallen away, and the windows were covered with torn sheets splotched with three years' worth of uplifted soil. Children ran the streets, dirty and hungry; some had simply been abandoned.

"We are getting deeper and deeper in dust," the *Boise City News* wrote.

On May 23, 1934, Bonnie and Clyde were ambushed outside a gang member's family home in rural Louisiana, their bodies pummeled with lead from rounds of Browning automatic rifles. Bonnie died in a red dress, her favorite color. She was twenty-four. The papers had a field day with pictures of the former Texas Ranger with his bloody prey, and then it was back to the dreary routine of life in a dusty fog.

Buildings that had been fresh-painted in Boise City's blush of youth stood decrepit and raw. A town that had been named for its phantom trees now looked nearly treeless. The train station where suitcase farmers had poured into town stood windblown and empty. The grain silos had not been stuffed with fresh wheat for three years, and dust blew up against the sides of hollow barns and hardened, forming caked barriers. The defiance, evident at the start of the Depression when the county proudly turned down relief, was gone. In its place was a sense of doom, as if No Man's Land were being punished by God. Some ministers told people they must have done something wicked to deserve these awful times. The newspaper conveyed this sentiment as well; civic chauvinism disappeared from the pages of the *Boise City News*. The paper ran a front-page drawing of the Grim Reaper with a death grip over No Man's Land and began a piece on the storms with a citation from Ezekiel:

"Behold, I have smitten my hand at thy dishonest gain which thou has made."

Hazel Shaw did not think she had come by anything — her little nest in the funeral home, the new baby girl — by dishonest gain. The ministers were referring to the wheat bonanza, which seemed eons ago: all the people buying new cars, dancing late, drinking bootleg hooch, purchasing washing machines on credit, plowing up more ground to keep up with the unnatural float of grain prices — up, up, up, more, more, more. Hazel was religious, but her God was not full of vengeance. Her God was hope. Hazel lived across the street from St. Paul's Methodist Church, a reminder that the Lord was in her neighborhood at all times. At night after she had finished draping the windows in fresh sheets and sweeping out the dust, Hazel rocked baby Ruth Nell to sleep, telling her things would soon get better, the sky would clear again. It was an early winter on the High Plains, the blue northers charging down in October. Some trees never leafed out that year; it was a fall without color, just as it had been a spring and summer of gray.

One morning while Hazel rocked her baby, she saw in the pale light a small coffee box on the steps of the church across the street. She walked outside to her front porch and took a second look. There was a coat thrown over the box. She went inside to start the day's chores and forgot about it. Ruth Nell's crib was in the one corner of the bedroom that Hazel tried to keep spotless. She scrubbed it down daily, washed the baby's blankets. She gummed the windows up fresh.

The store in town sold a five-hundred-foot roll of house-sealing tape for thirty-five cents, promoted through an ad that read "Mrs. House-wife, Keep That Dust Out by Sealing Your Windows with Gummed Tape." Her chores done, she visited with her Grandma Loumiza, the original Lucas homesteader who lived south, near Texhoma. Grandma Lou said she'd never seen the land so mean-edged. It was a danger to breathe, and Grandma Lou was starting to show it, coughing until she fell to the ground. A widow for two decades, she was field-tough, able to do any chore a man could do on her homestead. But these fits of hacking were debilitating.

That night, a light snow mixed with dust began to fall, leaving a dirty, frothy covering on Boise City. Hazel noticed the coffee box and the coat still on the church steps; they had been there all day. The next morning, with the temperature well below freezing and several inches of brown snow on the ground from the snuster, Hazel looked outside: the coat and box had not been moved. She walked across the street to the steps, brushed back the snow, stripped away the coat. There was a baby inside, blue-faced, barely moving, perhaps no more than four pounds, no bigger than a garden squash. Hazel rushed home and tried to warm the baby, holding her close and rubbing her. She heated milk and got some hot fluids inside. Her husband summoned the minister, a doctor, and the sheriff. The baby had been out in the cold for at least forty hours, wrapped in nothing but a blue flannel diaper and covered by the coat. The doctor rubbed the baby with oil, then wrapped her in several layers of blankets. Sheriff Barrick did not seem surprised by the discovery. He had a drawl, slower each year, that seldom shifted to higher gear unless he was truly irate. This veteran had seen a lot in the gas-choked trenches of Europe during the Great War, but what he had investigated in the land around his home county of late were new lows for Cimarron County. People were abandoning their children — not in great numbers, mind you, but enough to make the sheriff feel a sense of shame for his fellow Oklahomans.

Nationwide, the 1930s was the first decade in United States history when the number of young children declined. Never before had the birthrate, at less than twenty children per thousand women of child-bearing age, been so low.

As the baby's temperature rose, the infant started to cry. Color came to her cheeks. Hazel thought it was a miracle, a baby resuscitated to life after being out in the cold, the dust, and the snow. But it was horrid, as the sheriff said — and, she had to add, *evil* — to think that people would just walk away from a baby, leaving it alone on the church steps in the frigid, dirty air. This ain't the worst of it, the sheriff said. One family had abandoned all three of their children; they were too poor to feed them, said it was inhumane to hold on to the kids. The infant that Hazel found was eventually adopted by a couple east of town. A short time later, word came that the coffee-box baby had died of something that was killing both children and old people throughout the High Plains — dust pneumonia.

13

The Struggle for Air

I N THE WINTER OF 1935, everybody in the Osteen dugout had a
cough, raw throat, and red eyes that itched at all times, or trouble
getting their breath. The family — Ike, his brother, and two sisters, and the widow living inside a divot in the prairie of Baca County
— had tried to seal their home, stuffing rags into wall cracks, gluing
strips of flour paste–covered paper around the door, taping the windows and then draping damp gunnysacks over the openings. Wet bed
sheets were hung against the walls as another filter. But all the layers
of moist cloth and flour paste could not keep the wind-sifted particles
out. The dugout was like a sieve. When their Red Cross masks got
so clogged it was like slapping a mud pie over the face, they rigged
up sponges to breathe through, but the general store in Springfield
couldn't keep up with the demand and ran out of sponges. The plow
that Ike had used to make money in the wheat boom was almost completely buried. Going to the outhouse was an ordeal, a wade through
shoulder-high drifts, forced to dig to make forward progress. They
tried parking the old Model-A on different sides of the dugout or atop
the dunes as a way to keep it from getting buried. In March, the worst
dusters yet came from the north. The storms blocked the sun for four
days, although it was never completely dark, and packed winds strong
enough to knock a person down. It forced the Osteen family inside for
three of those days and smothered the Model-A. Ike listened to the in-
cessant crackling of static electricity around the windmill. Poking his
head out of the hole, he saw currents running down the windmill and

along a wire — a blue flame. Wasn't nothing; his friend Tex Acre said the static at his place was so strong it electrocuted a jackrabbit. Saw it with his own eyes.

With each new duster, hope that the Osteen half-section could deliver some measure of relief to the family slipped away. For days, they were not sure on what side of the horizon the sun rose and on what side it set. A black blizzard in February carried such a punch it knocked telephone poles down. By the spring, Osteen's mama wanted only to see her son get through school, and then move to town. Ike was holding on, trying to attend school on the days when the storms would allow his mule to stumble through the sifting dunes. Sometimes he would ride all the way to the schoolhouse only to find it closed on account of the dusters. Every school in the county was closed for a week in March. At one school, children were trapped just before the afternoon school bell, unable to go home. They spent the night holed up behind the thin walls of the wood-frame building, cold and hungry. Stories like that made parents give up on school. It was too risky, and they did not see any reason for it. Life's ambitions and dreams had dried up; people held to a few, desperate desires — a longing to breathe clean air, to eat, to stay warm. School was a luxury.

Ike considered dropping out. There was supposed to be work on a government road job, paving a line across southern Baca County into New Mexico, work that a boy could get if he could lie about his age. He also thought of hopping aboard the train and heading west, seeing what California was all about. He and Tex Acre had talked about lighting out for some place that had trees and water. But Ike's mother said it would break her heart if he left before making it out of high school. She needed at least one child to bring some light into the dugout. He signed up to help with the senior play, *Mail Order Bride,* staying after school in the tiny gym to work as a stagehand. But in midspring, just days before dress rehearsal, practice came to a sudden halt — the play was off. Cots were hauled into the school gym and placed in tight rows. The Red Cross was converting the gym into an emergency hospital. It soon filled with wheezing, fevered people, including some of Ike's classmates. Nine people died. One of the victims was seventeen, Ike's age, a classmate who had hoped to graduate with him that spring.

One dirt-filled day blended into another. Starting on the first day of March, there was a duster every day for thirty straight days, according to the weather bureau. In Dodge City, Kansas, the Health Board counted only thirteen dust-free days in the first four months of 1935.

People were stuffed with prairie topsoil. In a report delivered to the Southern Medical Association, Dr. John H. Blue of Guymon, Oklahoma, said he treated fifty-six patients for dust pneumonia, and all of them showed signs of silicosis; others were suffering early symptoms of tuberculosis. He was blunt. The doctor had looked inside an otherwise healthy young farm hand, a man in his early twenties, and told him what he saw.

"You are filled with dirt," the doctor said. The young man died within a day.

Prairie dust has a high silica content. As it builds up in the lungs, it tears at the honeycombed web of air sacs and weakens the body's resistance. After prolonged exposure, it has the same effect on people as coal dust has on a miner. Silicosis has long been a plague of people who work underground and is the oldest occupational respiratory disease. But it takes years to build up. In the High Plains, doctors were seeing a condition similar to silicosis after just three years of storms. Sinusitis, laryngitis, bronchitis — a trio of painful breathing and throat ailments — were common. By the mid-1930s, a fourth condition, dust pneumonia, was rampant. It was one of the biggest killers. Doctors were not even sure if it was a disease unique from any of the common types of pneumonia, which is an infection of the lungs. They saw a pattern of symptoms: children, infants, or the elderly with coughing jags and body aches, particularly chest pains, and shortness of breath. Many had nausea and could not hold food down. Within days of diagnosis, some would die.

Desperate parents pleaded with the government men to help their families escape. Their children were being strangled by dust. In a month, a hundred families in Baca County gave up their property to the government in return for passage away from land that was killing them. Roosevelt had not yet settled on a plan to relocate people, but there was money available, in piecemeal relief efforts, to help folks forced to move.

The Red Cross declared a medical crisis across the High Plains in 1935, opening six emergency hospitals, including the one in Ike's school gym. But in the homesteads of Baca County, No Man's Land, and southwest Kansas, many people in dire need of care could not get to the medical centers. Secondary roads to withered farms — none of them paved, most of them barely graded — were impassable in the first months of 1935 because of blowing drifts. And the chill was a force of its own. February was the coldest in forty years. People were stuck in drafty, dust-swept homesteads, meat-locker cold, coughing dirt into their pillows. Fighting for their lives, the sick rode mules or horses over the chop of the dunes to the hospitals. In Beaver County, adjacent to Cimarron, three hundred people were diagnosed with dust pneumonia. Nearby in Liberal, Kansas, nine people who came into the medical facility died of the same thing. In March, one out of every five people admitted to all hospitals in southwest Kansas said they were choking on dust. The next month, more than 50 percent of admissions were for dust-related respiratory ailments.

Jeanne Clark, whose dancer mother had left New York for the High Plains to get help for her own respiratory ailments, came down with a high fever, chills, and chronic cough in her home just north of Baca County. She was put in the emergency hospital in Lamar, Colorado, in a room with wet bed sheets draped over the windows. The former haven for lungers had turned lethal. Jeanne's mother had begun to look for a way out of this maelstrom. She had gone from Broadway's bright lights to a small town where she was starved for light and a clear day, and had been thinking of ways to get back to New York when her little girl came down sick. Jeanne was an only child. The doctor said they did not know if she would live to see Easter Sunday 1935. She slept most of the day, awakened occasionally by her father's cigar smoke. She loved seeing her daddy, but the smoke made her scream.

The Red Cross advised people not to go outside unless they had to and then only with their respiratory masks. Even rail travel was hazardous. A train from Kansas City to Dalhart had to stop several times when passengers complained they were choking. The train came to a halt, idling in an effort to let the dust settle enough so that people could scoop out the passenger cars. Another train in Kansas was derailed when it plowed into a dune that had formed in just a few hours. Despite the Red Cross warning, people *had* to go outside. They lived outdoors; the outdoors lived with them. It was one and the same. They had no choice. High Plains nesters were more intimate with the elements than perhaps any other people in the country. They knew black dust came from Kansas, red from eastern Oklahoma, a yellow-orange from Texas. And sometimes all of Kansas, Oklahoma, and Texas seemed airborne at once: black, red, and orange converging. The sunlight that filtered through these dusters took on eerie hues — sometimes even green. People knew that when the wind blew from the southwest, the duster to follow would go through a range of colors — everything but the golden light they remembered from the first days of breaking the sod. If the dust clouds were high from the south, somewhat thin, they would take the shape of moving mesas, topping out at better than two miles above the ground. And when dusters came from the north, the clouds boiled up like thunderheads and usually carried a heavy load. These black northers were the most hated. Life in the galloping flatlands was a pact with nature. It gave as much as it took, and in 1935 it was all take.

14

Showdown in Dalhart

DRIFTERS, LUNATICS, AND BANKRUPT shopkeepers filled
the courtrooms in Dalhart. On many days, the slow grinding
of the law against people who could no longer stay afloat was
the only business in town. Uncle Dick Coon took title to a pool hall
that was one of the oldest hangouts in town, foreclosing on a debt of
$612. The court awarded Coon four pool tables, four domino tables,
twelve chairs, five cue racks, four sets of dominoes, and two cigar
cases. Banks foreclosed on red bulls and black steers, on tractors,
combines, water tanks, windmills, light fixtures. Simon Herzstein
tried but could not find a way to reopen his store in town. By 1935,
Herzstein was three years behind on city taxes. He had stayed open
through days when not a single shirt sold before finally calling it quits.
After Herzstein was foreclosed on $242 in back taxes, the City of
Dalhart had title to a piece of space long-occupied by the leading
clothier on the southern plains. It became another empty hole in a
sagging town.

The sign at the edge of Dalhart — "BLACK MAN DON'T LET THE
SUN GO DOWN ON YOU HERE" — was strictly enforced. In February, a norther came through the High Plains, sending the mercury
plummeting to seven degrees. The hazy, arctic air hung on for a week.
When two black men got off the train in Dalhart, hungry and nearly
hypothermic, they looked around for something to eat and a place to
get warm. They found a door open in a shed at the train depot. Inside

was some food and shelter from a cold so painful it burned their hands and feet like a blowtorch.

"TWO NEGROES ARRESTED": the *Dalhart Texan* reported how the men, aged nineteen and twenty-three, had sniffed around the train station, looking for food. They were cuffed, locked up in the county jail, and after a week brought out for arraignment before a justice of the peace, Hugh Edwards. The judge ordered the men to dance. The men hesitated; this was supposed to be a bond hearing. The railroad agent said these men were good for nothing but Negro toe-tapping. The judge smiled; he said he wanted to see it.

"Tap dance," Edwards told the men.

"Here?"

"Yes. Before the court."

The men started to dance, forced silly grins on their faces, reluctant. After the tap dance, the judge banged his gavel and ordered the men back to jail for another two months.

As the ground took flight through the middle years of the Dirty Thirties, the courts had to contend with a new type of mental illness — the person driven mad by dust. Texas, like most states, had a civil procedure for committing people to involuntary confinement in a state institution. County courts had jurisdiction. A young judge, Wilson Cowen, impaneled a jury of six to hear a story that was common on the High Plains: a young woman found wandering the streets, muttering incoherent pleas. Cowen was deeply troubled by these insanity trials. He had been elected in the summer of 1934, despite his youth (he had just turned thirty) and his inexperience (he had been in Dalhart for only five years). While running for judge, Cowen roamed all over Dallam County and saw firsthand how the dirt-packed winds were taking the life out of the place. He drove for days without seeing a single green thing. He saw farmhouses without a chicken or cow. He saw children in rags, their parents too frightened of dust pneumonia to send them to school, huddling in shacks shaped into wavy formations on the prairie, almost indistinguishable from the dunes. He had been a judge less than a year when he was assigned the case of a mother of young children, the thirty-five-year-old widow found on the streets. Bankrupted by the wheat bust, the woman had lost her husband to dust pneumonia, leaving her without a man or a penny to her name. Her children were hungry, dirty, coughing, dressed in torn, soiled clothes. Their house was nearly buried, and inside centipedes and black widows had a run of the place. The worst thing was the wind. It never stopped. One day, the woman simply snapped.

"Dust is killing me!" the woman shouted. Her voice echoed through the redbrick fortress of the Dallam County Courthouse.

Cowen tried to talk to her about what had happened and the steps she could take to recover. The judge told her about the relief house, just opened in town, Doc Dawson's operation. The Doc was broke. All the money he made at the sanitarium had been put into the land, and the land gave back nothing. What was left for him was service, the impulse that had driven the Doc all his life. With a donation from Uncle Dick, he opened a soup kitchen known as the Dalhart Haven, serving hot beans from a big pot and black coffee, sometimes hot. Dunes were spreading all around the Panhandle, sifting and lengthening, transforming the old XIT lands to desert before the eyes of a panicked citizenry. The Doc's ambition had ebbed to a few goals: live through the dusters, keep the soup kitchen running.

And so Judge Cowen suggested to the shrieking woman, perhaps she could find temporary relief at Doc Dawson's Dalhart Haven.

"Dust is killing me!" she shouted again. "It's killing my children."

Privately, the judge told friends some hope existed if only the government men could find a way to tame the dunes and if the skies could spare some rain. Cowen was encouraged by talk among some of the government men about trying to control the prairie with contour plowing. *Conservation* — that was the new word coming from Big Hugh Bennett. He had sent one of his soil scientists to Dallam County, and the man told farmers they had been "practicing suicidal production" on the land. If the government was going to help, people would have to promise, in writing, to change their ways, would have to act as one. But getting a community consensus looked like a hard thing to do at a time when most people were still in shock at the collapse of their lives and their beloved piece of Texas dirt. This tomorrow land was running out of tomorrow people.

"Dust is killing us all! God help us."

The court heard how the woman's shack was nearly a tomb under the topsoil, and her children were close to suffocating. An expert told the judge that the woman had lost her ability to care for her children or herself. After half a day's deliberation, the jury agreed. Resisting the tug on his heart, Judge Cowen signed a certificate committing the mother to the insane asylum at Wichita Falls, Texas. Her children were given to the state. Cowen was thirty-one years old when he heard that case. More than fifty years later, it still bothered him.

There were times in the two-room shack shared by five members of Bam White's family that Lizzie White nearly snapped as well, when the pain was too much. The shack had no electricity, no running water.

"The wind," she would say, shaking her head, a haunted look on her face. "Oh, the wind, the wind."

They worked and ate by the light of a kerosene lamp. Keeping the dust out was impossible. Even fresh-cleaned clothes, hanging outside to dry on the line, were at risk. When a duster rushed through, she had to hurry and get the laundry off the line, because there was usually just enough oil in the blowing sand to soil the clothes. Lizzie swept five, six times a day. She had her boys shovel dust in the morning, after it piled up outside the door. Sometimes a big dune blocked the door, and the boys had to crawl out a window to get to it. The dust arrived in mysterious ways. It could penetrate like a spirit, cascading down the walls or slithering along the ceiling until it found an opening. Of course she taped windows and doors, draped everything in wet sheets, turned the pots over, covered the sink. But there it was floating in the kerosene lamp's light, after supper, free-floating. Just the sound of the prairie wind could make her stomach tight, for she knew what would follow. And the sight of her children, these hungry kids, their noses never clean. She kept them out of school on days she feared they might get caught in a blinding duster. The dust pneumonia scared the life out of her. Her sister, who lived to the south, had caught it. Came up with the fever and powerful body aches and had trouble breathing, as if her air passages had been cut off. Came up with the coughing all night and day till she broke three ribs. Fever shot up, and then she died before she could find her way to one of the emergency hospitals.

Young Melt's job was to tend the garden, hauling water in pails to a square of ground out by the side of the shack. It was not much to look at, except for the watermelons. They grew big and green, and the Whites counted the days until they could cut one open and submerge their faces in the sweet, wet fruit. Midsummer, amid a string of dusters, the static electricity was crackling like firecrackers. In the evening, when the dust clouds drifted through, Melt went outside to check the garden. He had watered it that morning, but now it was dead, killed by the electric currents of the duster; the leaves were black and the vines collapsed. The static had singed the foliage of the watermelon plants.

Not long after the garden died, the children came home and found Lizzie White buckled over in a corner. She was crying, her face in a towel. The boys looked into their mama's red eyes, felt the towel moist with hot tears.

"What're we gonna do, Mama?"

Lizzie White could not muster a teaspoonful of optimism for her children.

"It's up to your daddy," she said. "I can't live like this anymore."

Between selling his skunk hides and a few odd jobs, Bam White spent most of his time in 1935 with old XIT cowboys. They talked about holding a reunion of the biggest ranch in the Lone Star State. Maybe stage a rodeo, pool some cash in town for a purse. Bam no longer dreamed of hiring on at a ranch. Place where he'd worked when he first came to Dalhart, Mal Stewart's spread west of town, had blown away. It was all sand, like most of the old XIT. The way the cowboys kept their tomorrow days alive now was to rope off a section of Denrock Street on a Saturday night and hold a square dance. Bam didn't care for dancing anymore; every joint in his body cried with some ache or another brought by a lifetime of breaking horses and chasing cattle. What he did now was call the dances, setting the time with the musicians.

Bam White spent other days kicking around on what was left of the James's place. Old Andy James, his heart was broken by the death of his family's grand slab of Texas. For so long, the James boys had the run of the Llano Estacado. They were part of the country, a proud family. The patriarch had come to the grasslands in 1898 but died before he could stake his claim. The boys and the widow lived in a two-room dugout before establishing a ranch that went from north of Dalhart to south of Boise City — second in size only to the XIT. Their diamond brand marked cows that had been fattened on the thickest carpet of mid-America. And the stories these boys could tell: skinning cattle by hooking a team of horses to the hide was one that always made people's eyes light up. They had lived through grass fires that rolled over the prairie like devil's breath and witnessed half a dozen times when the Cimarron River swelled up and raged through the country. More than once, blizzards killed off half their herd, and somebody was always sick or bleeding from a run-in with barbed wire after too much corn whiskey.

Now the James ranch was in tatters. Much of it had been sold to keep the bankers at bay after cattle prices collapsed in the last decade. The paper-chasers were one thing, but the James boys could not fight the dust storms. Andy James never got sick much and never complained; once, he had a few teeth pulled by a dentist with only the numbing aid of a bottle of hooch. But the black blizzards got to him that year, and it affected everyone who was close to him. The swagger was gone even from his son, young Andy, the horseman who used to brag to Hazel Lucas about eating his "mighty crunchy" grasshoppers. Bam had never seen a cowboy so blue as old Andy. Everybody's ranch was in the same condition, blowing away.

A meeting was called in the Dalhart Courthouse. About 150 men and women who used to ranch, or still held title to land that had been good grass for cattle, packed the room. Andy sat and listened while complaints were stacked high. Then he stood to give his piece. His family, he reminded everyone, had come to the High Plains at the start of the new century and initially chose four sections of land — 2,560 acres — of this country's sod because of one thing: the grass. There were no farmers when the James family started their ranch. The whole area was covered with grama, curly mesquite, and bluestem that were waist-high in wet years. Andy James's daddy said the land would never be plowed up. A season's time on the James ranch was all a person needed to fall in love with the grassland. Over the years, Andy had seen places with more trees, places with more mountains, places with more water, more people, all the things that the Panhandle didn't have, but he always came home to the ranch because it was paradise. And even though the family lost much of their spread in the cattle bust, their soul was still in the land. Andy hated what the farmers had done, tearing up this good earth. He hated the nesters for digging straight lines in open pastures and prospecting for wheat like drunken miners in a gold rush, and then for walking away from it and letting it blow. What they'd done was a crime against nature. But Andy could not live with hate and regret; it wasn't right, this bile and bitterness, and it kept him up at night. Not long ago, Andy went out to the ranch to have a good long look. It sickened him. The cottonwood trees planted by his mother — dead. The grass that had stretched from sunrise to sunset — gone, not a blade in the ground. Fences smothered by dust. Roads buried under drifts. Tumbleweeds and sand piled as high as the courthouse, a castle of dirt.

"This is a terrible way for us to treat our land," he said at the meeting. He hacked up the prairie silt until his windblown face was red and he doubled over in pain.

There followed a couple of hisses from some nesters. They aimed the gothic death stare at Andy. Does he think he's got a monopoly on righteousness? Others started clapping and whistling: yeah, boy, you tell 'em. Andy James had spoken a truth. He ended with a call to listen to the government men, give 'em a chance. Yes, it was not a cowboy's way to depend on somebody else, especially the government. But this was their only hope, this soil conservation idea that Big Hugh Bennett was trying to get people to agree on. Bennett's men had proposed turning a big stretch of swirling prairie in Texas into a demonstration project of how to hold down the earth, the largest such project in the country. But it would require a majority of people in the county to approve of the plan. If things went right, they might get grass back in a few years' time. And with grass, cattle would follow. The country might spring back to life.

"Bullshit!" came a shout.

But Andy James had won over the crowd. They elected him and Mal Stewart, the rancher who had hired Bam White, to write a letter to Bennett in Washington and let him know they were good to go. Bennett had told Congress that fifty-one million acres were so eroded they could no longer be cultivated. It would take a thousand years to rebuild an inch of topsoil. What could be done — now — was all theory. But theory was better than another day in the howling dirt. Texas was a unique disaster, for the programs Big Hugh had up and running elsewhere were all designed to stem water erosion. Wind was the problem of the High Plains. The two cowboys sent a letter: folks in the Panhandle had agreed to do something about the airborne earth in Texas. Just show us how.

In early April the two black men who had been sitting in the Dallam County jail for three months were brought back to the courthouse for trial. The railroad agent again told how he found the men, on the coldest of nights, looking for food and shelter, and looking in a place that happened to be property of the Rock Island Railroad. The judge asked the men if this was true and they said, yes sir, we were hungry and cold and saw that little haven of warmth and food and we pushed open the door and helped ourselves to something. With this admission, the judge found the pair guilty of criminal trespass and sentenced them to 120 days in jail. But again he wanted one more thing.

"Dance," the judge said. The two men obliged, and as the *Texan* reported the next day, the tap-dancing Negroes made for a good laugh for judge, prosecutor, and the Rock Island Railroad agent.

The paper's editor, McCarty, had become frustrated by the image that the rest of the country was getting of his beloved High Plains. He could never build an empire on sand. His cheerleading had not lagged through dusters that tore at the town like crows feeding on a corpse. He ran a double-spread picture of his town looking its Sunday best. "Beautiful panoramic view of Dalhart shows it as a city of homes where living is a real pleasure," he wrote. The real estate ads were more honest than the journalism. People offered to swap their land for a truck. One realtor wrote: "We've had hell here, and it has been no place for suckling babes or tender-hearted softies."

To McCarty, it was bad enough that people had sent a telegram to Washington a year earlier, begging for help, saying they were "fighting desperately to maintain our homes, schools, churches." That brought the kind of attention that McCarty could not stand, making his neighbors look like failures. Fox Movietone News had been around for a couple of weeks, filming mountainous dusters as they swept through the High Plains on an almost daily basis, with maps pinpointing Dalhart and Boise City as the dead center of the worst storms, based on charting of windblown soil done by the government men. It was McCarty's nightmare: his town held up as a howling wasteland on thousands of movie screens across America, a netherworld for the lost. The black blizzard that covered Dalhart in half an inch of what looked like dirty snow was captured by the Movietone News crews and sent out to theaters, where the pictures played before regular features like *The Gay Divorcee*.

McCarty buried news of that storm deep inside the paper in a single column, and instead promoted a plan of action. The *Texan* announced a rabbit roundup to exceed all others for slaughter. A few days later, six thousand rabbits were killed as people spread out over a wide swath of penned land. This time guns were allowed and there was "an ammo truck for anyone who runs short," as the paper reported. And if this wasn't evidence that the people of Dalhart were not going to passively sit by and accept the fate of transient land, there was more to come. Using his column, called "Cactus, Sage and Loco," McCarty put the best face on the dark winter of 1935. These Movietone News features going out of Dalhart were a slander, he said, as toxic as idle gossip.

Earlier, during the cold snap that had driven the two black drifters to seek warmth, McCarty wrote that the worst was over. But a month later, an even colder norther rolled through, and the temperature fell to six degrees Fahrenheit. At the same time, a monstrous dust storm broke the routine of smaller dusters. It blanketed all of the Texas and Oklahoma Panhandles, southern Colorado, and southwest Kansas. Dalhart was hammered. The dust was coarser and heavier than the usual flour-light silt. It felt like gravel. It shattered windows and swooshed down chimneys and ran along the walls and buried the streets like a winter blizzard. In the morning, footprints and car tracks were imprinted in the dust. A baby boy, aged eighteen months, died one day after that storm.

"A TRIBUTE TO OUR SAND STORMS": McCarty declared it was time to stop treating the dusters like a Biblical plague, time to give them praise. The newsreel people and the traveling reporters from the big city dailies and the magazines — they had it all wrong. The dust storms were majestic, in their way, even beautiful, he wrote. Instead of cowering in the sand, people should look skyward in wonder. Some of his readers thought McCarty had gone mad.

"Let us praise nature and the powerful god that rules nature," he wrote. "Let us in centurion tones boast of our terrific and mighty dust storms and of a people, a city and a country that can meet the test of courage they afford and still smile." He urged citizens of Dalhart to "view the majestic splendor and beauty of one of the great spectacles of nature, a panhandle dust storm, and smile even though we may be choking and our throats and nostrils so laden with dust that we cannot give voice to our feelings."

The new approach was welcomed by those who were sick of being told that the end was near. The idea that nesters should never have broken the southern plains and planted towns was absurd, McCarty felt. He scoffed at the suggestion of Secretary of the Interior Ickes that people should be relocated to land less hostile to human habitation. A person needed only to go inside the Mission Theater, ignore the lies from the newsreels, and see what this country was really like. There, the movie *Cimarron,* a tale of the Oklahoma land rush (filmed in Hollywood), was playing. It featured heroic sodbusters more to McCarty's liking. Outside the theater, these dusters were part of a freakish spell of weather — an epic trial, yes — but the Texas Panhandle would come back, strong, and look like the admirable place in the movie. McCarty's tribute generated more mail and publicity than anything he had written in his six years as editor of the *Texan.* The complimentary letters were prominently displayed, including one that compared McCarty to some of the greatest American writers of all time.

"Your composition in Friday's paper styled 'A Tribute to our Sandstorms,' in my humble opinion is one of the most beautiful specimens of elegant rhetoric I have seen in contemporary literature. The beautiful imagery, choice figures and excellent diction of this article are beyond question. The reverent spirit which pervades the whole, and the poetic appreciation for nature are worthy of its excellent style. One would search long and with great care before finding in Hawthorne, Poe or Irving paragraphs of greater literary merit."

Unfortunately the letter was unsigned, leaving the impression that McCarty himself had penned the anonymous tribute to his praise of savage dusters. But McCarty was on to something. He had tapped into the resilience of people who wanted to do something other than club rabbits, pray for rain, and wait for the gates of hell to open for them.

"I enjoy a storm," McCarty wrote a week after the defiant column. "I like to see old gnarled and scarred trees silhouetted against the sky, defiant of the winds, ready for any storm that may come. I like to see men and women, scarred with the battles of life, proven on its toughest testing ground and ready for all that comes their way."

From the worst conditions came the strongest men, he concluded. "Our country has been beaten, swept, scarred and torn by the most adverse weather conditions since June, 1932. It is bare, desolate and damaged. Our people have been buffeted about by every possible kind of misfortune. It has appeared that the hate of all nature has been poured out against us." He made light of Easterners who whined when the big duster dropped its load on the population centers in May 1934 — "scaring the wrist-watch cavemen of the East to death."

From praise of the dust storms, McCarty moved on to praise of the people who endured the storms. Yes, Americans were soft, as he said last Fourth of July, except for these High Plains nesters. They were no wristwatch cavemen.

"A TRIBUTE TO OUR PEOPLE": "Spartans! No better word can describe the citizen of the north plains country and of Dalhart," he began this piece. "Bravery and hardship are but tools out of which great empires are carved and real men made Spartans."

The "Spartans" seemed to respond. People from five counties in the Texas Panhandle met in Dalhart in March, holding a "rally to fight dust," as the *Texan* put it in a headline.

"More than 700 sturdy Panhandle citizens, wind-whipped and dust-covered, voted to stand by their guns and once more make this county blossom as the rose," the newspaper said. How to make it blossom was a question left unanswered. Hugh Bennett had received the telegram sent by the cowboys, and his soil conservation service now had a blueprint to hold the land down. The project would cover only a fraction of the three million acres in the Panhandle that were badly torn up. But they had started something, which was better than sitting by idly as the sky carried their homesteads away.

The larger battle was not over the beauty or savagery of sand, or the endurance of the people, but what to ultimately do with the land and the families living in its midst.

"It is not a pretty picture but there is a certain satisfaction in staying with it," McCarty wrote.

People had been lured to one of the last open spaces left on the American map by extravagant claims of water and prosperity. Was it too late to simply call them back, to admit that the nesters had been duped and the land raped? McCarty thought that by turning the argument around — by saying that dust storms were nature at its glorious extreme and the people living amid them virtuous — he could keep the towns intact. The government was still considering how — or even if — the prairie grass could be stitched back in place. McCarty was against any attempt to re-grass or depopulate the southern plains. Such ideas, he said, could only come from "armchair farmers." A Spartan would stay put.

McCarty's boosterism could not hold the storms back, nor curb the danger to people who felt like miners trapped in a deep shaft, nor stop the deaths. The plague took more lives of the Spartans. A week after the Rally to Fight Dust, a young Dalhart mother, Murrel Sanford, died of dust pneumonia. She was twenty-six and left behind a baby who was dying of the same ailment. Four feet of dust on the main road into Dalhart from the south trapped cars, preventing them from getting back into town. Other drifts completely buried abandoned farmhouses. Another black blizzard reduced visibility in town to a single block. It was not quite dark, but the streetlights were on, and the town was wrapped in an eerie haze. In mid-March, another child died in Dalhart, just a few days after his first birthday, of dust pneumonia. McCarty's paper played up dusters in other states, while minimizing the ones in his town. He reported how a hundred families a month were fleeing Cimarron County, just over the state line to the north.

"Even wagons were pressed into use as the coughing, choking humans fled before the fury of the stifling dust," the paper reported on April 11. At times, McCarty seemed to gloat in the storms of others — dust schadenfreude.

"KANSAS TAKES LEAD
DISASTROUS STORMS SURPASS TEXAS VARIETY"

Wire service photos showed shoppers in Kansas, otherwise fashionably dressed, with dust masks over their mouths, and dead, skeletal cattle, looking like fossils in the sand. And it was true: the dust in Kansas was falling in heaps; a team of soil scientists calculated that during the storms of March and April 1935, about 4.7 tons of dust per acre fell on western Kansas during each of the blizzards. The tonnage not only crushed trees, broke windows, and dented the tops of cars, but the ceilings of houses were collapsing as well. The pressure was not on pitched roofs but on the flat ceiling inside, beneath the roof, after dust filtered in and settled. The head of the Kansas State College of Agronomy said not even steady rain could save the parched wheat lands in southwest Kansas. The land was too far gone. The recent dusters in Dalhart, McCarty's paper explained, were the fault of all this swirling earth from other states.

"FOREIGN DUST PROVES PANHANDLE IRRITANT": "It is the dust blowing in from other states, notably Nebraska, Iowa and Colorado, that is irritating the nose and throat of Panhandle residents," the story reported. The Spartans of Texas were a stronger breed than the dust victims of other states. "The sand and dust storms are worse in Oklahoma, Kansas, Colorado and other states than they are here or else they are a bunch of sissies up there bawling their eyes out because of a new experience which grew old to most of us in our child-hood," McCarty wrote.

By April, McCarty was at his most defiant. He ran a front-page challenge: "GRAB A ROOT AND GROWL."

Dalhart citizens, he wrote, had endured "the furies of hell turned loose." But the worst was over. He had predicted the same thing in February, and several times in the previous year, 1934. But now he had a feeling in his gut that better times were ahead, and he wanted his to-morrow people to act like it.

"Sure, things are tough, the dust is terrible, the wheat is gone, the prospect for a row crop is diminishing and all hell's broke loose but we know what is back of this county. We know what it will do when it gets half a chance. We know that it will rain again and the High Plains always bounces back like Antaeus of mythical fame, stronger after each fall."

To McCarty the dusters were an adventure. "Grab root and growl — hang on and let's see how this all comes out."

A growling *could* be heard in town, from stomachs. Dalhart, lo-cated in the southern half of the American breadbasket, could barely feed itself. More people sought refuge in the kitchen that Doc Dawson was running out of his old sanitarium building. Some days, two hun-dred people waited in line: Mexicans who lived in the shanties near the Rock Island roundhouse, drifters who had just stepped off the train, and longtime Dalhart residents who had not seen a paycheck in three years. The Doc made his big pot of beans and brewed up five gallons of black coffee. Doors opened in late afternoon. People had to remove their hats, wash their hands, and after eating, clean their tin plates in a communal hydrant. Nobody could go through the line more than once. This daily queue of gaunt, emaciated people was not what Uncle Dick Coon had envisioned when he decided to build his empire in Dalhart. But Dick had a soft spot for people broken by dust and poverty, even as his foreclosure actions moved through the courts, and he did not leave the house without his hundred-dollar bill inside his pocket. He never forgot the horror of Galveston, the town buried by a wall of water twenty feet high, winds of a hundred and fifty miles an hour that shredded houses, more than six thousand people killed, their bodies strewn for miles, their homes reduced to matchsticks. Uncle Dick was the Dalhart Haven's quiet backer. With Dick's money, the Doc was able to buy dried beans, potatoes, and coffee. Otherwise, the Doc himself might have been waiting in line, tin plate in hand, in another town. He and his wife had nothing left.

The Red Cross organized a shoe drive. They asked people to go through their closets, find shoes that were too small, too tattered — it did not matter. They collected several hundred pairs in a hotel room at the DeSoto donated by Uncle Dick. A Mennonite cobbler was enlisted. Old belting material was picked up at the railroad depot, and tire casings were collected. Over several weeks, the shoes were torn apart and put back together, with fresh soles. Dalhart now had daily beans and remade shoes for the asking. It was enough to hold people in place while the government men figured out some way to hold the soil in place. But what they really needed was rain. By March, less than half an inch of precipitation had fallen for the year. 1935 was shaping up as a drier year than 1934, which had been the most arid on record in many parts of the High Plains.

Town leaders solicited ideas on how to force moisture from the sky. One popular method was to kill a snake and hang it belly-side up on a fence. In southwest Kansas, dead snakes were hung for miles on barbed wire, their white-scaled stomachs facing the brown sky. They baked in the sun until crisp. No rain came. A better method, more scientific according to the rain peddlers, was aerial bombing. The concussion theory dated to the first century A.D., when the Greek moralist Plutarch came up with the notion that rain followed military battles. Napoleon believed as much and fired cannons and guns at the sky to muddy up the ground between him and his attackers. Civil War veterans who wallowed in cold slop believed that ceaseless, close-range artillery fire had opened up the skies. In the late 1890s, as the first nesters started to dig their toeholds on the dry side of the one hundredth meridian, Congress had appropriated money to test the concussion theory in Texas. The tests were done by a man named Dyrenforth. He tried mightily, with government auditors looking over his shoulder, but Dyrenforth could not force a drop from the hot skies of Texas. From then on, he was called "Dry-Henceforth."

Government-sponsored failure didn't stop others from trying. A man who called himself "the moisture accelerator," Charles M. Hatfield, roamed the plains around the turn of the century. A Colonel Sanders of rainmaking, Hatfield had a secret mixture of ingredients that could be sent to the sky by machine. In the age before the widespread use of the telephone, it was hard to catch up with the moisture accelerator after he had fleeced a town and moved on.

In 1910, the cereal magnate C. W. Post became obsessed with commanding rain down on a swath of West Texas land that he owned. Post was hoping to plant a model community, hundreds of small farms, on two hundred thousand acres he had purchased with the family fortune. It was flat, featureless, sunbaked. And if God couldn't give his land rain, Post figured he could grab it himself. He became an expert on rainmaking, if a self-proclaimed one. A disciple of the concussion theory, Post ordered his ranch hands to make a kite strong enough to carry up to two pounds of dynamite. The cowboys were taken aback. Kites? Yes. He wanted 150 of them. Post was going to give the concussion theory its best chance at proving out — by carpet-bombing clouds from kites. The failures in the past, he believed, were due to poor delivery systems. Post took the train down from the Midwest and examined what his ranch hands had rigged up for him. The kites seemed sturdy enough. He loaded six of them with dynamite. But just as Post was getting ready to launch his aerial agitators, it started to rain. Hard. He and his men dove for cover. The next year, 1911, he returned with a new plan. This time, no kites. He had procured several small howitzers such as those used by the Army and tailored them for rainmaking. At his command, charges were fired into the sky. The clouds thundered with explosions. Nothing. No rain fell. Post died two years later, his Texas sod still empty of model homes, still dry, the concussion theory just that.

By the time of the 1930s drought, older nesters recalled the rich, steady rains that fell twenty years earlier — twenty-five inches and up, every year — and again attributed that to the daily bombardments in

Europe. If they could not bring the big guns to the High Plains, they could attempt something on a smaller scale. The experiences of Napoleon, Dry-Henceforth, and the cereal magnate had been lost on town leaders in Dalhart. They were desperate.

The hat was passed around Dalhart, as was done with a dubious plan to find a final solution to the rabbit problem. Hard as it was to give even two bits to the rain effort, it was the kind of investment that could save a farm or a business if it paid off. Uncle Dick was among the first to buck up. He flashed that C-note, making some think he was going to pay the lion's share, before he put it back in his pocket and found a smaller denomination. A rainmaker named Tex Thornton was hired to squeeze the clouds. Thornton's specialty was explosives; he promised that a combination of TNT and solidified nitroglycerin would do the trick. It had been tried at Council Grove, Kansas, and broke the drought, Tex claimed. Tex was paid three hundred dollars. Of course he would have to get the dynamite and TNT high enough into the clouds to do any good, and for that, he would need a little more money. The hat was passed again. They paid him another two hundred dollars. People in town made plans for a street dance. Everyone was invited to a potluck picnic, music from some of the old XIT cowboys, a big celebration to welcome back rain. Tex Thornton promised vertical water by the first week of May. Dalhart was on its feet.

15

Duster's Eve

S HE STARTED TO COUGH that winter, a baby's ragged hiccup, and it never stopped. Though Hazel Shaw had sealed the windows and doors and draped an extra layer of wet sheets over the openings, the dust still found Ruth Nell in her crib. It was oily and black some mornings, covering the baby's face. Her lips were frothed and mudded, her eyes red. She cried and coughed, cried and coughed. Hazel lubricated her tiny nostrils with Vaseline and tried to keep a mask over her face, but the baby coughed or spit it off. A doctor took tests, listened to the hurried heart. Ruth Nell was diagnosed with whooping cough. You should probably leave, for the life of your baby, the doctor advised.

South forty miles in Texhoma, Loumiza Lucas was tucked under quilt layers inside the family home. The matriarch of the Lucas clan, Hazel's grandma, was coughing hard, just like the baby. Loumiza was eighty years old, a widow for twenty-one years, with nine children, forty grandchildren, thirty great-grandchildren. There was yet no Social Security.

"It is hard to be old and not have anything," a widowed North Dakota farmer's wife wrote the president in 1934, in a letter that was typical in its pleading tone. "I have always been poor and have always worked hard, so now I am not able to do any more. I am all worn out but am able to be around and I thank God that I have no pains."

Loumiza was in pain. The dust filtered into her home like a toxic vapor. She stopped eating. She grew weaker. Every time she brought her teeth together she tasted grit. Her bedroom was a refuge but not a pleasant one. It was a dusty hole in a homestead. She could not be moved because the risk of travel exposed her to the wind-borne sand. Her family begged her to eat. She withdrew deeper under the pile of quilts. The windows were sealed so tightly that light from her beloved land was completely blocked. It did not matter: she hated what No Man's Land had become. It was better to remember it as it was when she came into this country, arriving by covered wagon to Texhoma, and north to a half-section of their own, her and Jimmy, in the free kingdom of No Man's Land. That high bluestem in the corner of the county, tall as the reach of a scarecrow, that carpet of buffalo grass, and Lord what the rains could do in a good year — it was what the land was supposed to look like.

Grandma Lou seemed more worried about her youngest great-granddaughter, the baby Ruth Nell, than her own health. She waved off the questions about her diminishing spirit and asked about Ruth Nell, and she prayed. She clutched the one Bible she had carried throughout her life, a tattered thing that had traveled across time and terrain. As the dusters picked up, some of Lou's friends and even some of her own family believed the terrible storms were a fulfillment of Biblical prophecy — a sign of the final days. But Lou knew better. There was nothing in her Bible that said the world would end in darkness and dust.

Two days before Ruth Nell's first birthday, Hazel and her husband decided to flee, breaking the family apart for the health of the baby, as the doctor had recommended. They had to get out now or risk the baby's life. This year, 1935, had been one duster after the other and April showed no sign of letup, no rain in the forecast, four years into the drought. At the end of March, black blizzards had fallen for twelve straight days. During one of those storms, the wind was clocked at forty miles an hour or better — for a hundred hours. The *Boise City News* said it was the worst storm in the history of the county. Schools closed, again. An emergency call went out: come get the children and take them home. The schools would reopen when it was safe. Boise City looked ghostly, shuttered from the storms, hunkered down like an abandoned outpost in the Sahara. All the windows were cloaked in brown. Cars that had shorted out on the static were left in roads or ditches, and they soon were covered and became lumps in the sand.

Hazel hurried along her plan to get Ruth Nell out of Boise City. She arranged to stay with her in-laws in Enid, Oklahoma, well to the east. But just as they were ready to depart, a tornado touched down not far from Enid, the black funnel dancing around the edges of the very place where Ruth Nell was to find her refuge. It was a gruesome thing, ripping through homes, throwing roofs to the sky. Now what — stay or go? Hazel and Charles felt they had no choice but to go. It was more dangerous living in Boise City, and if they waited much longer, they might not get out of town. The coffee-box baby haunted Hazel, the little blue-faced infant left in the cold who had died of dust pneumonia.

Sheriff Barrick said the roads out of town were blocked by huge drifts. The CCC crews would no sooner dig out one drift than another would appear, covering a quarter-mile section of road. A caravan of Boise City residents who had tried to leave earlier in the week with all their belongings loaded into their jalopies was pinned down at the edge of town, and they were forced to return. The volume of dirt that had been thrown to the skies was extraordinary. A professor

Digging out fence posts, Cimarron County, Oklahoma, 1936

at Kansas State College estimated that if a line of trucks ninety-six miles long hauled ten full loads a day, it would take a year to transport the dirt that had blown from one side of Kansas to the other — a total of forty-six million truckloads. Better days were not in the forecast.

Hazel made it south to Texhoma, where she and Ruth Nell could ride the train to the eastern part of the state. If the baby could take in some clean air for a few weeks, living with her grandparents, she might shake this horrid cough. The journey to Enid was not easy. A few weeks earlier, a train full of CCC workers slid off the dust-covered tracks and rolled, killing several young men. Hazel's train sputtered its way east, stopping frequently so the crews could shovel sand from the tracks. Hazel tried to stay positive, but it looked awful outside: all of the Oklahoma Panhandle blowing and dead, no life of any form in the fields, no spring planting, no farmers on the roads. By the time mother and daughter made it to Enid, the baby's cough was no better. Her little stomach must have been in acute pain from the hacking, and she might have fractured a rib from coughing, for the baby cried constantly. At times, Hazel cried along with her and prayed intensely, hoping for relief. Arriving in Enid, Hazel rushed Ruth Nell to St. Mary's Hospital. The doctors tried to clean out her lungs by suctioning some of the gunk, but the baby would not settle. She coughed and cried, coughed and cried. The doctors confirmed Hazel's fears — Ruth Nell had dust pneumonia. She was moved into a section of the hospital in Enid that nurses called the "dust ward." The baby's temperature held above 103. She could not hold down milk from a bottle; it came back up as spit and grime. The doctors wrapped the baby's midsection in gauze and loose-fitting tape, as a way to hold in place the fractured ribs and diminish the pain in the stomach muscle. Still, Ruth Nell coughed and cried, coughed and cried.

"You must come," Hazel phoned her husband from the hospital in Enid. "Come now. Ruth Nell looks terrible. I'm so afraid."

Charles got in his car and plowed through the dust, trying to make his way east. Just getting to Guymon, one county over, proved hazardous. He had his head out the window the whole way, as he had done a year earlier during Ruth's birth, but this time the sand blinded him. He wore goggles and a respiratory mask but they clogged quickly and he was forced to remove them both. Once the car veered off the road and tipped, and it seemed like he was going to crash it again. He decided to drive along the ditch, with two wheels below grade and the other two wheels on the road. It was the only way to move forward through the haze and be sure of his direction. It was nearly three hundred miles to Enid, a drive of two days, moving slowly along the ditch. He kept going at night, with the headlights on. In order to drive halfway in the ditch, Charles had to bring up the chain that usually dragged below the car because it picked up too much debris — mostly dust-encrusted tumbleweeds. Without the chain, though, his car had no way to ground the static. What he needed was a lull between dusters. He got his wish during the first hundred miles. But midway into his journey, he drove into a duster and the static shorted his car. He was stranded.

He kicked the vehicle, coughed up a fistful of gunk, and shook the sand from his hair. He lubricated his nose with Vaseline and waited for the duster to pass, imagining his baby girl gasping in the hospital. After nearly an hour, the black blizzard dissipated, and Charles was able to restart the car.

By the time Charles made it to St. Mary's Hospital, he was covered in dirt, his face black. He went to the dust ward. Hazel was crying. Ruth Nell had died an hour earlier. She knew by the look on the doctor's face when he came to her with his hands up.

"I'm sorry — your baby is dead."

Back in No Man's Land, Hazel's Grandma Lou stopped coughing. She had been running a fever for several days and could not hold down food.

"How's the baby?" she asked. "How is Ruth Nell? Any word?"

Her son had not heard. Loumiza turned away and closed her eyes. She would not see the homestead green again, would not see any more of the starving land. She slipped under layers of quilt and took her last breath, dying within hours after her youngest great-grandchild fell. The family decided to stage a double funeral for baby Ruth Nell and the Lucas family matriarch. They would hold a ceremony at the church in Boise City, then proceed out of town to a family plot for burial on Sunday, April 14, 1935.

16

Black Sunday

T HE DAY BEGAN as smooth and light as the inside of an alabaster bowl. After a siege of black and white, after a monotonous jumble of grit-filled clouds had menaced people on the High Plains for seasons on end, the second Sunday in April was an answered prayer. Sunrise was pink with streaks of turquoise, a theatrical start. The air was clear. The horizon stretched to infinity once again, the sky scrubbed. There was no wind. The sun infused every gray corner with a spring glow. Nesters crawled out of their dugouts and shanties, their two-room frame houses and mud-packed brick abodes, like soldiers after a long battle. For once, they did not have to put on goggles or attach the sponge masks or lubricate their nostrils before going outside. They stretched their legs and breathed deep, blinking at the purity of a prairie morning, the smell of tomorrow again in the air. The land around them was tossed about and dusted over, as lifeless as the pockmarked fields of France after years of trench warfare. Trees were skeletal. Gardens were burned and limp, electrocuted by static from the spate of recent dusters. Still, the day had enough promise to remind people why they had dug homes into the skin of the southern plains, and some dared to entertain a thought on this morning: perhaps the worst was over.

Where to start? Windows were unsealed and opened wide, the heavy, dirt-laden sheets removed. Some windows had been sealed so tightly with wind-hardened dust that they would not budge. It was spirit-lifting to actually let clean air and sunshine inside. Going room to room with a scoop shovel, it was easy to fill a large garbage can with dirt. Roofs had to be shoveled, ceilings as well. Some ceilings had collapsed. Many were sagging. People cut holes overhead, crawled up, and pushed dust through the opening. Bed sheets, towels, clothes could be washed and allowed to dry in this sun, and they would smell of the plains on its best day. Outside, the cows would get a good scrubbing and drink from holding tanks without taking in grit. The cows looked so worn down, having lost patches of hair to the dust, their skin raw and chapped, their teeth chipped by chewing sandpaper with every meal, their gums inflamed. Chickens were due a run of the yard, fluffing sand out of their feathers. A horse might get its nostrils cleaned and find a stretch where it could gallop without sinking up to its knees in drifting sand.

A "grand and glorious" rabbit drive, as the *Boise City News* called it, was back on after a month-long delay because of dusters. A preacher had warned people they should not club rabbits on the Sabbath, that they would rouse the Lord to anger. But today the weather was flawless, a chance to kill maybe fifty thousand rabbits. And it seemed to some nesters like the perfect way to vent their frustration over a collision of bad days — forty-nine dusters in the last three months, according to the weather bureau.

Roy Butterbaugh, a musician by trade — sax and clarinet — who had bought the *Boise City News* on a lark a few years earlier, thought it was time to leave behind the bonds of this broken earth. He wanted to fly. The dusters had made him claustrophobic. Oh, to stretch out, to get above the dead ground and float in the blue and the sunshine. A friend had a little single-engine airplane at the edge of the town, next to the dirt strip that served as a runway. It did not take much to talk Butterbaugh into going for a spin in the clean air.

Church sounded right. This was Palm Sunday — a week before Easter, the start of the holiest time on the Christian calendar. God had to be in a forgiving mood or else why would the day be so wondrous? With weather like this, No Man's Land needed only a couple of good rainstorms and fields would once again be fertile, said a minister in his Sunday sermon in Boise City. But they had to pray in order for this to happen. Some who wanted to go to church were too embarrassed by how they looked. Little Jeanne Clark, who had just left the hospital in Lamar after a long bout of dust pneumonia, only had dresses made of sackcloth, with the onion brand names printed on the side. She could not go to church in such a thing; the other children would laugh at her.

In Baca County, Ike Osteen did extra chores around the dugout. After being cooped up so long in the pocket of home, Ike had a burst of energy. The dusters had been so thick through February and March that the half-section looked unfamiliar. He was seventeen now, a young man with an itch to get on with life. He wandered about the 320 acres of Osteen family ground, trying to find a familiar landmark. The orchard was dead and covered. A dune, perhaps six feet high at the top, had formed along the length of the tree line. It looked like a wave frozen in place. He saw prints in the sand from jackrabbits and heard a sound that had just arrived for the first time this withered spring — birdsong. Where would they nest? Maybe find a corner of the barn that had not been dusted. The garden space, where the Osteens had grown lettuce, tomatoes, carrots, sweet potatoes, and corn for popping, was under a drift grave. Implements and machines were buried. Ike found the tops of cultivator wheels and a horse-drawn buggy used by his late daddy. But only the tops. He thought of digging them out, but he would need more help than he could get from his two sisters and brother in the dugout. And where had all the topsoil gone? What state now held the Osteen farm? In places where dunes had not piled up, Ike found a couple of arrowheads. As he picked at the hardened dirt, he thought it might be an Indian burial ground, laid bare by the winds. He could see the outline of graves, and they made him wonder what the Comanche would do if they rose from the dead and found the buffalo grass gone and the land destroyed.

Using the scoop shovel, Ike cleared away enough sand to reveal the doors into the fruit cellar. His brother hauled water inside for baths. With the windows open on a windless day of perfect clarity, everyone in the dugout could get a good soak without worrying about the water going brown. After it cooled, the bathwater was not wasted. It was used to nurture an elm tree, just about the only thing still alive on the Osteen homestead. The outhouse was a roof above the sand. Drifts piled nine feet high against the walls. At least the dugout was not completely buried. Over at Roy Beightol's farm, a few miles away, the house had been drowned by dusters, and the family forced to flee. Only the shingles of the roof were visible.

After he had cleared a path from the dugout to the outhouse, Ike turned his attention to the Model-A, which he called Old Henry. After shorting out in a duster, Henry had not been driven for some time. It was all Ike could do to keep it from being buried during the month of March. Ike took a flat contact file to burned spots on the points in the distributor. He wore them down enough so that the engine fired. Now he had a way to get back to school. Of late, because of the difficulty of riding a mule or driving Old Henry to the Walsh High School, Ike had been staying all week in the village; he and his buddy Tex Acre were boarding with his grandma in Walsh. He came home only on weekends. For twelve years, Ike and Tex had been best friends, and the wonder was that they were still in school. All the times the train passed by, carrying their dreams out of Baca County, it had been hard to resist. They had to get through just April and May, and then they

Black Sunday, southern Colorado

would be free. Ike picked up Tex and drove over to Pearl Glover's house to give her a ride back to school as well.

They all agreed: it was the best day of the year. Shirtsleeve weather, temperature in the eighties. The three high school seniors drove with the windows down, the warm air in their faces, the spotless sky overhead. They talked about getting their gym back and resuming practice for the senior play. The Walsh High School gym had been a makeshift hospital for a month now, run by the Red Cross. But with the weather so nice and only the slightest breeze out of the southwest, Ike, Tex, and Pearl expressed hope that their gym would become a theater again.

About eight hundred miles to the north, people in Bismarck, North Dakota, started calling the weather bureau. A high-pressure system had been sitting over the Dakotas, and it was tussling with a cold front that had barreled down from the Yukon. With the clash of warm and cold currents, the air turned violent. Winds screamed over the grasslands, carrying dust so heavy that visibility was less than a hundred yards. The Dakotas had been pummeled by numerous dusters during the Dirty Thirties, but this one was bigger and stronger, packing a tremendous load of sand. In two hours' time, temperatures plunged more than thirty degrees, heralding the cold front's advance. By midmorning, the windblown soil slid down over South Dakota and was advancing on Nebraska. The weather bureau was flooded with questions:

What happened to the sunlight?

Why is it so dark?

Was this a twister? A series of twisters? Something new and horrible?

Where did it come from? What was the forecast? Where was it going? How long would it last?

Will we get enough air?

What should we do? Flee? Hide?

The weathermen were as confused as the callers. The storm that had moved out of the Dakotas a year earlier and blanketed New York, Washington, and ships at sea gained strength because it rode the jet stream and its high-level winds to the east. This duster was moving south with the cold front, but it was darker by far than anything ever seen before on the prairie. Some people compared it to a wall of muddy water, boiling up and then down on the earth. No air reconnaissance had picked it up; the nearest weather bureau measurement plane, used in the daily forecast of 1935, was out of Omaha, hundreds of miles east.

An Associated Press reporter from Denver, Robert Geiger, was traveling toward No Man's Land with photographer Harry Eisenhard on that Sunday morning. The route took them from Denver to the southeast, away from the mountains, over the high, browned prairie, through Arapahoe, Elbert, Lincoln, Cheyenne, Kiowa, and Prowers Counties, to Baca. They planned to go on to Boise City, Guymon, and Dalhart. There had been nothing to indicate a massive duster was on the way, but black blizzards were nearly impossible to forecast. The newsmen were simply looking for more anecdotes about the storms that were killing the southern plains. With black blizzards blowing through almost daily, Geiger's stories were getting good play across the nation. The pictures sent out by the wire service during that winter and early spring told as much, if not more, than Geiger's prose: people with masks and flashlights, navigating the perils of small-town main streets, cars dodging the drifts and haze of a country road, storefronts boarded up, schools closed, cattle lying dead in the dust.

When the big roller crossed into Kansas, it was reported to be two hundred miles wide, with high winds like a tornado turned on its side. In Denver, temperatures dropped twenty-five degrees in an hour, and then the city fell into a haze. The sun was blocked. That was just the western edge of the storm. The front end charged into Kansas carrying soil from four states. Near the town of Hays, where Germans from Russia had settled fifty years earlier, a small boy who had been playing in the fields with a friend dashed for home. He got lost in the midday blackness; confused, he circled back. The next day he was found dead. He had suffocated, half a mile from home.

A telegraph inquiry around 2:30 P.M. came by Morse code from northern Kansas to the railroad depot in Dodge City, Kansas, about 140 miles northeast of Baca County.

"Has the storm hit?"

The reply came a few minutes later, tapped from the Dodge City depot.

"My God! Here it comes!"

Dodge City went black. The front edge of the duster looked two thousand feet high. Winds were clocked at sixty-five miles an hour. A few minutes earlier there had been bright sunshine and a temperature of eighty-one degrees, without a wisp of wind. Drivers turned on their headlights but could not see ahead of them, or even see the person sitting next to them. It was like three midnights in a jug, one old nester said. Cars died, their systems shorted out by the static. People fled to tornado shelters, fire stations, gyms, church basements. There was a whiff of panic, not evident in earlier storms, as a fear took hold that the end was near. A woman in Kansas later said she thought of killing her child to spare the baby the cruelty of Armageddon. A weather bureau station agent wrote in his journal that the duster extended east and west for as far as the eye could see. It was lighter at the top, coal black at the ground. As it advanced, it seemed to recirculate, picking up fresh dirt and then slamming it down, in rolling fashion.

Ed Stewart of Elkhart, Kansas, ran outside and mounted his camera at the edge of town, pointing it north. As the biggest duster ever seen rolled into town, he clicked off a series of pictures. In the first frame of the sequence, the storm moves up behind Elkhart. Houses and small outbuildings and a car or two are visible in brilliant sunlight. They are dwarfed by the thick, heavy clouds creeping up behind them. Above the rolling front, the sky is still clear, highlighting the contrast. In the next frame, the clouds turn ink black as they swallow the town. By the middle frames, only telephone poles in the forefront are still visible; they soon disappear. The last pictures show a darkness of deep winter night — hole-in-the-ground black. The AP team, riding just ahead of the duster, was also getting pictures, but their shots were taken farther away from the front. The AP team drove into Baca County and headed for Boise City.

Just below Elkhart, in the northern fringe of No Man's Land, several hundred people were massed in a field for the rabbit drive that had been promoted by the *Boise City News*. They had driven from

Black Sunday, southern Colorado

Guymon and Boise City, and many came not out of civic duty but hunger. With cattle gone, no wheat in the ground, chickens running blind and hungry, people in No Man's Land had started to can rabbit meat to store in their cellars, along with the pickled tumbleweed. If meat was sealed tight in the canning jars, it would keep. The rabbit drive drew a huge crowd. People moved the animals along a V against a fence into a pen, where they were clubbed with bats, chains, and wrenches.

Ike Osteen was five miles away from his homestead, with Tex and Pearl, when he noticed rabbits and birds fleeing south. This he had never seen: a desperate migration, the birds screeching by his car, the rabbits in a sprint, all headed in the same direction. It was curious because there still was no wind, and the early afternoon was as luminous as the morning had been. He looked north and east, scanning the horizon of the broken land of Baca County on a rare day when a person could see into forever. Then he saw it, a few minutes past 4 P.M.

"Looks like it's gonna be a booger," he said to Tex.

They drove on another mile before realizing it was more than a booger — it was the mother of all dusters. The birds were now thick in the sky, the rabbits struggling to find hard ground on which to get some traction. Ike felt the static shoot through the inside of the car.

"Hey!" He touched Tex, and the shock was strong enough to knock him back. He felt like he had grabbed a power line, a live wire.

"Pull over," said Tex Acre. "Let's make for that house up ahead."

The Model-A quit on him. They got out of the car and took a quick look at the mountain advancing toward them, black and boiling. The farmhouse, owned by the Elmer Coulter family, was close by. The three teenagers made a dash for the farm. The Coulters were standing out front, watching the roller advance. Mrs. Coulter was on her knees praying.

"Hurry! Get inside!"

Every spike on a barbed-wire fence was glowing with electricity, channeling the energy of the storm. Ike and his friends were a few yards out when the dirt got them. It came quicker than most dusters and was deceptive because no wind was ahead of it. Not a sound, not a breeze, and then it was on top of them. They were slammed to the ground and engulfed by a wall, straight up and down, the dust abrasive and strong, boiling up, twisting. The noise was ferocious, a clanking, scraping sound. They could not tell up from down, one side from the other. Without their dust masks or goggles, Ike and his two schoolmates were blinded, and they struggled to breath. They crawled forward, clawing at the air, and found the farmhouse door. The Coulters let them in and slammed the door. It was black inside. Elmer Coulter lit a kerosene lamp, but the weak glow only extended a few feet, like a flashlight with dying batteries. They sat on the floor with towels over their heads and mouths. Tex was on one side of Ike and Pearl was on the other. He could hear their voices and feel their hands, but he could not see them. He could not see his own hand in front of his face.

In Boise City that morning, a double funeral was held at St. Paul's Methodist Church. Then it was time to bury two wooden caskets: the tiny one holding baby Ruth Nell, and the bigger one with the body of Loumiza Lucas. Hazel was struggling with her feelings of deep grief on this incongruously beautiful day. God had taken her only child and her grandma on the same day. The minister's words helped, some-what, but Hazel could not force her emotions into a tidy place. She had put on a face of dignity, wearing her white gloves, with hugs and thank yous to all the relatives. The tears came. She tried not to give in to the despair that owned No Man's Land. The church had been packed, more than two hundred people, not just the extended Lucas clan that lived all over the Oklahoma Panhandle but also much of Boise City, dear friends. Faye Folkers, the brightest student Hazel had taught, was there. She was a senior, same age as Ike, getting ready to graduate if the high school could stay open long enough for her to get a diploma. Sunday was her seventeenth birthday. After the funeral, she was going out with a friend for a drive.

The funeral procession started for Texhoma, a long line of Model-As, Model-Ts, and pickup trucks following the hearse that carried Grandma Lou, all moving southeast in the embrace of the spring sun-shine, the wind just a whispery breeze. The plan was to proceed over a dirt road forty miles to Texhoma and bury Lou next to her husband, Jimmy, near the ground they had worked so hard to cultivate, the place where members of the Lucas family became landowners for the first time. Hazel and Charles stayed behind. They had wanted to bury their baby in Boise City, at the little cemetery at the edge of town. They were part of Cimarron County, more than most. Hazel had rid-den horses over the land when it still had its grass. She knew most of the families and had taught many of their children. She had fallen in love with Charles at a Boise City track meet. They married in town, moved away and then moved back, started a business. They had no intention of leaving, even if No Man's Land seemed cursed. They wanted to bury their baby here, but the Boise City Cemetery was so drifted — sand covered the crosses and tombstones of departed pio-neers — that there was not a decent place to put a body in the ground. Hazel and Charles decided to bury the body of their baby in Enid, where his family lived, and wait until Monday to go east.

The procession was on the road by 3 P.M. The family estimated it would take three hours to get to Texhoma, giving them enough time to bury Grandma Lou an hour before sunset. The hearse carrying the old woman's body and the line of cars moved slowly over a road intermittently covered by drifts and pockmarked with ruts. Every car dragged a metal chain to ground the static, and these tails kicked up dust so that the Lucas funeral procession looked like a line of small clouds moving along a narrow road. After an hour, the caravan of grief came to a halt; a drift on the road blocked further advance. Lucas men with shovels got out and started digging, still dressed in their best clothes.

In the northern part of No Man's Land, Joe Garza was taking advantage of the clear day to find some stray cattle. Born on the Lujan ranch, Joe had learned to break broncos and cajole sheep before he was big enough to get a seat at the ranch dinner table. His world was the open ground of Oklahoma's far corner, the mesas of New Mexico and north into Colorado, riding horses over the old Santa Fe Trail, moving sheep, sleeping under the stars. Joe Garza was thirty-five years old this spring and alone in the world. His father had just died in Clayton. Joe worked for food and a roof over his head, which was portable: a horse-drawn wagon with a small cabin built into it. He knew the High Plains were broken, that nature was dead or had disap-

Black Sunday, Baca County, Colorado

peared. The creek near where he had been born, just down the slope from the ranch, was dry. And the grass that had fed Lujan sheep and cattle since the days when only the Comanche dialect or Spanish was spoken was under layers of sand.

On Sunday, Joe and another ranch hand, Ernest, rounded up a few stray head of cattle and shooed them over to a camp the wranglers kept near a creek bed. Along the way, they passed a sheepherder from the Lujan ranch, the Guyago boy, moving animals. He was too young to be out here alone, Joe thought. The day was clear enough that Joe had decided to sleep outside, though it would get down near freezing at night. Joe was cooking a pot of pinto beans over the fire, lying on his back, whistling away the Sunday afternoon when he saw birds fly by his camp. They screeched as they headed south, like they were sick or wounded. The cows acted funny as the birds moved by. Joe got up and walked over to the horses, which were tied to a stake. Joe's horse was pawing at the ground, nervous and sniffing like he knew something. His tail flickered and snapped with an electric crackle and the hair on his hide stood up, alive with electricity. Joe had seldom seen the horses so jumpy. He untied the harness and let the horses go. He knew they would come back. The Lujan ranch was the only place for miles where an animal could reliably get water and feed. If the horses wanted to run a bit on this glorious day, let 'em be. He went back to his early afternoon supper, the beans slow cooking over coals.

"Joe . . . look at the sky!"

He turned to the north and saw what looked like the leading edge of a fast-moving cloud. Joe walked up the side of the dry creek bed to get a better look, the spurs on his boots making it hard to move fast. When he got to the top, his heart went into a gallop. An enormous formation faced him — a tidal wave of roiling black — just a quarter mile away. He slid down the embankment and made for the little shelter atop his wagon. In an instant, the duster showered down on them, dirt streaming through the fine openings of the little cabin. Joe and Ernest stuffed rags into the openings and reached to find a kerosene lantern. They lit the flame, but it went out; there was not enough oxygen in the space to keep it alive. Joe lay on his stomach, a shirt over his head, the air snapping like gunfire, coarse sand swirling. Like other cowboys at the Lujan ranch, Joe was used to the dirt and wind. What scared him now was the blackness, as if the sun had been shot out of the sky. And it was cold.

Joe moved closer to the wall, shivering.

"Listen," he said to Ernest. "You hear that?"

He cupped his ear. It was a high-voiced cry. An animal? Horses didn't sound like that, even when they whinnied in despair. A cow? No bawling cry of a starving hoofer ever made that noise. A lamb? Not this bleat.

"I heard a holler," Joe said. "I'm going outside."

"You're gonna get killed."

"I'm going outside."

Joe stuck his head out, made a megaphone with his hands and shouted into the black void of the storm. He heard something in return. He shouted again. The voice came back.

"Keep on shoutin'. I'm gonna find ya."

He edged toward the voice, stumbling with his spurs. He fell to the ground, crawled forward. After forty-five minutes, he was close enough that the voice was next to him. He could not see a thing. He reached out and searched with his hands, trying to draw an image by sense of touch.

"Who's that?"

It was the Guyago boy, the sheepherder. The child was crying when Joe finally touched him. The boy said he was caught on the naked ground when dust descended on him and knocked him down. He thought he was going to be buried alive. He had crawled along the dirt, yelling, hoping his voice would reach somebody.

"Heeyyyyyoooooooh!" Garza yelled for the other ranch hand, back at the shelter. He hollered for some time, moving slowly in the direction where he thought the wagon would be, holding the boy's hand.

"Heyyyyyyooooohhh! Out heeeeeere!"

Finally, a voice came back.

"Joe! This way. . ."

Using the voice of Ernest as a guide, Garza and the boy crawled back to safety. Inside, Ernest had lit the kerosene lamp; there was now enough oxygen to keep the flame going. But they could not see each other's faces.

The funeral procession, about fifty people in all, was six miles out of Boise City, still a ways from the Lucas family plot in Texhoma. They had spread out some to let the dust from the chains dragging behind car axles settle. About 5:15 P.M., they saw the heap of half-mile-high dirt casting a shadow before it was on them, and it was so big, so dark as to scare some in the procession into thinking there must have been an explosion somewhere, that a mountain range had blown its top. The cars were in the flattest part of No Man's Land, a place where a bowling ball on hardpan was at its angle of repose. From this perspective, the mourners got a broad, expansive view of the Black Sunday duster. The wall looked like it ran for several hundred miles, east to west. The top was mostly flat, only slightly jagged at one end. The front was advanced by columns, which billowed ahead of the main storm, as if clearing the ground. The Lucas clan argued over what to do. Some people wanted to turn the caravan around and go back to Boise City. Others, mainly older family members, thought it disrespectful to turn tail on the day of Grandma Lou's burial. As the roller approached, options disappeared. Like a wagon train on the old Santa Fe Trail, the cars in the procession closed ranks with the hearse in the middle and faced south, so the storm would not hit the engines first.

"Who's got water?"

"Next to the radiator."

C.C. Lucas always kept drinking water in canvas bags. They poured water into scarves, shirts, and handkerchiefs, and tied them on. The children were told to crawl under the cars and keep the damp clothes on their faces. Everyone fell to the ground or got inside a car. As the big duster had bullied its way south, it had picked up more power and more density. There was probably no better source of pulverized sand than the arid, wasted wreckage of the High Plains on this afternoon in April. The earth went black. People saw flashes of electricity around their cars, the only light in the void. When it hit, the duster covered the hearse roof and the tops of vehicles, and blew granular bits against the windows and scoured the road beneath the cars where people were hiding. It was dark for more than an hour.

Around 6:30, the winds diminished enough so a person could stand without getting knocked down. As the coarse air thinned some, people were able to see their hands and then to see another face. But that presented frightening images for the children — the adults scared, with blackened faces, tears muddied.

They had to get back to Boise City. To stay out in this open road, with the black blizzard pounding them, could mean death. Headlights were turned on, and cars turned around to face north. Some cars would not start. With no visibility and a deep ditch on either side of the dirt road, it would be difficult to drive back to town, but people in the procession felt they had no choice. Half a dozen men stripped off their coats and joined hands. This flank of Lucas mourners would walk the road as a guide, followed closely by the hearse and the other cars. In this way, they groped their way back to Boise City.

The rabbit drive northeast of town was in midswing when the duster hit. Hundreds of people had herded several thousand rabbits against a fence. They moved closer for the killing, bashing heads with clubs and sticks when "that thing," as one man called it, lumbered near. Point your finger at it, someone said, and you would poke a hole in it — it was that thick. It's purple! No, it's closer to the inside of a dog — the blackest black. People dropped their clubs and scrambled for their cars. See now, this is God's wrath for killing bunnies on the Sabbath, just like the preacher said. A pickup truck full of teenagers sped for home. It veered off the road, the driver blinded by the storm, and fell into a ditch. The kids huddled under a blanket, waiting for the air to clear. Holding hands, they walked slowly, swatting at the black air, seeking a schoolhouse they had just passed. A hand felt a wall. The school was locked. One boy crawled through a window and opened it. It was cold inside, with the sun gone, the black norther upon them. They broke apart a desk and built a fire in the potbellied stove, waiting for light to return.

At the Folkers homestead, some chickens mistook the dark for nightfall and went inside to roost. Others clucked and jittered in a circle, their eyesight taken by the duster. Gordon and his mother, Katherine, worried about Fred. The old man had gone out with a friend, two miles away on the open land. Katherine and her son crouched low inside their house, unable to get a lantern going. That morning, Katherine had opened all the windows and cleaned the house, top to bottom. It had not been so free of dust in three years. This home, which had been the high point of the Folkers's progress in No Man's Land, now seemed a trap, a cave where the ceilings and walls slowly crumbled. The drought had so calcified the wooden window sashes that they had shrunk, opening space for fine dust to get inside. The Folkers had stuffed the cracks but earlier today had removed the towels for cleaning. Black dust showered along the walls and trickled through the ceilings.

The AP team traveled over the state line into Oklahoma, just ahead of the wall of dirt, but it was closing on them. Though wind speeds were estimated at one hundred miles an hour at the roof of the roller and sixty miles at the ground, the duster itself seemed to have slowed a bit, based on government notations of when the storm hit a certain place. By early evening, the formation was moving about forty miles an hour. The newsmen crossed the bridge over the anemic Cimarron River and aimed for Boise City. Just north of town, near the farm of Herman Schneider, they stopped their car. Eisenhard took a picture of the duster as it rose up behind the Schneider farm.

"What a swell picture," he said.

Black Sunday, Liberal, Kansas, 1935

The shot ran in newspapers all over the world, one of the few news service photographs taken of Black Sunday as it unfolded. Geiger estimated the cloud's height at several thousand feet. And while he initially thought it was black, he wrote in his notes that it appeared to be blue gray as it rolled over Cimarron County. In front of it were columns of dust, which looked like smoke, slightly lighter than the main duster. They got back in the car and sped ahead, trying to outrun the cloud, up to sixty miles an hour on the dirt road. It was not fast enough. They saw the road narrow like a tunnel before it disappeared altogether. Geiger slammed on the brakes and turned on the car lights. They sat in the black. After half an hour, they tried to move forward. Geiger braked again, swerved, trying to avoid a family of five that was standing in the road, looking for help. The car went into the ditch, just missing the people.

They pushed the car out, packed the family inside, and resumed as the blizzard lashed at them. In Boise City, the Crystal Hotel was filling up, and there was no way to see who was who or where to go. People crowded into the lobby, a room where bright-faced suitcase farmers once spent their earnings on the biggest steak on the menu. A crowd of scared, dusted exiles gathered around the weak lights of kerosene lamps. They wanted news. What was going on? Where had this come from? When would it end? What did it mean? Geiger had no answers. He wanted only to get back to Denver in time to get the AP pictures out. His car had shorted out. He offered fifty dollars to anyone who could drive him back to Denver.

Thomas Jefferson Johnson was walking home from the Lucas double funeral when the storm hit. Johnson was tall and tough, a homesteader who came west in a covered wagon from the Ozarks and established a dugout on a quarter-section. Johnson was just half a block from home when the blizzard overwhelmed him. He fell to the ground, fumbled for something to hold on to, tried to get his bearings. It was worse than either of the twisters he had lived through, worse than hailstorms that destroyed his crops in the past, as if all of No Man's Land was heaved up and collapsed. Felled by the duster, he crawled forward, crossing the road on his belly. Disoriented in the blackness, he moved on his hands and knees one way, which he thought would lead him to the house. But it led another way, and he never found it. The heavy sand blew up his nose and got into his eyes, burning. He crawled about six blocks away from the house, fumbling over hard ground and drifts, until he found a shed. It felt as if hornets had stung his eyeballs. Heavy sand was lodged under the lids and against the eyes. He rubbed them for relief, but that only wedged the dirt deeper. When Johnson's family found him later in the evening, his eyes were full of black dirt and he said he could not see. He went blind on Black Sunday, and his vision never recovered.

A few doors away from the Johnson house, Hazel Shaw was packing for the next day's burial of her baby when light was snuffed from the house. A four-year-old niece, Carol, was staying with them for the afternoon, playing around the little apartment attached to their funeral home. Hazel reached out blindly, trying to find the child. Every time she touched a doorknob or metal object, she was jolted by electricity.

"Carol . . . ? Carol! Where are you?"

Hazel had not slept since she took her dying child east a week earlier. The dust pneumonia, the struggle for life in the hospital, the mean, swift deaths of the baby and of Grandma Lou, and the funeral this afternoon — it had been one slap of sorrow after the other. Through it all, she had tried not to break down. But now, with her little niece missing, it was too much. She bumped into walls and knocked over dishes trying to find the child, the tears coming as the dust swirled through the house, her face streaked with black. What had she done to deserve this? Charles grabbed a large flashlight and went outside. The flashlight was worthless; the beam was able to penetrate only a few feet in the heavy silt of the black blizzard. He called for the child but heard nothing but the squawk of birds. Charles fell to his belly and shimmied along the street. There was slightly more visibility at ground level; the cloud seemed to hang just above the earth. Using this crawl space, Charles moved along the street, counting his arm lengths as a way to measure distance. When he got to a place that he estimated to be the approximate distance of the niece's house, he turned and crawled up to the door. He jabbered, his voice panicky, searching for faces.

"I . . . we . . . we lost Carol. She's gone! She was playing out front in the yard and then she was gone."

"No. No. It's all right. Is that you, Charles?"

The voices in the dark delivered a flash of good news. Carol was safe. The little girl was with them. She had run home when she saw the cloud creep up on Boise City.

Half a mile away, Roy Butterbaugh, the Boise City newspaper publisher, had just climbed into the seat of the little airplane at the edge of town, his buddy in the pilot's seat. They saw the duster approach and decided not to fly. But as they walked away from the dirt airstrip, the curtain fell on them, and they turned, racing back the other way to the airplane. The blackness caused them to stumble. On the ground, they crawled forward to the plane. They got inside, closed the doors. The plane was latched to the ground by guy wires, but it bucked in the fierce winds, rocking hard.

In the cockpit, the two men were just a few inches apart but could not see each other's face.

Another pilot, the aviator Laura Ingalls, had managed to get aloft before the storm. She was flying over the Texas Panhandle in a Lockheed monoplane, attempting to set a new nonstop flying record for crossing the continent. The plane was sleek with low wings, very

Dust storm approaching Johnson, Kansas, April 14, 1935

fast. Ingalls was approaching the Oklahoma border when she spotted the moving mountain of dirt. It stretched so far she could not see the rear of it, and it looked several hundred miles wide. Even at its top, where the wind should not be able to hold so many coarse dirt particles aloft, the formation was dark, a deep purple, she thought. Ingalls gunned the engine, ascending for cleaner air. She climbed to 23,000 feet. By then it was obvious: no way could she expect to leapfrog over this duster. She turned the plane around and scouted for a place to land, the record on hold.

"It was the most appalling thing I ever saw in all my years of flying," she said later.

The Volga Germans had gone outside after church services, taking in the sun and clean air. Their churches stood, though the paint had been blasted away by the dusters. Their houses, many made of brick and two stories, were monuments to craftsmanship, thrift and order. Above all, the Germans prided themselves on keeping their homes clean. On the Volga, there were laws against unswept sidewalks and unkempt front yards, punishable by lashings in the village square. To have the insides of these New World homes trashed by dusters, to have the walls and ceilings leak dirt, week after week, for years on end, was too much for some of the women. The land around Shattuck on the Oklahoma-Texas border had betrayed them. After four years of drought, the Ehrlichs were out of grain. George Ehrlich, the original settler, had lost his ambition when the grief took hold of him following the death of his little boy, Georgie, on the road near his house. It fell to Willie, his only surviving son, to keep the homestead going. On this Sunday, Willie had his calf out for a walk, looking for grass in a dried-up creek bed. He was wandering the land with his sister and her husband when black columns approached from the northwest.

"You better save that calf," Willie's sister said, pointing to a ravine near a fence line. "Looks like it's gonna be a terrible rain."

They had lived on the High Plains long enough to know that when a swollen, dark cloud formation burst and fell on dry land, the runoff could pump up a slit in the earth. Flash floods took almost as many lives as did prairie fires and twisters.

"That's no rain cloud," Willie said.

He had the calf in his arms when the dirt cloud hammered them. Knocked to the ground, Willie coughed up dirt, hollered for his sister and brother-in-law, and felt around for the animal. He rose to his feet and walked just a few steps before he fell again. The fence line was nearby. Willie found the prickly tumbleweeds balled up along the lengths of cedar and followed the line, figuring it would lead to the barn. Hand over hand, he moved along the fence, splinters jamming his palms and elbows, inching along until he ran out of wood. He was where the barn had to be. He knew every inch of this land. And yet, he reached out in space and touched nothing. Ehrlich stumbled along and felt a hay bale — he was in the barn after all. The storm had blown open the door. He huddled in a corner and waited until near midnight, when some shape and shadow returned to the world. He never found his calf.

After they had cleaned all four hundred square feet of their house, giving the two-room shack a shine like it had not seen since they moved in, and after each of the three children had taken a bath, the White family in Dalhart got ready for evening church services. Sure, they wore clothes handed out by the government, and shoes that had been restitched by the Mennonite cobbler brought into town by the relief ladies, but they were clean for once. Bam put on a shirt that smelled of springtime and waxed the tips of his handlebar mustache. Lizzie had been talking for years about moving out of Dalhart, and these last months had nearly broken her. When the wind blew straight for twenty-seven days in March, accompanied by dusters more reliable than rain, Lizzie started to crumble. She cried until the warm, salty mist of her tears muddied with dust, and she talked every day about a place where they could find a pool of cool water, a grove of flowering trees, air that would not throw shards of earth at the family. But they were stuck, like other Last Chancers. Bam was old, in a place where the years could dent a man well before his time was up. What could a gnarled cowboy do in a broken land? He dragged home meat sometimes from the government cattle kills, and he coaxed eggs from hens. He planned to get some corn and hay going.

Their feisty son, Melt White, had just found out from an aunt about the Indian blood in him. At first he tried to deny it to himself. Indians had all been run off the Llano Estacado, and nobody had a nice word for them. The kids at school gave him a bad time about his skin. They called him "Mexican" and "nigger." He knew now he was Indian because his daddy said it was so and that's why they could ride horses better than most, and also why the old man could not handle liquor. Cherokee, Irish, and English on his daddy's side, Apache and Dutch on his mama's side. He'd been told it was a disgrace to be part-Indian, especially Apache — they were the meanest, sorriest tribe in the world, that all they wanted to do was drink and fight, his relatives said. Melt was a teenager and starting to think about getting out.

"I'm just a boiled-up Indian," he told a friend. "I don't belong here."

He wanted to go someplace where he could ride horses like his daddy had done. The family house was a bare huddle of boards and tarpaper: no trees, no lawn, the garden dead from static electricity.

Melt was outside when he looked north and saw a long line of black drawn across the prairie. It seemed like it was a mile high and moved quickly. Just ahead of it, the sun lit up the brown fields of Dallam County and the streets of Dalhart. Birds flew low, in a straight line, next to swarming insects. He ran inside.

"We ain't gonna be able to go to church," said Melt.

"Why's that?" his daddy asked.

"Come outside and have a look."

Bam White needed only half a look. There was no time to give the storm a proper stare. He hurried back inside the house.

"Close them windas!"

They wetted down bed sheets that had just been cleaned and covered the windows. Most dusters blew sideways, the dirt seeping through the walls in horizontal gusts. This one showered from above, the black flour slithering down the walls. In the darkness, while fumbling for the lamp, Bam hit his knees on the edge of the stove. The electric shock hurt worse than the knee slam. Melt touched his nose with his fingers, just to reassure himself that his hands were still connected to his body. He could not see his fingers.

Half a mile away, Doc Dawson had been sitting on the porch swing with his wife. It was truly summerlike that afternoon, the temperature in the upper eighties. Every window in the house was open. The blizzard fell on Dalhart about 6:20 P.M. A Rock Island Railroad train that was approaching the terminal came to a sudden halt; the conductor had doubts about continuing in the soup of black. Cars died on the main street in front of the DeSoto Hotel and offices of the *Texan* and the Coon Building. Uncle Dick Coon was getting ready for a Sunday meal. He never saw the food. Drifters who had just finished eating beans at the Dalhart Haven mumbled in confusion. A nine-year-old boy walked in a circle, crying, less than half a block from his house. He screamed: "Help me, please! I've gone blind."

John McCarty was reading a book when the page went black. He felt his way outside, glanced back at his house, three feet away. It was gone. Using a heavy flashlight, he found his way to the newspaper office. A Teletype was sending a story from Kansas about a duster people were calling "The great grand daddy of all dust storms." He reached out to find the window of the building, which looked out onto Denrock. He knew the streetlights had to be on, but he could not see a thing. Heavy black sand settled inside the office. This storm McCarty would not praise. There would be no paean to the might and beauty of nature. Just days earlier, in advising his readers to "grab a root and growl" and hang on for better times, McCarty had predicted that the worst was over. Now he readied a page one headline for tomorrow's paper: "SUMMER DAY TURNED INTO NIGHTMARE."

A woman in southern Dallam County called the newspaper in Amarillo to alert them that the biggest duster of all was rolling south.

"I am sitting in my room and I cannot see the telephone," she said.

Inside a blackened room in Pampa, Texas, 110 miles southeast of Dalhart, a twenty-two-year-old itinerate folk singer thought up the first line of a song about the world coming to an end. Woody Guthrie was with several people clustered around a single light bulb; the glow was so weak it looked like the end of a cigarette. For the last two years, Guthrie had been wandering around the Texas Panhandle, doing odd jobs, hopping trains. While working at a root beer stand that sold corn whiskey under the counter, he'd picked up the guitar during idle times and learned how to strum a few chords. As he watched the Black Sunday duster approach, he thought of the Red Sea closing in on the Israelites.

"This is it," said one of the people in the room, citing Scripture. "The end of the world."

Guthrie started humming. He had the first line of a song, "So Long, It's Been Good to Know Ya."

It took an hour for the Black Sunday duster to travel from the border towns to Amarillo. At 7:20 P.M., the biggest city in the Texas Panhandle went dark, and its 42,000 residents choked on the same thick mass that had begun its roll in the Dakotas, clawing the barren plains, charring the sky in five states, producing enough static electricity to power New York, a fury that has never been duplicated.

17

A Call to Arms

BOB GEIGER'S DISPATCHES and Harry Eisenhard's images ran in newspapers everywhere, providing words and pictures for a story that many urban dwellers still could not believe: midnight at noon, a duster that wiped out the sun! Earlier black blizzards had gone unrecorded, bringing horror to the prairie and chipping away at lives but known only to people stuck in the isolation of the High Plains. And for the first time, a term entered the nation's lexicon. It came from another of Geiger's dispatches, a throwaway phrase that was part of a larger point he wanted to make.

"Three little words, achingly familiar on a Western farmer's tongue, rule life in the dust bowl of the continent — if it rains." The three little words did not stick as much as the two, and thereafter, headline writers, politicians, and newsreels referred to the airborne part of the southern plains by its new name: the Dust Bowl.

In the first days that followed Black Sunday, people tried to explain it. The weather pattern that produced the storm was not out of character, especially for early spring. A mass of polar air had moved south from Canada, colliding with the dome of high pressure over the plains. As the heavier colder air pushed down a prairie lane, it drove the winds and caused the extreme, sudden drops in temperature. The winds were part of the landscape — always had been. Ever since the first Anglos dug a blade into the grass, they made jokes about the lashing currents. Newcomers wondered if it blew all the time. The standard answer was that the wind would shriek for ten days and then blow like hell for another five. The drought was in its fourth year, and it was the worst in at least a generation's time. But long dry periods were as much a part of the Great Plains as the grass itself. What was different in 1935 was that the land was naked. If the prairie had been held in place by adequate ground cover — grass, or even the matted sprouts of wheat emerging from winter dormancy — the land could never have peeled away as it did, with great strips of earth thrown to the sky. There were ancient dunes all over the plains, such as Nebraska's Sand Hills, but they were anchored by grasses like prairie sand reed, native species that were a perfect fit for a big neighborhood of tough winds and unforgiving sun. The soil had been so pulverized by the dusters of 1933, 1934, and early 1935 that it was easy to lift. And fresh-formed dunes added reinforcement for Black Sunday clouds. With every new reach for the ground, the storm became heavier, thicker, darker.

By Monday, the remains of Black Sunday were blowing east and south into the Gulf of Mexico, greatly dissipated at last but still carrying enough prairie residue to postpone daily life, if only for a few hours. For days, Congress had been sitting on Hugh Bennett's plan to save the Great Plains from itself. He wanted money and human support to go well beyond the scope of the demonstration projects that were up and running. He wanted something *permanent,* to ensure against wipeouts and to try and restore the grass. There were plenty of doubts, even as Bennett attempted to make his case like a trial lawyer in final argument. Witnesses testified about towns with a foot in the grave, farms abandoned, land that had not produced a crop in four years, families sick and hungry, schools closed, and the only hope a miracle from the president or rain from stingy skies. Bennett had been trying to draw a big picture, to impart some sense of the magnitude of the collapse of the plains. It was not just black blizzards, starving cattle, and an exodus of hollow-eyed people. The human stories, each sad in their own way, were part of a larger tragedy: the collapse of a big part of mid-America. One hundred million acres had lost most of its topsoil and nearly half had been "essentially destroyed" and could not be farmed again, Bennett said. Think about the size, Bennett said: an area stretching five hundred miles north to south and three hundred miles east to west was drifting and dusted; two thirds of the total area of the Great Plains had been damaged by severe wind erosion — an environmental disaster bigger than anything in American history.

Within the Roosevelt Administration, there were conflicting views on what was happening. A Harvard geologist told the president that an irrevocable shift in nature was underway, that the climate itself had changed, the start of a cycle that would take a hundred years or more and leave the southern plains a "desert waste," as Secretary of the Interior Ickes noted in his diary. The Agriculture Department said the cycle was shorter — this was the fourth year of a projected fifteen-year epoch — and classified it as a severe drought, not a shift in climate or geology. Still, a dry period of that duration could mean dozens, maybe hundreds, of towns in Kansas, Nebraska, Colorado, New Mexico, Texas, and Oklahoma would disappear, falling off the map as quickly as they had been stapled to it. It could mean that a big section of the United States that had once been labeled the Great American Desert would revert to its earlier designation. The cattle slaughters and payments to prevent people from planting more wheat had brought prices up, but government-subsidized scarcity had done little to restore the overall farm economy. The system was broken, just like the land. The debate was whether to start from scratch, with radical new methods of farming, or to give up on the southern plains altogether. Roosevelt was still fascinated by the idea of planting millions of drought-tolerant trees in the dusted-over flatlands, creating a huge protected zone. He was waiting for the report on its feasibility. The shelterbelt project could be a noble calling, Roosevelt argued, for a payroll of young, uniformed CCC workers motivated by an almost wartime urgency to save America's heartland, giving it the "lungs" of a transplanted forest.

Ickes continued to make the case against offering people more incentive to keep farming the Dust Bowl. At times, Ickes was an idealist, the designated dreamer of the New Deal. "Utopian goals? Utopian indeed," he said in response to a reporter's question two years into the administration. "We are a spiritual people, and life for us would not be worth living if we did not have this urge to reach for what will always seem beyond our reach." But he was also a practical pol, schooled in Chicago's street-tough trenches. His sharp elbows belied his scholarly look. As interior secretary, he was emperor of the outdoors, in charge of a public domain nearly the size of Germany. In his view, the land was spent; the drought was simply the deathblow. It was hard to tell people that their earnest agricultural toil had brought them great woe but Ickes did, even when his bluntness got him in trouble. He also went after politicians who were using New Deal relief plans to build regional empires. The Kingfish, Senator Huey Long from Louisiana, had told Ickes he could "go slap down to hell" for criticizing him. Ickes's response was in character:

"The trouble with Senator Long is he is suffering from halitosis of the intellect," he said. "That's presuming Emperor Long has an intellect."

Hugh Bennett took a different tack, using country charm and playing off the sheet music of history. Big Hugh was one part science and one part showboat. He had backed off trying to shame people into action and no longer singled out the United States as the biggest abuser of the land the world had ever known. Using the public-works dollar, people could build ponds and holding tanks. They could form community farming districts where everyone would agree to practice a strict set of conservation rules, rotating crops, fallowing land, abandoning tear-up-the-earth methods of plowing. They could stop the spread of dunes by building natural barriers. Big Hugh had come a long way in the two years since Roosevelt hired him. At first, the government looked at the wreckage of the plains in the same way it viewed the great Mississippi River flood of 1927, or a tornado or hurricane, for that matter — a natural disaster requiring relief. The Red Cross and the government worked to get people out of harm's way, to provide cots, food, shelter. In 1933, Bennett had been given five million dollars in relief funds to jump-start his fledgling Soil Erosion Service — a temporary agency with a limited scope: relief. But as the dusters picked up in ferocity, Bennett was one of the first in Washington to try and convince people it was not just another natural disaster or an epic drought. It seemed like something caused by man, a byproduct of hubris and ignorance on a grand scale. Maybe some of it could be reversed. But to do so, people would have to think anew about how they used the land. It could not be done in a piecemeal fashion.

Bennett worked Congress, trying to persuade them to create a permanent, well-funded agency to heal the land. He wanted there to be local control, with the first nudge coming from Washington. In his mind, every farm community would set up a soil conservation district and look at their region as part of the fabric of local ecology. Big Hugh was an imposing figure, notes stuffed in his pockets, hair uncombed, blue eyes bulging, his glasses coming on and off as he waved his big, dirt-soiled hands, citing everything from Pliny's descriptions of Roman terracing in *Natural History* to Thomas Jefferson's recommendations on contour plowing. There was much skepticism about spending tax money on such a venture. Weren't there enough New Deal public works and farm relief programs to help those sorry folks stuck in the High Plains? Yes, but Bennett wanted money specifically for a plan to hold the ground down for generations to come. It had to go beyond relief and triage. But didn't this go against the grain of the yeoman farmer? The sod was broken by strong men, working alone, who never got a dime or half a thimble of advice from some agency operating out of Washington, D.C. They were the toughest sons of bitches on the planet. What could some soil expert from the city know that a nester who had poked his ground for fifty years didn't know?

"If God can't make rain in Kansas," one congressman asked, "how can the New Deal hope to succeed?"

Bennett conceded that FDR had no plans to take on the work of God. His idea was much simpler: change human behavior, not the weather. "One man cannot stop the soil from blowing," he said. "But one man can start it." He also noted that the people in the desperate zone were begging for guidance. These tough farmers were on their knees, hands extended to Washington. Here was a telegram from ranchers in Dallam County, Texas, asking for a soil erosion project. Here were others from Kansas, Oklahoma, Nebraska. Just show us the way, they pleaded.

Still, many politicians thought other parts of the country needed more help. More than two million people had found government public works jobs, which paid a minimum of twelve dollars a week, putting bandages on the wounds of American life. But nearly twenty-five million were still without regular income, relying on part-time jobs, private charities, or black-market income. For African Americans, the unemployment rate was 50 percent. Throughout the South and in some places in the North, notes were posted on job sites that read, "No jobs for niggers until every white man has a job." It took an executive order from Roosevelt in May 1935 to open up the public works ranks to all races. Nationwide, per capita income had fallen from $681 in 1929 to $495 in 1934. The ranks of landless farmers had swollen to an unmoored army. Between 1930 and 1935, there were 750,000 bankruptcies or foreclosures on farms. In the tenant-farmer areas in the South, New Deal scarcity payments stuffed the pockets of landowners but forced sharecroppers onto the open road. Shattered lives littered the land from sea to sea. Why should the dust-ravaged plains get special attention?

Others thought the nesters of the southern plains were too dumb, too inbred, too thick to deserve more help. "They are simply, by God's inscrutable will, inferior men," wrote H. L. Mencken, one of the most influential columnists in the land. The best thing to be done would be to sterilize them, he said.

Bennett had been in touch with weather stations in the South. Black Sunday had changed everything. The storm's detritus — or perhaps it was a new duster — was moving east, picking up dirt in other states, even if it no longer had enough force and density to blot the sun. Bennett had been scheduled for another round of testimony before the Senate in midweek. After checking with the progress of the eastbound roller, he asked for a delay. The storm that blanketed New York and Washington one year earlier had been an eye opener. As Bennett told an aide, "When people along the eastern seaboard began to taste fresh soil from the plains two thousand miles away, many of them realized for the first time that somewhere, something had gone wrong with the land."

He wanted them to get another taste. On Friday, April 19, five days after Black Sunday, Bennett walked into Room 333 of the Senate Office Building. He began with the charts, the maps, the stories of what soil conservation could do, and a report on Black Sunday. The senators listened, expressions of boredom on the faces of some. An aide whispered into Big Hugh's ear. "It's coming."

This prompted a broad diversion, more on Pliny and Jefferson, jokes about his own farm and how hard it was to maintain the place. Keep it up, the aide told Bennett again, it will be here within an hour, they say.

Bennett told how he learned about terracing at an early age, about how the old ground on his daddy's place in North Carolina was held in place by a simple method that most country farmers learned when they were young. And did he mention — yes, again — that an inch of topsoil can blow away in an hour, but it takes a thousand years to restore it? Think about that equation. A senator who had been gazing out the window interrupted Bennett. "It's getting dark outside."

The senators went to the window. Early afternoon in mid-April, and it *was* getting dark. The sun over the Senate Office Building vanished. The air took on a copper hue as light filtered through the flurry of dust. For the second time in two years, soil from the southern plains fell on the capital. This time it seemed to take its cue from Hugh Bennett. The weather bureau said it had originated in No Man's Land.

"This, gentlemen, is what I'm talking about," said Bennett. "There goes Oklahoma."

Within a day, Bennett had his money and a permanent agency to restore and sustain the health of the soil. When Congress passed the Soil Conservation Act, it marked the first time any nation had created such a unit. Immediately, 150 CCC camps were reassigned from the Forest Service to Bennett's renamed Soil Conservation Service to augment the few troops he already had on demonstration projects. They would work "to the task of ending the waste of our land," as Roosevelt said, dispatching his restoration army. In all, about 20,000 people were sent to the southern plains. They came from the cities, from universities, from farms in other parts of the country. The president signed the act before April had ended, the worst month for those stuck in the blowing dirt.

But the administration was of two minds about what to do, for

Roosevelt also created, at the same time, the Resettlement Administration. The purpose was to give loans, averaging about seven hundred dollars a family, for people to start anew or to buy land for the same purpose. Though he was still reticent about encouraging a massive exodus, Roosevelt signed Executive Order 7028, granting federal authorities the power to buy back much of what it had given away in homesteads over the previous seventy-three years. The executive order was a stunning reversal of everything the government had done with the public domain since the founding of the republic. To some people who had staked their lives to land once heralded by the government as a source of "health, wealth and opportunity" and remembered when it paid for trainloads of nesters to the agricultural frontier of the arid lands, it smelled like one thing — a push to depopulate the plains.

In Dalhart, John McCarty took a fresh vow, in public: this will not stand! His anger burned through his prose and carried his voice. If they want to kick us out — we'll show them! McCarty announced formation of the Last Man Club, himself as president, open to anybody who agreed to stay put. No matter how hard the dust blew, no matter how deeply people were buried in sand, they would not retreat. His people were Spartans. They would hunker in their dust bunkers "until hell freezes over," he said. And then they would skate on the ice over hell. He printed enrollment cards that read:

> Barring Acts of God or unforeseen personal tragedy or family illness,
> I pledge myself to be the Last Man to leave this country, to always be
> loyal to it, and to do my best to cooperate with other members of the
> Last Man Club in the year ahead.

A person signed their name at the bottom, next to McCarty's signature, and was given a number. Last Man Number One was Ealy Moore, a rawhide-skinned former XIT trail boss now reduced to telling stories about the long-gone grass. Uncle Dick Coon, now said to be the only wealthy man left in town, was Last Man Number Two. The third man to join was Texas governor James V. Allred, who had been enrolled by Uncle Dick on a visit to the capital. It was a political stunt, but it worked, spreading the word of this defiant band of nesters in the middle of the Dust Bowl. Doc Dawson, destitute, suffering from ill health, running the soup kitchen, was Last Man Number Four. It wasn't just geezers, McCarty noted. Wilson Cowen, the young judge, was Last Man Number Thirty-One. If this elite group of citizens, Spartans whose mark on the land was as clear as the stakes originally planted by the Comancheros a hundred years earlier, wasn't evidence of the iron will of those in the middle of the Dust Bowl, what more proof could a person ask for?

A week after Black Sunday, banners went up around town: "RALLY TONIGHT — LAST MAN CLUB." McCarty's speeches were filmed by newsreels and sent to theaters across the country. He still looked like a young Orson Welles, with his athletic build and shock of dark hair. Behind him was a larger banner of the Last Man Club.

"Are we gonna stay here till hell freezes over?" he thundered.

"Yes!"

"I ask you again: how long are we gonna stay here?"

"Till . . . hell . . . freezes . . . over!"

The cheers spilled onto Denrock Street, where the dirt from Black Sunday had yet to be shoveled away, and onto cars stuffed with children, dishes, pots and pans, a few rickety chairs, and other belongings, families fleeing the lethal dust. Even as Judge Cowen joined the Last Man Club, he knew many people had to leave town or face death. "Exodusters," they were called. One Dalhart family asked the judge if he might buy them a tire to get them on their way. Other families with a cup or a hat in front of their belongings begged for gas money to launch them west. But hadn't they heard about the signs at the California border, warning Exodusters to turn back, that there was no work in California? Maybe. But there wasn't anything to hold a person to Texas, either. In Texas, per capita annual income was $298 — half as much as California. Judge Cowen ordered a Dalhart filling station to grant people leaving town ten gallons of gasoline — worth about $1.90 — and one secondhand tire. The offer was open to Dallam County residents only. It was the least they could do, the judge said, for somebody who had survived the blowing dirt of the last four years.

Over poker and drinks at the DeSoto Hotel, people carped at the handout of gas and tire. Deserters, they called those who packed up and left. No guts. Why should Dallam County give them anything? The people who decided to stick it out, to grab a root and growl with McCarty, were fired up by all the attention that came to the Last Man Club. They were Spartans — goddamn right! — but they had one big question: what would they do while growling?

For starters, they could kick some rain from the clouds. Tex Thornton, the former wildcatter, now full-time rainmaker, had his tool kit of explosives, his payment from the city, and was ready to start bombing the skies to bring moisture down on the Panhandle. He certainly had the endorsement of McCarty, who believed that all the shortgrass prairie really needed was a little rain and then the country would rise again.

"If you get a chance, meet Tex Thornton," McCarty wrote. "Tex handles this soup TNT and nitro-glycerin like it was so many sticks of wood. He is a real fellow."

McCarty urged people to join his Last Man Club quickly.

"I'm going to close the membership list with the first big rain because after we get a genuine soaker everybody will be wanting to stay and those who have gone away will want to come back."

His writing served a dual purpose, for McCarty was not only editor of the *Texan,* but he was now also director of the Chamber of Commerce, which had hired Thornton. Tex was waiting for just the right conditions before he worked his meteorological magic. By early May, he was ready and set up operations four miles out of town. The first evening, with a curious crowd watching, Thornton fired off his TNT rockets, one charge every ten minutes or so. Some of them carried as much as ten sticks of dynamite. The wind and dust blew as usual, obscuring Tex himself as he went through his rounds. After a few hours, people trickled home. In town, people could hear the thunder from Thornton's pyrotechnics well into the night. Doc Dawson wandered outside every half an hour, craned his neck, looking to the sky. Wind and dust. No rain.

The next day, Tex resumed his bombing. A smaller crowd showed up this time. Tex fired off a couple of duds, which blew up in the ground, creating his own dust storm that chased the crowd away.

"Gotta work on that," he said. "Needs some tinkering."

The fireworks continued through the afternoon and into the evening. Dawson strolled around town, taking in the sorry state of Dalhart as it tried to rally itself with aerial bombings and a Last Man Club. The acts of defiance felt good, but the town looked pathetic — no leaves on bare trees, dunes piled high on the sides of buildings, houses chipped to gray wood, the sand plowed like snow at the edge of town. Dawson would "howdy, neighbor" to people he had known since he pulled into the startup town in 1907, and they would "howdy" back. But a second exchange usually ended in details of something dark: news of a loved one suffering from dust pneumonia, a looming bankruptcy. People were at their breaking points. Almost everyone was sick with a variation of duster lung siege.

Thornton started up again the third day in the afternoon. Towns east of Dalhart complained that Tex was only sending more dust their way and asked him to stop.

"Just about got it right," Tex said.

The sky took on a beige look, which deepened to cinnamon brown as the wind carried a fresh duster into town. Tex aimed his explosives at the dust clouds, firing round after round until the thickening duster forced him into retreat at the dinner hour. After supper, with the winds taking a breather, Thornton was back at it. He attacked the sky until nearly midnight. The *crack crack* of explosives kept the Doc and most of Dalhart from sleeping. Dawson wandered outside in his nightshirt, held his hands palm-side up. Wind and dust. No rain. The sky looked eerie, light flashing at the base of dust clouds from the big calcium flares that Tex had sent up.

On day four, Tex Thornton rested. The forecast, as indicated by the barometer, called for colder temperatures, little moisture in the air — nothing fat enough to bomb. As for his failure to date, Tex said he needed only a bit of refinement. The problem was that he had to get his explosives directly into the belly of the clouds. He produced small gas balloons for precise aerial delivery and announced resumption of the rainmaking tomorrow morning, at a new location out of town. Tex tethered his balloons to a kite string, loaded them with bombs, and set them aloft. He came equipped with a special dust suit and mask, designed to keep him in place no matter what the sky threw back at him.

As the temperature dropped, low clouds moved in. There were reports of snow in Clayton and other parts of New Mexico, just to the west. Tex continued firing at the sky until dark. That night a light dusting of snow fell, one tenth of an inch. McCarty was ecstatic. It snowed the next day as well, changing to sleet with warmer temperatures. Of course, it also snowed in Denver, Albuquerque, and Dodge City, places that had not felt a rumble from the hands of Tex Thornton. Still, a grateful citizenry thanked the rainmaker from Amarillo. He had done his job. Some even thought the drought was over. They massed that night for a final rally on behalf of the Last Man Club.

"How long are we gonna stay here?" McCarty asked.

"Till hell freezes over!"

"That's right. Till hell freezes over!"

Tex tipped his hat, packed up his weather balloons, his nitro, and his TNT, and went on his way. "I did the best I could," he said. "I'm mighty glad for the people of Dalhart."

Optimism did not follow the snow flurries forty-eight miles north into Boise City. The town was reeling after Black Sunday, stripped bare. A few days after Hazel Shaw buried her baby, she returned home to the empty funeral home and the one-bedroom apartment. The crib haunted her. The church across the street glared back, housing an angry God. Grandma Lou finally had been laid to rest in Texhoma after the funeral procession had retreated back to Boise City, hunkered down for the night, and then resumed the march to her grave the next day. All things in No Man's Land, the landmarks of Hazel's life, had lost their meaning. She felt alone, staggered by depression. The questions, tinged with guilt, played over and over: Could she have done something to save Ruth Nell? Should she have tried to flee earlier? Why did they stay in Boise City so long, with the power of the storms building every day, the dirt so deadly?

The wind found any openings, carrying fresh black and brown powder into the apartment, rekindling the doubts. She busied herself with chores, but at times she simply broke down. It seemed useless: the repetitive tasks of cleaning a surface or a curtain or a floor that would sprout a new growth of prairie whiskers within half a day. She drove to homesteads of other Lucas family members and got further depressed. The roads were a hazard. But she felt so claustrophobic, so cornered; she had to see some green, to find clear sky, to escape the trapped enclosure of the dusted apartment. There was nothing that spring to indicate the new season: not a sprout or sprig of new life. The dead cattle, some with their eyes frozen and glazed over with sand, were pinned in grisly repose against fences holding tumbleweeds and dirt. Her uncle C.C. cut open the stomach of one dead cow that had wandered onto his land. His autopsy found the stomach packed so solidly with dust that it blocked food from getting any further. Other postmortems found the same thing: animals dead from starvation caused by internal suffocation. The dust was killing everything in No Man's Land.

By late 1935, more than a thousand people, about 20 percent of the population, had pulled up stakes and left Cimarron County since the start of the drought four years earlier. They crowded into horse-drawn wagons or Model-As with worn tires, the paint long ago chipped away, and headed east to Missouri and beyond to the Carolinas, or north to Denver, to the Snake River Plateau of southern Idaho, or eastern Washington State, or west to California. Ezra and Goldie Lowery, living on their canned thistles and yucca roots at the homestead outside Boise City, vowed again to hold on, despite the horrendous year they had suffered. Their daughter, Odalee, a senior and high school classmate of Faye Folkers, started the school year with mumps on her left side. She was out for a week, then went down with mumps on the other side of her neck. In November, she came down with the measles and was quarantined for three weeks. By February, a month when there was seldom a day without a suffocating dust storm, Odalee was diagnosed with scarlet fever. She was quarantined for another two months, and the family was forced to flee the homestead. They returned on April 14, Black Sunday. Her father remained defiant.

"We may have to eat rattlesnake," he said. "But I'm not leaving."

A month later, Odalee graduated. She was class valedictorian.

Some of Hazel's friends who had joined the exodus, filing west with migrants from tenant farms in Arkansas and eastern Texas and Oklahoma, reported back in letters that California was no better than Cimarron County. No matter where they had come from, or if they had some schooling or owned land, they were called the same thing: *Okie.* It meant being no better than a throwaway rag. At least in No Man's Land, people had family and friends to help them through or were able to swap a service for a dozen eggs or a shank of ham, and people looked you straight in the eye, with respect.

Signs in the Central Valley of California made clear how people felt about the new arrivals. One sign read: "OKIES AND DOGS NOT ALLOWED INSIDE."

Over the next two years, 221,000 people would move to California, most of them from Arkansas, Oklahoma, and Texas. But only 16,000 came from the actual Dust Bowl. A majority of people in the most wind-bared and lacerated counties in the southern plains did not move, or they relocated only a few hundred miles in one direction.

Hazel and her husband, Charles, were ready to get out. Yes, they had their little mortician's business. But families could not afford to pay. The Shaws would dress, help to ritualize, and bury a loved one, and then get paid in grocery scrip, or chickens, or a promissory note, or a little cash that was not nearly enough to cover expenses. The future was a black hole. Even Sunday visits to other Lucas family members were no longer an option — the sheriff warned people not to drive unless they had an emergency. Three weeks after Black Sunday, a pair of cars smashed head-on, killing the drivers. They were going only fifteen miles an hour when they collided, but the dust was so heavy it blinded the drivers. With every day, Hazel felt more buried, more depressed. Her hometown, which had rejected any relief help when the dry years started, now turned to Washington in desperation. Boise City had no pride left, no options, no future. The Cimarron County commissioners sent a telegram to the White House:

"80% OF RESIDENTS IN COUNTY IN DIRE NEED OF IMME-DIATE RELIEF TO SAVE THEM FROM SEMI-STARVATION."

18

Goings

THE OSTEEN DUGOUT broiled in the heat. In May, the temperature rose to 105 degrees, the highest the mercury had ever been that early in the year in Baca County. Once again, Ike and his brother Oscar carried buckets of water from the stock tank and threw it over the dugout. When the water hit the tarpaper roof, a hissing sound came from the Osteen home. Only a single elm tree was alive, sustained by water from baths and dishwashing. Inside the dugout, the sheets of mud that hung from the windows were worse than bars inside a prison cell, a reminder that the dust was always there, and they were trapped with it. Cramped as it was, the Osteens tried not to touch each other because of the static, the same kind of electrical energy that caused the windmill to spout a flame from a trailing wire and barbed-wire fences to emit blue sparks. But Ike and Oscar were always rubbing elbows, the connection sending a sharp, painful jolt. Ike's mother was thinking about moving the girls to town, to some little place, doing odd jobs. She had fed her family in part by canning meat from the government cattle kills. You could can anything, she always said.

It seemed like all of Baca County was ready to fold. Three miles from the Osteen homestead, the little village of Richards had shrunk to a post office. When Ike had attended grade school there, the town had two general stores, a cream and egg station, a couple of shops, and a fine cluster of homes. Richards would be gone before the decade's end; it had the smell of death on it, and the dusters themselves

236

seemed to sense it. Baca, so heavily plowed in the 1920s, was one of the most blown-away counties in the heart of the Dust Bowl; more than 1.1 million acres were so eroded they probably would never support a crop again, in the view of the government men. Not long after Black Sunday, a wire service reporter toured a Baca County mail route with a postal carrier. The mail had been delayed for nearly a week because the train could not get through to Springfield, the county's biggest town. They came upon homesteads where people had not seen a fellow human for weeks. At one location, a lone woman was shoveling dirt from a front walk; she was shoeless and hollow-eyed. When the mailman approached, she dropped the shovel and clutched his arm. She said she had been marooned for days.

"What's happened?" the woman asked. "What's going on in the outside world?"

The reporter asked her why she didn't leave.

"I'd like to," the woman said. "But I can't." She said the land was all she had; she thought she would die in a city, not knowing anyone, unsure how to feed herself.

Most Baca residents would have starved without the government. With nearly 50 percent of the county on relief, it wasn't considered a weakness to get help from somewhere else, because the land itself had given up. A church sent a telegram to the wire services in Denver, asking the entire nation to pray for rain in the far southeast corner of Colorado. They set the day of prayer for May 5. It didn't rain that day, nor the next day, or the day after. On May 8, a bundle of bruised clouds appeared on the horizon, rumbled with thunder, then let loose a gully-washer. It rained fast and furious, but the water hit bone-hard ground and drained to long-dry indentations in the earth, filling ravines until they rose in a muddy torrent and smashed sheds and took a horse and then disappeared. It was as if it had not rained at all.

In the summer of 1935, FDR launched the Second Hundred Days, one of the great thrusts of domestic change ever seen — zero to sixty in an eyeblink, by government time. Roosevelt signed the Social Security Act to ensure that the pensionless elderly would not starve, started the Works Progress Administration to keep the government payroll rolling, and backed the National Labor Relations Act, which enshrined union rights in the workplace. The farm economy was improving: income higher by 50 percent, crop prices up by 66 percent since Hoover had been turned out of office. Roosevelt took credit, saying the government cattle and hog kills and the plowing-under of surplus land had moved the market by creating a forced scarcity. The Supreme Court disagreed, at least on agricultural reach; they declared FDR's control of farm economy unconstitutional. The government could not *be* the market. Roosevelt was outraged. He accused opponents of "deliberately trying to mislead people by misrepresenting — no, why use a pussyfoot word — by lying about the kind of a farm program under which this nation is operating today."

But his Resettlement Administration was left intact by the ruling, and the government found plenty of takers, not so much for the loans to stay put as for money to leave. Those who did not own land — or had come as suitcase farmers during the wheat boom — took a thirty-five-dollar grant from Resettlement to move on. One day a boy would be sitting next to Ike Osteen in school, same as always, and the next day the seat would be empty, the boy gone for good. It was no shame to give up on school. Among the nine children in the Osteen family, Ike alone had stayed with the books to his senior year. His brother Oscar didn't see much use for education. Even after Black Sunday, when most of the next year people stopped counting on the future as a way out, Oscar Osteen held out hope of making something from the family land. They had a couple of mules, a barn, the buried tractor. There was always a chance Oscar could wake up one morning and the dunes would be gone, unveiling fields ready for planting, a little orchard, ground for growing broomcorn and popcorn, wheat and alfalfa. You never knew. Ike was more of a realist; if there was something for him in the homestead, he couldn't see it. In 1911, his daddy had hauled lumber by horse-drawn wagon from Elkhart, Kansas, thirty-two miles away, to build the barn and prop up the walls and roof of the Osteen dugout because he believed in transformation by hand. Build it, shape it to your will, and things would happen. In his day, horse freighters on their way west would overnight at the Osteen barn, bringing gossip, material goods, and fresh bits of human insight to lonely homesteads. Even at this young age, Ike sensed that Baca was never meant to be plowed and planted. He loved the land and part of him wanted just to stay put and fight. He was not a quitter.

The Red Cross moved the cots out of the school gym and the students set up chairs for graduation in May 1935. School had always been easy for Ike, even though he got in trouble for pranks, and he missed many days because the dusters kept him home. He was asked to make a little speech as class salutatorian. Only one student had better marks. Graduation day was sweat-your-pants hot inside the gym, but they could not open windows or even the doors for long to catch a breeze because the sand would swirl inside and make people gag. When Ike was called to the front to give his speech, the room went quiet but for the coughs of people who could not hold the soil down. He took a moment to scan the audience and find his mama in the crowd. She was red-eyed, wiping her face. Ike started in with his talk about how the future had to be better than the past, but that even with the black blizzards and the broken land and all the people leaving, Baca County was a great land, and he would always have fine memories of this little school on the prairie. He paused again because his mama was crying now; sitting there in front, she could not hold back the tears. Ike finished by thanking teachers who had seen him through, paid in grocery scrip.

Outside, after the ceremony, a hot wind blew, and Ike's mama brushed the tears from her eyes. She kissed her youngest boy.

"Congratulations," she said. "You did what no Osteen has ever done."

Ike handed his diploma to his mama.

"You take this," he said.

"Why?"

"That piece of paper says I have completed twelve years of education."

"Yes."

"But I want you to know something, Mama: I still don't think I'm smart as you. Not one bit."

Later in the year, Ike's mother turned her back on the dugout for the last time and moved into town with the two girls. The other children were gone, drifted away. She said the boys could split the homestead if they wanted it or sell it to the Resettlement people. Do whatever. After giving a quarter century of her life to raising nine children on the High Plains, she was done with the hole in the ground.

Ike took up the homestead topic with his brother.

"You want it?"

Oscar shrugged. "I don't have no other place to go."

"You're staying, then?"

"I guess. But I can't see how this could support two families. It ain't like it was in Daddy's day."

"Then it's yours," said Ike. "The place is yours."

"You want something for your half?"

"Nope. It's yours, Os."

"Well, all right then."

A few days later, Ike packed a bag with some dried meat, a couple of biscuits, a canteen of water. He walked one last time over the dirt floor of the dugout, looked in disgust at the muck clinging to the browned sheets over the windows, at the stove that had kept him warm through so many nights, fueled by cow turds. Above ground, the place was nearly buried. The fence line formed a barrier of snagged tumbleweeds and dust.

"What you gonna do, Ike?"

"Don't know."

"You leaving, then?"

"Yep."

"For good?"

"Don't know."

"Where you going?"

"Don't know. Not far, probably. Gotta find some work." He had heard there was a job in Springfield, on the railroad line by the Cimarron River.

"I'll see ya, then."

"Yeah. See ya."

Ike walked away from the homestead with just the clothes on his back and his bag of food and water, waded through the dunes, past the nearly covered outhouse, the barn with the wall of sand on one side, the windmill and its crackling static, the muddied trough of the stock tank, past the lone surviving tree — *goodbye to all that* — and out to the open country, the land that had been so full of ancient mystery, these secrets of the conquistadors, these Indian burial grounds, this place of ghost grass and ghost bison. He just kept walking.

19

Witnesses

H E STARTED HIS DIARY on New Year's Day, 1936. If Don
Hartwell was going to be buried under this sea of dust, he
wanted to leave something behind. He and his wife, Verna,
had lived through four years of drought, four years without a crop,
four years of deeper debt. Black Sunday had nearly snuffed out the
farm for good, the winds blowing with the force of a tornado, followed
later in the spring by a flash flood that nudged his house off its foundation, and then a summer of dusters that buried the corn and alfalfa
he had been able to raise in the floodplain. At age forty-seven, Hartwell was not going down without a fight, but if the elements finally
beat him, he wanted a record of his struggle; maybe it would serve as a
warning to some future nester. The problem with history was that it
was written by the survivors, and they usually wrote in the sunshine,
on harvest day, from victory stands. So Hartwell started his diary at
the darkest hour. This would not be a narrative of courage, grit, and
the good cheer of God-fearing people who had chased away the Indians, killed the bison, and produced the biggest wheat crop the world
had ever seen. Don Hartwell had no intention of being the toast of
the Chamber of Commerce or even of being invited to their regular
luncheon. His story was not *Little House on the Prairie,* but one
farmer's life on the Kansas-Nebraska border during a decade when
homesteads became graveyards. And he kept his diary secret, never
showing it to anybody, not even his wife.

"You hear a great deal about the 'noble pioneers' building up the country, and to a certain extent this is probably true," he wrote in the introduction to the diary. "But the women and children of those times were the ones who faced the real hardships and privations. Women's place in those days was in the home, which usually meant having 2 kids every 3 years and doing as much work as 2 ordinary men and living amid conditions which would cause a common hobo to breathe the open air and face the open road with 'thanksgiving.' The men were, in many cases, drunken, or ingrown religious fanatics who were worse to live with and deal with even than the drunks."

Hartwell's family had come to Nebraska in 1880, and it was never explained why. "My mother didn't like Nebraska and she despised my father's folks (not without some justification). I remember I used to tremble at night after one of their quarrels, too nervous to sleep." School was difficult. "I want to say right here that innocent childhood is generally anything but that — lying, stealing, inordinate cruelty (especially to animals) utter selfishness, homosexuality, masturbation, and various other sexual activities, sometimes even murder, are some of the activities of 'innocent childhood.'"

His father died in 1934, a year when Nebraska got just fourteen inches of rain, the lowest amount since 1864. The old man had raised hogs and cattle on a piece of land he claimed near the town of Inavale, Nebraska, not far from Willa Cather's childhood home in Red Cloud, where the Republican River drains a broad table of the prairie, several hundred miles northeast of No Man's Land. The town flourished during the wheat boom, with a lumberyard, a meat market, two general stores, a bank, a pool hall, a school, a post office, and a small music hall. Its decline started with the crash in farm prices, and it was further staggered by the Depression and drought. The bank closed in 1932, never to open again, and took the farmers' deposits down with it. Hartwell worked his little family farm outside of Inavale, in the sliver of Nebraska that was identified by the government as being a part of the larger Dust Bowl. He earned spare change playing piano at dances and lodges along the Republican River, and his wife brought in extra income making dresses for people in town. They had no children. Hartwell wrote every day. A selection of his thoughts shows his drift in the worst years.

Jan 6

Did you ever see a middle aged man working for his board on a farm?

Feb 8

Last night was one of the worse nights I have seen in this country in many years, a terrific gale of blowing snow and 15 below zero. We moved our bed out in the dining room beside the stove, the first time we ever did that. The horses in the N. pasture seem to be alright today, although we have no barns for them anymore.

Feb 14

I have often thought of sending valentines (as who hasn't) but I never have.

Feb 21

I haven't much ambition anymore. When one sees all he has slipping away, his ambition seems to gradually go along with the rest.

Feb 29

Well, ordinarily today would be Mar. 1, but this year gives us one more day to hold to the place which has meant so much to me in life and tradition in the last 35 years, from the scent of the wild plum bush and the violets and the blue grass in April, to the little dry thunder showers in June which break away late in the afternoon, with the meadow larks singing and the wild roses which seem to be brighter and smell sweeter when wet with rain than any other time.

Mar 7

A horse sale was held at the stock yard in the afternoon. I sold one of ours. There are six left now, I don't know how long I can keep them. When one has to buy all the grain he feeds and has very little to buy with, it is uncertain. The 'stock yard' at the R.R. is a bare, deserted looking place.

Mar 15

Mostly cloudy, cold, heavy dusty looking clouds and rather chilly
s.w. wind. Very dry everywhere. The alfalfa sowed in the field w. of
the feed yard is about all dead.

Mar 17

This is St. Patrick's day so every one is supposed to wear something
green or act that way. It was pleasant in the afternoon, but cold,
dusty s.w. wind in the afternoon.

Mar 20

Spring began today at 12:58 pm we heard it announced over the
radio. Spring's coming was an important event to me years ago.
Spring and summer was when I really lived, especially in May and
June when the flowers were in bloom, the fruit trees, the grass getting green along the creeks, the frogs singing in the evening, and
there was the possibility of a 'big rain' which seldom comes. Fair
today, dry dusty NW wind.

Mar 21

Very dusty, windy, mean.

Mar 22

Very dusty, warm strong s.w. wind at times dead still at 4 pm the air
and sky filled with dust, the sun only faintly visible all day.

April 8

These dust storms are getting serious in this country, fences in some
places almost entirely covered. Further W. and S. much land is entirely ruined. And no rain in sight.

April 15

The air is filled with dust . . . The whole country is rapidly becoming an area of shifting dust and sand, blowing South one day and
North the next. Fences, in some places, are covered with drifting,
blowing dirt.

April 20

At 2 p.m. a terrific wind and dirt storm from the No. Impossible to see much or do anything, a few clouds, but so much dirt and wind you can't see them.

April 28

I got the piano Davis used to have in the pool hall in the afternoon. I don't know how long we will keep it — how long we can.

May 21

15 years ago the whole Republican R. bottom was a vast expanse of alfalfa and corn fields. Now it is practically a desert of wasted, shifting sand, washed out ditches, cockle burrs and devastation. I doubt if very much of it can ever be reclaimed.

June 2

I wish I knew where we will be a year from now.

June 15

Vic C., Artie and the kids left for California this morning. They say they are coming back, but I don't know. Many are leaving the country. Drouth, hard times are driving many out.

June 27

I took a thermometer out in the W. corn field today, at the ground surface it registered 142!

July 4

Today is one of the worst storms I ever saw, even here. It is 100 degrees and a S.W. wind and dust of gale proportions at times. Red Cloud 'celebrated' today but it was such a terrible day we didn't go anywhere.

July 14

I have cultivated corn every summer since 1908 but I wonder sometimes if I will ever cultivate any corn on this place again.

July 15

102 degrees. Corn and every thing is mostly destroyed . . . It is really too hot, dry, discouraging and devilish to do anything. Over 2500 have died in this 'great middle west' of the effects of this Hellish weather and country since July 1st.

July 21

I have seen a good many bad years in this country, more, in fact than any other. But I never saw any worse than this one. Corn is practically all destroyed now, pastures are as bare as January.

July 30

Charlotte Lambrecht was in this afternoon. Charlotte is quite the stickler for morals and temperance, nearly all of us go through that stage at some time in our life. Too many times life slips apart and we find that is all we have left to us.

July 31

July was the worst month (so far) of the worst year ever known.

Sept 1

Well, another summer is about gone, and I wonder, some times what we will be doing a year from now. I always dread to see summer go, no matter how bad it is. Winter with its sickness seems to last so long.

Sept 10

I took down 3 pigs to the sale in the afternoon they sold for $12.05 or about $4 each. These sales are remarkable. An old can and kittens sold for .05. Ducks sold for .30 each. One horse sold for $11 another for $7.

Sept 19

I finished mowing the Russian Thistles on the place W. of Stickneys. I would like to be some place or see the time when something would grow besides Russian Thistles.

Oct 2

I listened to the 'World Series' baseball game over the radio. The
N.Y. 'Yankees' beat the N.Y. 'Giants' 18 to 4. One can hear the ball
game in N.Y. City from the radio (wireless transmission) in his own
home. You can hear the crack of the bat and the ball hit the catcher's
glove. Who would have thought it possible 25 years ago!

Dec 3

Verna & I went to R. Cloud today and took down another shoal to
the sale. She brought $9 and weighed 120 pounds. Mrs. Vance &
John (her son) rode back with us. John was returning from jail from
one of his periodic 'drunks.' But drinking is about the only recre-
ation left around here & you have to do that by yourself.

Dec 25

I believe today is the warmest Christmas morning I have ever seen
. . . We swept & dusted & made some candy in the forenoon. We
had dinner by ourselves at home.

While Don Hartwell was scribbling descriptions of daily life on a
dusted-over piece of ground, others were trying to record similar details with cameras. It was a son of Kansas, Roy Emerson Stryker, who
came up with the idea of creating a record of American decay for the
files of the Farm Security Administration. The motives were not jour-
nalistic: Roosevelt was running for a second term, facing an increasingly hostile Supreme Court, and having documentary support for
conditions that called for programs deemed radical and un-American
by critics could be invaluable. But as it turned out, perhaps by accident or perhaps because of the talent that Roy Stryker hired, the government photo unit proved to be one of the lasting and most popular
contributions of the New Deal, far outliving its propaganda purposes.
The wire services had moved pictures of Black Sunday and other big
storms, but their lenses had been aimed at the sky. It was rare to see
the lines in a sandblasted face, or look into the eyes of a broken nester,
or see a woman nursing her child slumped next to a jalopy loaded
with all her worldly goods. Stryker sent his photographers out to the
heart of the Dust Bowl to get the faces of the desperate. He told his

shooters that they should do more than drive by and hustle back to the city. They should taste the dirt, get to know the people, live with the dusters. A kid from New York City, Arthur Rothstein, was just out of college, twenty-one years old, when Stryker sent him to Kansas, Texas, and Oklahoma in the spring of 1936. It was like sending George Catlin on one of the first explorations of the West, for Rothstein returned with images that most of America had never seen.

Outside Dalhart, he shot a picture of a lone car running just ahead of a black blizzard on an open road; the car is dwarfed by the dark cloud on its tail. In Boise City, Rothstein found a town slouching away from the sand pummeling, its buildings unpainted, the windows brown, so much dirt floating around that it was impossible to tell a

No Man's Land, photographed by Arthur Rothstein of the
Farm Security Administration

street or front lawn or sidewalk from the drifting prairie. All that was visible in a picture he took of one abandoned house was a rooftop and stovepipe poking through the sand, like the scope of a submarine rising above the sea. Roaming through No Man's Land, Rothstein stopped his car outside the shack of Arthur Coble's family. Coble was digging out fence posts and hauling water to a couple of starving cattle. When a sudden wind carried a wave of soil up from the south, Coble and his sons fled for shelter. One of the boys, Darrel, had been a student of Hazel Lucas Shaw's when she taught for grocery scrip in Boise City. Rothstein's picture caught father and son, face into the wind, running for cover to a ramshackle, half-buried outbuilding; it looks as if the very earth is swallowing them. Just the tops of fence posts are visible in the foreground, and the background is shapeless beige. It became one of the most significant images of the time.

Another documentarian, Pare Lorentz, wanted to tell a larger story, not just take snapshots of those trapped by the dead land. His idea was to film a narrative: how and why the Great Plains had been settled and then brought to ruination. Like a fable. Lorentz had never made a

Abandoned farm in Cimarron County, Oklahoma

film before, but he was sure of his vision. Hollywood was not. He was turned down by every major studio. But in 1935, after Stryker set up a documentary division, Lorentz found a backer for his film — the United States government. Now Hollywood took notice and did everything it could to stop him. The studio heads did not want government competing on their turf, for Lorentz planned to make a documentary that would play commercially in theaters across the country. Opponents said it was a dangerous thing for the Roosevelt Administration to be getting into the business of telling stories through pictures. They feared it would be propaganda. Lorentz said he wanted only to tell a story that needed to be told: as one arm of the government tried to save the plains, another arm would try to show how people had created the problem. After much debate, the film was given

Hugh Bennett talking to farmers in Springfield, Colorado

the green light. It would be one of the most influential documentaries ever made, the only peacetime production by the American government of a film intended for broad commercial release. To assuage critics, Lorentz said he would accept nothing but his salary of eighteen dollars a day. He ended up paying for some of the production out of his own pocket.

Lorentz and his crew moved to the High Plains, catching dusters as they tumbled across the land, getting chased off the road, living with the grit, hearing the same story told over and over, in varying forms: the boom, the bust, the dust. They filmed in Montana, Wyoming, Colorado, Kansas, Oklahoma, and Texas. When he arrived in Dalhart, Lorentz found monstrous dunes and a town trying to rally itself even as it was swallowed by dirt. The most horrific footage of dusters came from the Texas Panhandle. Lorentz had been filming without a script, which angered his cinematographers, who complained of his peripatetic direction. He wanted *everything* in the frame. But as he filmed around Dalhart, a central image began to take shape: that of the iconic plainsman who first tore at the prairie earth. He asked around town if there was an old cowboy in these parts, somebody who still kept a wagon or a horse-drawn plow. People gave him the name of a couple of XIT hands. Those old boys had plenty of stories to tell but no horse-drawn plows. Then somebody tossed out the name of a little man with a handlebar mustache who lived in a two-room shack with his family at the edge of town — fellow by the name of Bam White.

White was everything Lorentz was looking for. He had a pair of tired-looking horses that he kept around to pull his wagon. He had an old plow, which was covered by drifts. He had a face with the hard years, heat, and gusts etched into it. Lorentz hired Bam White to hitch a horse to his plow and pull it in the fields. White was puzzled: that's all you want? Lorentz paid him twenty-five dollars for his effort. To White, it was two months' pay for two hours' work — more money than he ever earned in so little time. Bam White, silhouetted against blowing soil, became the lasting image of the film that Lorentz made: *The Plow That Broke the Plains.*

The film treated the Great Plains as a mythic place in a lost world.

It opened with a map showing the immensity of the flatlands. This land had been paradise for bison and cattle. "Grasslands," the narrator says in poetic idiom, "a country of high winds and sun, high winds and sun." This Eden was never meant to be farmed as intensely as it was. "Settler, plow at your peril," the sodbusters were warned. They tore at the land with industrial-age armies of tractors and threshers, consuming the grass like locusts. When the rains stopped, the land blew, the sky filled with dirt. The score, composed by Virgil Thomson, who grew up in Missouri, was as powerful as the pictures. The music swelled with the first wondrous images of the prairie and turned dark and menacing, like the soundtrack of a Hitchcock thriller, when the land raged against the people.

The Plow That Broke the Plains showed alongside *It Happened One Night* at the Rialto Theater in New York. In Dalhart, it opened at the Mission Theater, where just a few years earlier a son of the southern plains, Gene Autry, had appeared in his first picture, *In Old Santa Fe*. Now the story on the screen was about a real cowboy. Bam White took his family; it was the first time young Melt had ever seen a movie. The boy kept staring up at the screen and then back at the little man sitting next to him — his daddy, bigger than life, bigger than Gene Autry in the movie posters still hanging in the lobby. The film moved Bam to tears. He always thought there was a reason why his horse had died in Dalhart, marooning the family on this wedge of desolate ground. Now he saw the answer, there for all the world. In March 1936, the film played at the White House and the president of the United States looked into the hard, sun-seared, dust-chipped face of Bam White, the wanderer, the Indian half-breed who was thereafter the visage of the High Plains at its lowest point.

20

The Saddest Land

A T THE START OF 1936, Hazel Lucas Shaw was five months pregnant, with a fighting chance to bring another child into the world. But whether there would be a world — a home in No Man's Land — was a bigger question. The government men held a summit in Pueblo, Colorado, moving the debate from the marbled comfort of Washington, D.C., to the war zone itself. They heard grim numbers about the enormity of the disaster. More than 850 million tons of topsoil had blown off the southern plains in the last year, nearly 8 tons of dirt for every resident of the United States. In the Dust Bowl, farmers lost 480 tons per acre. Where it had gone — to the heavens, to the sea, to the mountainous edge of the plains — was anyone's guess. And what did it mean to lose 850 million tons of dirt in a single year? It meant 5 million acres in a coma, with little chance of being cultivated. It meant 100 million acres might never be productive farmland; no matter how much it rained in future years, the ground was too bare, sterile, or weighted with dunes. It meant that dust pneumonia was going to stalk schoolyards and sidewalks until the land was stabilized. It meant that some towns that were dying would not come back and were not even worth the effort of resuscitation. This had become evident with every fresh announcement. At year's end, the state of Kansas made plans to close four hundred schools.

"Unless something is done," the Forest Service warned in a report, "the western Plains will be as arid as the Arabian desert." But short of veiling the sun, cuffing the winds, or creating rain from thin air, what could be done?

Just as the grass had been stripped away, now the schools, churches, homes, and main streets that had been anchored to the overturned sod were being peeled off, piece by piece. The towns died without ritual. Broken Bow, Kansas, went from three hundred people to three. Inavale, where the diary-keeper Don Hartwell and his wife, Verna, had finished a Christmas dinner alone, lost one of its two stores at year's end, and the county shed 22 percent of its population. The debate at the dust summit was the same one that had raged in Washington, with fresh urgency: whether to encourage people to cling to the land, hoping for recovery, or to let the plains empty out, a retreat of defeated Americans. If they did nothing, it looked like the trends that had accelerated in 1935 would continue. Across the entire Great Plains, nearly a million people had left their farms from 1930 to 1935. Out-migration had started slowly, driven by depressed wheat and cattle prices in the northern plains. But it was drought and dusters that chased them out of the rest of the prairie, particularly in three states: Kansas, Oklahoma, and Texas. McCarty's Last Man Club was no stunt: more than two thirds of the counties in the Texas Panhandle were losing people by the close of 1935.

Roosevelt was torn. "You and I know that many farmers in many states are trying to make both ends meet on land not fit for agriculture," he said in one radio chat. "But if they want to do that, I take it, it's their funeral." But he also clung to an instinctive belief that there was a way for man to fix what man had broken. Even though his aides reminded the president that nobody had ever tried to prevent the collapse of an entire region, Roosevelt believed in the big restoration dream.

The summit ended with an expansion of existing plans and some smaller new measures in social engineering that would prove historically ironic. Bennett's agency went ahead full bore on a trial-and-error search for the best grass to reseed the dusted-over lands, and it started mapping out areas that could be reseeded. The basic challenge was finding a way to hold the ground down long enough for any seeds to sprout. On farmland that the government had purchased, fences would be cleared and buildings removed so that the drifts would have no place to pile up against. The administration agreed to buy an initial 2.25 million acres of used-up and dusted-over farmland. Despite the complaints of groups like McCarty's Last Man Club, the government men believed it was cheaper to buy people off the farm than to pay them relief to hold on to marginal land. One new idea was to give some of these lands back to the Indians. The natives had never wanted to farm on a grid; they asked only for grassland, which fed bison. Now the government decided to purchase up to one million acres for Indians who would agree to run livestock over the land after it had been rested for a few years. Some of this land was on old Cherokee ground in Oklahoma. In essence, the government would now be getting rid of cowboys to put back Indians.

Baca County became a prime target for re-grassing of the prairie. There were no forced sales, no use of eminent domain. The government paid $2.75 an acre to re-claim a homestead. That seemed a paltry amount, but there were no other offers. A person with a half-section could get $880 from the sale of their piece of dirt and start anew. This land might go back to grass; it might become a desert. It would be left to itself, after the windmills and stock tanks and fences had been dismantled, the houses torn apart and sold for scrap, the roads left buried. It was suggested that some people might want to move the dead from cemeteries in the worst areas; before long, it could be impossible to find the tombstones.

The journalist Ernie Pyle, one of the most influential writers of the day, toured the plains in the summer of 1936. He called the Dust Bowl "this withering land of misery." Driving through counties in Kansas that used to have a farm on every quarter-section, Pyle said, "I saw not a solitary thing but bare earth and a few lonely, empty farmhouses . . . There was not a tree or a blade of grass, or a dog or a cow or a human being — nothing whatsoever, nothing at all but gray raw earth and a few farmhouses and barns, sticking up from the dark gray sea like white cattle skeletons on the desert." It was, he wrote, "the saddest land I have ever seen."

Pyle never bumped into the ghostly figure who traveled the dusted roads of western Kansas, a man with a white beard and long white hair who carried a staff and called himself "Walking Will." Farmers would see him along a road, stop and ask him if he needed a ride. Sometimes he would get in; other times he kept walking. When he took a ride, it was not for long.

"Stop the car!" he shouted. "The Lord has instructed me to get out and go back."

Then he would walk over another stretch of road, repeating his pattern. In 1936 Kansas, he seemed to belong, a figure from an uncertain dream.

The *Atlantic Monthly* carried more of its "Letters from the Dust Bowl," written by the Holyoke graduate turned farmer's wife, Caroline Henderson. She lived in the northeast corner of No Man's Land.

"Wearing our shade hats, with handkerchiefs tied over our faces and Vaseline in our nostrils, we have been trying to rescue our home from the accumulations of wind-blown dust which penetrates wherever air can go. It is almost hopeless, for there is rarely a day when at some time the dust clouds do not roll over. 'Visibility' approaches zero and everything is covered again with a silt-like deposit which may vary in depth from a film to actual ripples on the kitchen floor." The letter was written June 30, 1935, two and a half months after Black Sunday. By March of next year, things had not improved.

"Since I wrote you we have had several bad days of wind and dust. On the worst one recently, old sheets stretched over door and window openings, and sprayed with kerosene, quickly became black and helped a little to keep down the irritating dust in our living rooms. Nothing that you see or hear or read will be likely to exaggerate the physical discomfort or material losses due to these storms. Less emphasis is usually given to the mental effect, the confusion of mind resulting from the overthrow of all our plans for improvement or normal farm work, and the difficulty of making other plans, even in a tentative way."

Her pen fell silent through the torturous summer. Only 8 of the 136 homesteads in her township were still occupied. One day she saw "an unpardonable sin" — a neighbor dismantling a well, hoping to sell the pipes as scrap. Her love of the farm — a fidelity of three decades

— had given way to a different emotion, raw loyalty. She would stand by the land as one stood by a dying spouse, but her heart was broken.

"It is just a place to stand on," she said of her farm.

For Hazel Shaw, the only plan she had for the next year was to bring a new life into the world to replace the one taken from her by the dusters. She went north to Elkhart, Kansas, for this birth. The memory of the drive to Clayton for Ruth Nell's delivery, and of her husband's battle with sand-vexed roads, was fresh. In Elkhart, the baby was born without trouble, a black-eyed boy. When he came into the world, his first cry — forceful and loud — sounded to Hazel like the most lusty cheer of life she had heard in five years. They named the baby Charles, for his father. He seemed robust, with good color, good size. At his baptism three months later, the baby grabbed the silver cup that the minister was holding and refused to let go. They all laughed: the boy had strength. Now, where to live? Most of Hazel's family, her mother, Dee, a network of siblings, cousins, aunts, uncles, young and old, were staying put in No Man's Land. Cimarron County was Lucas country, but in the last year it had killed Grandma Lou and baby Ruth Nell, and that made it impossible for Hazel to feel the same way about the land. Many of her relatives were scared; they had no idea what was going on or when it would end. They looked around and assumed that the far corner of Oklahoma was becoming a desert.

Summer temperatures were brutal. For two days in July and two days in August, the mercury reached 118 degrees, the highest ever recorded at that time in No Man's Land. August went down as the hottest of the century in Oklahoma. It was 117 degrees in Dalhart, 120 in Shattuck. There had been some rain but it came in bursts, big dumps from the sky that spilled over the hard ground and inflamed ditches into flash floods, and then it was all gone, and they went back to drought and temperatures above the century mark.

Throughout the heat wave, Hazel was desperate for a little cross-breeze in the apartment — some clean, moving air — so they could sleep at night, but she could not risk the dust getting to her new baby. Hazel kept the place so sealed up it was like living in a can. She would not take the baby outside except on the clearest of days. She draped a wet sheet over the crib, about two feet above the head of the baby. He was never in the crib without a dampened cloth overhead. Later, when Charles grew to a young man, he was claustrophobic and thought it had to be a product of his early months spent looking up at a dusted, wet sheet from a crib in a sealed apartment.

At the end of the year, she said goodbye to No Man's Land. Hazel put on her white gloves and brushed back tears but said tomorrow would bring good things to the young family, so it was not worth a long cry. She planned to leave with her dignity intact, like a lady. In 1914 at the age of ten, she had first seen the grassland, rising on her toes on the driver's seat of her daddy's covered wagon to get a look at this country. She would hold to the good memories. She and Charles and the baby moved to Vici, closer to the center of Oklahoma, near her husband's family. There would be a place, always, in Hazel's memory of the blackest days in No Man's Land. But it would shrink, because Hazel would force it down to size to allow her to live.

A hundred miles to the east, the Volga Germans tried to keep their community around Shattuck from crumbling. Strong men still wept, hiding their lapses like alcoholics sipping in secret. The men cried because they had never seen anything like this and had never before been without a plan of action. Always, they had been able to hammer at something, to dig and scrape and cut and build and plant and harvest and kill — something forceful to tip the balance, using their hands to make even the slightest dent during the bleakest times. Families spoke furtively of a mother or young bride who had gone crazy, walking away from her house only to be found days or weeks later stumbling around a town, lost. Just as they had fled the Rhine in 1765 and the Volga 120 years later, the Russlanddeutschen now talked of moving again.

Most days, George Ehrlich sounded like he believed he would live through this, but it could have been the brave, forced words of one who had seen it all. A German family could live on bread, beer, and wurst, the Ehrlichs told their Anglo neighbors. They got some money from the government, about seven dollars a head for cattle, which gave them enough to buy flour and sugar — something was always coming

out of the oven. A cousin would bring out the violin that had survived
the immigrants' trip through the hurricane in 1890, and there was music and warm bread and memories of the Volga at its best. But the
drought was in its fifth year, and it was taking its toll.

The Borth children were felled by dirt. The doctor came to Gustav
Borth's three-room house and examined them. Two of the kids had
fever, chest pains from coughing, sore ribs. Dust pneumonia was his
diagnosis. He said they had to get out of the High Plains or get to a
medical shelter. But the nearest hospital was full and the Red Cross
never made it to the German community with a triage facility. Gustav
moved Rosa's bed to the kitchen next to a cook stove heated by cow
chips. With enough cow manure as fuel, the Borths could keep her
warm. There was no room for another bed. Her brother was put in
the room with his parents. For three weeks, the kids hacked and spit
up dust, waiting out their illness. A girl of fifteen, Rosa fixed her stare
on the brown land outside the window; she never saw a bird or a
flower or a bee. If she could just find a single green weed, she decided,
it would be enough to make her happy.

With his children facing a mortal illness, his land dead and dusted,
Gustav thought of the Russian steppe often, and it was always better
in his mind than this place in America. He still went to church, half a
mile away, and the family tried to sing "Gott is de liebe" along with
the rest of the congregation, but they were nearly empty inside. Many
times they were too embarrassed to be seen in public, for Rosa was
clothed in dresses made of chicken feed sacks.

"Es ist hoffnungsloss," Gustav Borth said. *It is hopeless.* Usually, he
tried to keep the overt pronunciations of failure from his family. Like
the tears.

"Es ist hoffnungsloss."

Then the bank took his combine. During the glory years, the combine had allowed Borth to pile high his grain, his stacks of fibrous
gold. He moved the children hundreds of miles south to live with
cousins in Texas. Gustav was left with his homesickness for the Old
World, his sense of failure.

• • •

That spring, with *The Plow That Broke the Plains* playing in theaters, Dalhart found itself in the spotlight. There on the big screen was Bam White cutting up the best grassland in the world, the cause of this nightmare. John McCarty was livid. He denounced the film as a tool of the government, designed to drive people off the land. It went to the very character of the Panhandle pioneer that the editor of the *Texan* had long praised as the epitome of courage and foresight. If this kept up, Dalhart would die.

"It is purely a propaganda film," McCarty said. "It is bound to do more damage to our credit and our agriculture that it can possibly do good." McCarty urged people in neighboring towns to come take a look at Dalhart for themselves: see the defiance, feel the fighting spirit. Politicians in Texas joined McCarty in their outrage. Eugene Worley, a delegate to the Democratic National Convention in 1936, demanded that the government withdraw the film from theaters. "It's a libel on the great Texas panhandle," said Worley. Melt White went back to see the film again, staring up at his daddy moving along the horizon of the windblown land, with the stirring music, as a narrator said, "Forty million acres of the plains totally ruined by the plow."

The filmmaker, Pare Lorentz, was hardly the first person to blame misguided agriculture for the wreck of the plains. Seasoned XIT ranch hands and soil scientists such as Hugh Bennett had made the same case, in their way. The *New York Times* correspondent in the Midwest, Harlan Miller, saw the run-up and frenzy of the wheat boom, the town building and the suitcase farmers, the debt loads and the technological revolution, and he watched it all fall apart — the whole arc.

"Plowed recklessly during the World War and since, denuded of the vegetation which knits the earth against the onslaught of the winds, powdered by drought for years, these arid lands have taken wing," he wrote in a long piece for the *Times* on March 31, 1935, two weeks before Black Sunday. A similar story from a year earlier carried the headline: "PLOW SPELLED ITS DOOM."

A son of the Texas Panhandle reached the same conclusion. Doc Dawson's youngest boy, John, had left Dalhart in 1929 to start a law

career in Houston. He returned in the mid-1930s to help his struggling father and to see if anything could be salvaged from the land the
Doc had hoped would bring him a comfortable retirement. John was
startled and angered by what he saw. A letter from his mother just after Black Sunday had described "the blackest dark you ever looked
into," but her words did not prepare him for his reaction. The land
had become a moonscape, empty and hideous. During dusters, the
earth had a sickly smell. He found no wildlife, no grass, no trees growing outside of the few hardy locusts planted in Dalhart. The Last Man
Club and Lorentz's film were getting a lot of attention, creating an impression of a town engaged in a big struggle over the forces remaking
the land. But Dawson found that most of his neighbors were just
plain numb, worn down by the struggle to get through another day.
There was no economy, no buyers for goods in town. His mother
tried to keep up appearances and talked still of books and cooking a
Sunday meal and God. But she was distressed by the dust that showered down her walls, by the filthy streaks on the windows, the puckered faces she saw at Doc's soup kitchen, people in pain from hunger.
Five years now they had put up with it. Five years, with no end in
sight.

Still, the Doc told his son he had a feeling a little rain might finally
be coming their way. Six years earlier, when the boy first came home
from college, the Doc had taken him out to his land and scooped up
the earth. As he held it in his hands, he pronounced it the finest dirt
on the planet, capable of producing damn near anything. Now he said
he was exhausted, out of money and nearly out of time. His health
was shot. The Panhandle had to get one normal year of precipitation.
But what, exactly, was normal? Dalhart had been a town for only
thirty-five years, and weather records had been kept barely longer
than that. John Dawson was upset because he felt people had done
this to themselves. All of them — the nesters who had chased away
the cowboys, the real estate promoters, the people who subdivided
the XIT, and Dawson's own father, who carved up his own little piece
of the Panhandle only to have it become a collection point for tumbleweeds — shared some of the blame.

Government kept the town alive. Hugh Bennett came to Dalhart in

August 1936 to look over the biggest soil conservation project on the plains, called "Operation Dust Bowl." The plan was to slow the drifts by contour plowing, which created furrows and made it less likely for the earth to lift off in great sheets, and then plant it over with grass seed from Africa. The goal was to build a living thing from scratch, to create a place of interdependence, not a crop. Only God on the third day of creation might know the feeling. Bennett was also struggling to put the fledgling conservation districts together. The nesters had usually worked alone, one man against the land, and sometimes one man against another, each with his section. Bennett was trying to create what amounted to neighborhood civil defense committees of the soil. But people had to take the initiative. A soil conservation district would fail if only a few people went along with it. It was all theory, of course. But neighbors bitched about other neighbors not wanting to do their share, or shucking duties, or being sloppy or lazy or drunk or too religious or just plain onerous. Big Hugh got an earful.

At the same time, Bennett, as part of the team appointed by Roosevelt, was working on the investigation into the cause of the Dust Bowl. The administration had started a number of big initiatives but most of them were tentative, pending the conclusions of the Dust Bowl jury. The president wanted the report by summer's end.

McCarty went out of his way to impress Bennett, to show the president's man that Dalhart deserved its shot at redemption. See here: Uncle Dick Coon and his properties and that C-note in his pocket — hoo, boy, he's got big plans. And just look what a break they nearly got from Tex Thornton last year, after he busted up the sky with his TNT and nitro. All they needed were a couple of steady soakers, and the land would spring back, green and frisky. His town was a fighter. It was full of Spartans. It would lead the way for others in the High Plains. When a group of people from Guymon, which was nearly as smothered and gasping as Boise City and Dalhart, came for a visit, McCarty arranged for a handful of musicians to meet them. See here, he told Big Hugh: look how the town opens its arms. The musicians got up on a flatbed truck just as the boys from Guymon rolled in to see what one dusted town could learn from another. The wind had been blowing sand all day, making it hard to see, and then it shifted, bringing in a reddish dust from New Mexico. McCarty got on the flatbed and invited the Guymon visitors to come on up with him, join hands, and sing. They started singing "Old Faithful." The dust fell red and heavy, and when a weak rain was squeezed from the sky, it was liquid gunk.

". . . Old Faithful, we rode the range together . . ."

People fled for cover. But McCarty continued to sing from the back of the flatbed truck, holding hands with a bankrupt merchant from Guymon, showing everyone the spirit of Dalhart while clay drops fell and splattered his face, making it look as if he were crying tears of red mud.

21

Verdict

I N   A N   A G E when people who ran the country thought the great
rivers of America could be plugged to create a green promised
land in the Pacific Northwest and electrify the Tennessee Valley,
Hugh Bennett was encouraged to think big and think epic. When he
returned to Washington after the Dust Bowl summit and a tour of his
conservation projects, Bennett believed that the Great Plains could be
saved; it did not have to blow away and lose its people. But all the
marvels of concrete and rebar used elsewhere could not put back
what the winds and a swarm of one-way plows had done on the prairie. There would be no magical engineered solution. Some believed
so, of course. Congress authorized a plan to reverse the flow of water
under the Continental Divide, an attempt to create a hydraulic savior,
moving west to east through a tunnel. In Oklahoma, politicians were
still insistent on choking off the little flow of the Cimarron River to
create an impound of water near Guymon. Others thought the solution was to go deep, dig far below the surface, and mine the great
underground reservoir of ancient water, the Ogallala Aquifer. Deep
wells, drilled for oil or gas, had found a ready source of water five
hundred feet or below. Bring it up, many county leaders told Bennett
during his tour of the Dust Bowl. If rain would not come from the sky,
it could come from the ground. The Ogallala was there for the taking,
just like the grassland itself thirty years earlier. Bring it up.

Four million acres of farmland were empty, abandoned, with no
takers, not even Resettlement — whose mission was to buy back land.

From the start, Bennett thought the answer was getting people to treat the prairie soil on its own terms, a great plowup in reverse. Conserve what farmland could be saved through new methods of contour plowing, crop rotation, and soil conservation districts. For other lands, the ground could be seeded, and in time the southern plains would have its grasslands back. Perhaps. Bennett, whose graduate degree was in chemistry, was not given to policy speculation. He was a man of science: look at the facts, draw the right conclusions. But he was in new territory. They all were. There were no historic models.

Roosevelt had asked for an honest verdict: why had the Great Plains blown away? What made this land die? The crisis of the transient prairie had already cost Depression-strapped taxpayers an enormous sum — five hundred million dollars since 1933 — on remedial land projects, grants, loans, and relief. Before spending any more money, the president wanted to know if the plains could be saved, and if so, how. Roosevelt had also asked whether the arid flatlands should have been settled. Had it been a colossal mistake to allow homesteading on the land? Was the Jeffersonian small farmer, small town, agri-citizen model a horrible fit for the grasslands? Had this environmental catastrophe — the worst in American history — been aided by government?

The report of the Great Plains Drought Area Committee was delivered to the president on August 27, 1936. It was labeled "personal and confidential," signed first by Bennett, and then seven agency heads. An extended memo, *The Future of the Great Plains,* was due at the end of the year. But this shorter report showed where the committee was going. The conclusions were stark.

The climate had not changed. This refuted a theory Roosevelt had been mulling for some time: that the plains were in the first years of a hundred-year cycle of change. The plains had suffered a severe drought — no argument there — but dry times were part of prairie life, dating back eons. An accompanying map showed the president what was obvious to any student of American geography: the nation's midsection west of the ninety-eighth meridian, from the Canadian border to Mexico, received only twenty inches of yearly rainfall or less. This was simply not enough rain to raise crops, no matter how much "dust-mulching" or other dry farming gimmicks were promoted, and it was why banks for so long had refused to lend money in this arid zone. During the drought, the dry states had received anywhere from five to twelve inches annually.

"There is no reason to believe that the primary factors of climate, temperature, precipitation and winds in the Great Plains region have undergone any fundamental change," the report stated. "The problem of the Great Plains is not the product of a single act of nature, of a single year or even a series of exceptionally bad years."

What, then, was the cause?

"Mistaken public policies have been largely responsible for the situation," the report proclaimed. Specifically, "a mistaken homesteading policy, the stimulation of war time demands which led to over cropping and over grazing, and encouragement of a system of agriculture which could not be both permanent and prosperous."

For Roosevelt, who believed in human initiative aided by government goodwill as a guiding force, these words were hard to take. His most trusted aide on the land and a host of experts were telling him that *people* — not weather or bad luck — had caused the problem. What's more, in an additional blow to Roosevelt's humanitarian impulses, the experts said a big part of what ailed the prairie could not be fixed by man.

"The basic cause of the present Great Plains situation is an attempt to impose upon the region a system of agriculture to which the Plains are not adapted," the report stated. "The Great Plains has climatic attributes which cannot be altered by any act of man, although they may be slowly changed, for better or worse, by natural weather cycles which we cannot yet predict."

The report moved on to how the disaster had unfolded — a chronology of collapse. One chart showed how quickly the grass was overturned. In 1879, ten million acres were plowed. Fifty years later, the total was one hundred million acres. Grass was needed to hold the soil in place; it was nature's way of adapting to the basic conditions of the plains, the high wind and low rainfall. Buffalo grass, in particular, short and drought-resistant, was nature's refinement over centuries. The turf was intact for thousands of years, and then in two manic periods of exploitation — the cattle boom, followed by the wheat bubble — it was ripped apart.

"Thus there was not only a progressive breaking up of the native sod but a thinning out of the grass cover on lands not yet plowed."

But having placed the blame for the flyaway plains on the farming equivalent of a gold rush, Bennett and his colleagues did not then fault the individuals who brought the plow that broke the land.

"The settlers lacked both the knowledge and incentive necessary to avoid these mistakes. They were misled by those who should have been their natural guides. The Federal homestead policy, which kept land allotments low and required that a portion of each should be plowed, is now seen to have caused immeasurable harm. The Homestead Act of 1862, limiting an individual holding to 160 acres, was on the western plains almost an obligatory act of poverty."

This was the most damning indictment: the sacred Homestead Act, *almost an obligatory act of poverty!*

Technology and speculation came in for their share of blame. Wartime demand drove up prices, stimulating record production. The prices could not hold, leaving farmers to plow more ground as the only way to break even. And these bountiful years happened "at the beginning of a wet period which has apparently been terminated." Had farmers tried to settle the arid plains forty years earlier when it was more typically dry, they never would have broken ground.

"The dust storms of 1934 and 1935 have been visible evidence to nearly every American living east of the Rocky Mountains that something is seriously wrong. The extent of the erosion on the Great Plains has not yet been accurately measured. It is safe to say that 80 percent of it is now in some stage of erosion."

Roosevelt liked action plans, programs that could be carried out quickly, grandly mobilizing big forces toward a common goal.

"We are definitely in the era of building," he said in a speech, "the building of great public projects for the benefit of the public and with the definite objective of building human happiness."

But the report said there was no easy solution.

"This is a situation that will not by any possibility cure itself. A series of wet years might postpone the destructive process, yet in the end, by raising false hopes and by encouraging renewal of mistaken agricultural practices, might accelerate it."

And why should a city person care about this wreckage of lives and land?

"The situation is so serious that the Nation, for its own sake, cannot afford to allow the farmer to fail," the report concluded. "We endanger our democracy if we allow the Great Plains, or any other section of the country, to become an economic desert."

It was enough to keep Roosevelt up nights. Failed homestead acts. Settlers misled. A speculative frenzy. And now the retreat: ten thousand people a month leaving the Great Plains, the greatest single exodus in American history. He took to the airwaves, sounding pained and conflicted. In a radio chat on September 6, 1936, too early in the calendar to claim to be from his "fireside," he tried to inspire people to hold on.

"No cracked earth, no blistering sun, no burning wind, no grasshoppers are a permanent match for the indomitable American farmers and stockmen and their wives and children, who have carried us through desperate days, and inspire us with their self-reliance, their tenacity, and their courage."

It was an election year, and Roosevelt was extremely popular. Europe was tense, with Hitler consolidating power and fortifying his military in Germany, and the Spanish Civil War a staging ground for the larger battle to come. Consumed by its domestic crisis, the United States declared neutrality in the affairs of Europe. The Republicans ran a Kansan, Governor Alf Landon, the only GOP governor west of the Mississippi. Landon said Roosevelt had no idea how to fix the Great Plains and was taking the country in a radical direction. Most Americans felt otherwise: the election was a rout. Roosevelt carried every state but Maine and Vermont, winning the Electoral College by the largest margin ever, 523 to 8, and the popular vote by more than ten million, with 60 percent of the electorate. Late in his life, Landon was asked about the New Deal and its lasting effect on the country. He said it "saved our society."

The High Plains, like the rest of the country, had given its heart to

Roosevelt. People wrote to him as if he were an uncle, the one who always had an answer.

"Please do something to help us save our country, where one time we were all so happy," a plainswoman, Mary Gallagher, wrote.

FDR went back to Bennett and others at work on the larger report of the future of the dusted land. What was next? They had more of the same coming: the past had been a failure, nature was abused, the dust storms were the consequence, don't count on rain to save it.

"Nature has established a balance in the Great Plains," an early draft of the second report concluded. "The white man has disturbed this balance; he must restore it, or devise a new one of his own." Here was an echo of Aldo Leopold's groundbreaking conservation essay of 1933; they even quoted him, citing the interdependence of people and other species, earth and technology.

Bennett's agency was ready to start planting the first sections of new sod on the stripped land. But many questions remained: how could grass ever get started during a marathon of drought? What species would survive? How long would it take for the sod to build up, resilient as in the past? Were there enough nutrients in the soil for grass to take hold? Soil science was basic; agronomists could tell the makeup of soil, its composition, but no one had ever dreamed of recreating an entire ecosystem. The new grass would have to live or die on the nutrient-poor land, after it was settled with basic erosion therapy. The nesters had removed a perennial plant, a perfect fit for flat, wind-scraped land, and replaced it with a weak annual. The government bought 107,000 acres in a dead corner of Kansas that drained into the Cimarron River, just over the state line from No Man's Land, and designated it as the first patch in the rebuilding of the great American grassland. They planted a mixture: weeds to hold the ground down, grass from Africa, blue grama, bluestem, buffalo grass, and other flora. It would take time: ten, twenty, maybe fifty years before a big new swath of turf was in place again.

Roosevelt still wanted something dramatic, something quicker — a Grand Coulee Dam for the soil. His "Big Idea" of planting trees down the middle of America had taken on a life of its own after the Forest Service came back with a positive report. The president had been mocked since he first talked up his vision, a belt of trees a hundred miles wide, stretching from the North Dakota border with Canada to just south of Amarillo, Texas. Trees could not stop the dust. But they could provide shelter from black blizzards, enough so people could get a crop in. He hoped the project could accomplish three things:

Break up the wind.
Check erosion.
Employ thousands of people.

Some also said the trees would produce more rain, though this promise was never written into the enabling law. And in pushing for government-subsidized tree-planting on the flatlands, Roosevelt was harkening back to an earlier American law, the Timber Culture Act, which allowed people to claim a significantly larger homestead if they agreed to plant and maintain trees on a portion of the land.

A tree-planting crew was dispatched to Oklahoma, east of No Man's Land. Roosevelt's Big Idea was underway.

"This will be the largest project ever undertaken in the country to modify climate and agricultural conditions," said F. A. Silcox, chief of the Forest Service. He apparently had not read the warnings of the Great Plains report, the cautions against trying to remake the climate. The tree planters were CCC crews, young men hungry for work; an eleven-man team could plant six thousand trees a day. Nesters stared at these earnest New Dealers dropping saplings in the ruined soil, planting trees like crops in rows running north and south, filling the tanks of big gas-hauling trucks with water to give the trees a start. Damn fools, the nesters said. Nobody plants a tree on the prairie facing north and south. After a time, the crews shifted and planted rows running east and west, a more effective wind barrier.

Trees would bring people together, make it easier to live, some of the experts said — social change through hardwood. "We are going to improve living conditions," said Charles Scott, who was in charge of the shelterbelt program in Kansas. "We want to make conditions livable. We want to develop a rural sociability, a rural happiness, a rural contentment which we think such plantings will bring about."

The goal was to plant 180,000 acres a year, mostly on private land, which the owner would then take responsibility for. The trees were planted in strips up to a mile apart, up to a hundred strips within the width of the shelterbelt. Farming would take place between the strips. One government scientist who had been sent to the Gobi Desert to study what could grow on sterile soil came back with several species; another returned from the Sahara with suggestions. Adjustments were made based on advice from nesters. Into the ground went cotton-woods, honey locusts, hackberries, ash, walnuts, ponderosa pines, and Chinese elms. The trees held through that first winter, and by late spring of 1937, as the dusters started up with the ferocious seasonal winds, Roosevelt sent the crews out again. The president ignored the warnings of Hugh Bennett and others who said man could not alter the basic nature of the Great Plains. Bennett could have his fledgling new grassland and soil conservation districts, but Roosevelt bulled ahead with the idea that had most captivated him from the start. He dispatched his army to half a dozen states, to the most broken counties, the most barren farms, the driest land, with a simple command: plant trees, two hundred million of them, from the top of the plains to the bottom.

22

Cornhusker II

A T YEAR'S END, Don Hartwell was worried about his health, his long shadow of debt, the dead land, and about an America that still seemed lost seven years into the Depression. In his summary of 1936, he wrote in his diary that it was the driest year ever in Webster County, Nebraska. He wanted to spend New Year's Eve at a dance in the town of Red Cloud, to put behind him the past twelve months of misery. But a cold drizzle and then a norther packing dust and snow kept Hartwell and his wife at home near Inavale. They ate cornmeal and ham and went to bed early. On New Year's Day, he recorded in his diary the simple facts of life on the farm, the wind at twenty-two miles an hour, gas selling for twenty cents a gallon, which meant it took a full day's work at one of the government road jobs to fill up your tank.

"Many things of importance have happened," he wrote, "and we are also thankful for some things which did not happen."

Ike Osteen had walked away from his dugout in Baca County. Hazel Shaw had given up on No Man's Land after losing her baby to the dust. The German Borths had been forced to break up their family, sending the children south to escape death from pneumonia. But in the Republican River drainage of southern Nebraska, Don Hartwell tightened his grip on the land, holding on to it because he had nothing else. At the start of 1937, about nine million acres of former homestead land were orphaned in Nebraska. Hartwell was trying to fend off complete failure — losing the farm to the bank, losing his wife, all his

273

dreams dissolving. He still made a little money playing piano in towns on the Kansas-Nebraska border, banging out dance tunes till early morning. People liked favorites, old-timey songs, but Hartwell would often end a set with the words, "Don't know why, there's no sun up in the sky" from "Stormy Weather," and damn if people didn't care to hear it, Hartwell liked to play it.

Jan 10

Influenza is hanging like a pall over the country. Hundreds have died in the large cities & it is gradually closing in on this country. Smallpox was the popular disease last winter.

Jan 11

We have only 2 old sows, 6 fall pigs & 5 horses now & I doubt if we can get feed for them much longer. So — I don't know. I don't know whether we can even stay here this year. I wish we could see our way clear again.

Feb 14

Well, it's Valentine's Day again! I think everyone has a sneaking desire to send one to someone besides his father or mother or other 'accredited' associates & has still more desire to get one the same way, but few, oh so very few, ever do.

Feb 18

The air is filled with dust today. Very bad dust storms are reported in W. Kans., Okla. etc, but that is not unusual for the drouth dust & wind program of this country for the last 4 or 5 years.

I didn't get home from Superior until 3 a.m. so am rather tired.

Feb 25

In Chicago a man offered to give away his baby so he could keep his car and, of course, there is much righteous indignation. But at least he dares to be honest. I'll bet anything that thousands of others would do the same thing, if only they dared to and could.

Mar 4

It is fair and clear today, warm in the afternoon. I didn't get home till 2:30 this a.m. But I don't know yet for sure what we are going to do this year & I don't know where or how we can borrow any more money to keep going on this year.

Mar 6

I haven't felt extra well for the last 2 weeks. Our yard is bare as the road. I sowed blue grass last spring, but last summers drouth killed it out.

Mar 18

We are still wondering what we are going to do this year. We, like the rest have nothing left to mortgage to keep 'farming,' so I don't know. A terrible school house explosion at New London, Texas, 450 killed. Some of our tulips are coming up.

Mar 30

Verna & I went to Harry Chaplins sale. A big crowd was there. He, like many others, has lived here many years but also, like many others, is being forced out of the country by the continuous drouth of the last few years.

Apr 4

Some people live in hopes of 'something happening,' — I have always lived more or less in fear of it. And, contrary to popular belief, very many of the things we live in fear of DO happen.

Apr 10

I did some disking in the field W. of the feed yard in the afternoon. The first disking I have done this year. But we don't know from one day to another what we can or will do this year!

Apr 14

Partly cloudy & more or less dusty all the time. I did some disking on the W. bottom in the afternoon. But I don't know yet if & how we can stay here this summer, so it is not very encouraging to try to do very much. Very warm.

Apr 15

Well, my hunch concerning last year proved to be utterly correct. 1936 was one of the most complete failures ever known, even here. All the alfalfa & corn I put in last year was utterly destroyed by hot winds except a little fodder on the bottom.

Apr 16

The big alfalfa fields which used to be so common in this country are all gone now. Just bare, windswept infested fields remain.

Apr 24

Today is the worst so far this year. A mile gale from the N.W. & blinding dust. One can't do much & it doesn't look as though there was any use of doing much anyway. Wind, dust & drouth are getting worse every day.

Apr 30

April is ending! I wonder if we ever will live here another April.

May 20

The dust still hangs in the air & the drouth is getting worse all the time. I planted corn on the W. bottom. The heat & dust were stifling 1–3 p.m.

May 25

Well, I finished planting corn — until I start replanting it. It seems nothing grows for me even after I get it planted. The air still is sort of hazy & dusty but clouds gathered in the S.W. at 6 p.m. Verna and I went in the cellar for awhile.

May 29

Went to R. Cloud . . . We took our lawn mower & rake along & cleaned up the cemetery lots. . . . I went to Riverton to play for a dance — not many there. I doubt if I go again.

June 1

I finished re-planting corn today — I guess.

June 19

Today was as mean as one could ask for. A driving S.W. wind, dust coming in clouds from the river & at 6 p.m. a vague dusty cloud from the N.W., which passed with a few drops of rain. A crowd gathered for an out door picture show but none was held.

June 22

The drouth really got going today. I weeded the corn N. of the feed yard — but the horses have taken to giving out so I don't know just how I will get along. Bad luck seems to follow me.

July 2

I laid a thermometer on the ground at the base of a hill of corn today, it registered 137 degrees!

July 4

Today is Sunday & the 4th of July, a quiet combination in Inavale. A clear sky, a blazing sun. I swept & dusted in the forenoon. We had cherry pie for dinner. We didn't go anywhere. We used to years ago, but those days are gone — forever, I guess.

July 7

The drouth still continues its way of destruction & despair. First the alfalfa seed didn't come up because of drouth now nearly all the cane I sowed is destroyed & it is now starting to destroy the corn, corn is damaged about 20 percent.

July 14

Some Russian aviators flew from Moscow to California over the N. Pole today, that would be easy compared to raising corn in Webster C., Nebraska.

July 15

I placed a thermometer out in the field beside a stalk of corn, it registered 140 degrees! No wonder things burn! A carnival is in R. Cloud but I haven't been to one for a long time.

July 16

One small cloud formed in the W., another in the N.W. This one went S.E. & gave Red Cloud rain & hail, we got a light shower at 7 p.m. One of the horses got sick in the afternoon. I don't know — it seems as though we haven't much left to do much with.

23

The Last Men

P EOPLE SHUNNED BAM WHITE in Dalhart, blaming him for that picture show that made it seem like the nesters had killed the land out of greed or ignorance. They called him half-breed and traitor to Texas, even if all Bam did was guide a plow across a desiccated field as the documentarians filmed him. Most days, Bam didn't care what people said to him or about him. Gossip in town wasn't worth a cup of curdled spit. But it hurt when young Melt came home from school, fevered over what people had said about his daddy. Melt was proud of his father. Seeing him up on the big screen at the Mission Theater made him a bigger man. Bam, Andy James, and the old XIT cowboys knew they were right, that the nesters had ripped up the grass without a thought to what it might do to the natural order. That huge sand dune on the James ranch looked like a transplant from the northern Sahara, all misshapen, growing daily. The irony was that Andy was a rancher; he never got into the wheat game, and the desert dunes on his ranch were somebody else's dirt. More than 700,000 acres in Dallam County were seriously eroded, by the calculation of Hugh Bennett's men. It would not change a thing to say it wasn't so. Much of the land felt like the powdered residue left after an explosion.

Still, in the spring of 1937 in this place of next year people, it was hard to corral the impulse to put something in the earth. Nobody had money for tractor fuel, or hiring farm hands, or even for buying seed. The government handed out seed for grass and gave grants for gasoline, so long as people agreed to try a new way of tilling the ground. Bennett's project, Operation Dust Bowl, was in full swing. An army of CCC workers, aided by unemployed farm hands, was called to duty each morning from barracks on the High Plains, in a war against dirt. The CCC workers pushed the huge, creeping dune on Andy James's ranch around, trying to level it, and then making furrows so that the dust was shaped to offer the least resistance to prevailing wind patterns. The dune had been fifty feet high at one point, topping the roof of any barn, a monster that had grown to nearly a mile in length. They seeded a section of the exhausted ranch with African desert grass and cane. And while they did not say it would ever be a working spread again, they did say it might spring back to life, an awakening of green. In a few years, some grass might grow again without the help of the CCC, and maybe some wild plums in the draw will take hold, some sagebrush, maybe some tamarisk, and it could look in parts like it did when the James family had first come to the High Plains and pronounced it the most heavenly place on earth. If they could make it work here, Big Hugh said, they could do it anywhere in the Dust Bowl. Dallam County was the lab. Bennett started out working with 16,000 acres, but the project expanded quickly to 47,000 acres, with a goal of ten times that size. After so many years of destruction, of hearing how they had killed the land, people wanted to be a part of restoration. It felt good to be trying to heal something.

The Whites planted corn and some grass on the patch of ground outside their two-room house. There was a little section of intact sandy loam that had not been dusted over or ripped up. Bam had kept it in grass, and though it browned early and looked dead for most of the last six years, it held the earth down. Another part of the ground was as hard as cement. When Bam took his hoe and hacked at it, he could barely make a dent. He got his axe, called out to his boys to come have a look, and tried to split the armor of dirt. Only after repeated big swings could he make a slit. He ran the horse-drawn plow, the same one that was in the picture show, over some bundled-up dirt, and got it moved around enough to get some seeds in there. He planted alfalfa because he wanted a little hay to give his two horses, and because after it was cut the stubble would be left on the ground as a way to hold the ground in place. The rain came right in the spring, an inch one day, half an inch another, then ten days of sun, followed by a two-inch downpour. Bam told the children they might actually have something to show in the summer.

Doc Dawson took time off from his duties at the soup kitchen to give his land a final go. It looked so defeated: tumbleweeds snagged against the barbed wire, the surface shaped like an old brown rag. There were dunes ten feet high and hillocks of red dust from New Mexico and heaps of that sickly yellow sand that blew in from other parts of Texas. He followed the advice of the CCC crews, plowing in furrows so the wind would ripple instead of rip and lift, and he pushed the dunes around. He tried planting grass seed as well and drilled holes for corn and maize, which had always been easier to grow than a toenail.

People across the Panhandle had finally agreed to strict conservation, setting up sanctions for any landowner who let his property blow. It was out of character, not very Texan, to allow a committee of farmers and ranchers to determine whether one individual was not in compliance with the laws of nature, but then it wasn't very Texan to let the New Deal conservation men have the run of the Llano Estacado. But they had begged for the help, sending a telegram to Washington. Even Dalhart's lone banker, Lon C. McCrory, had joined in the plea for outside relief, saying, "We need somebody to save us from ourselves."

The remedial efforts did not keep cattle from dying or black blizzards from rolling over other parts of the Dust Bowl. In 1937, there were more dusters on the High Plains than in any other year — 134. To people who lived with death and gray land, it had become the palette of life, almost unnoticed. But to people who had been away or came to the Dust Bowl with fresh eyes, the sight of this sick land was shocking. A minister's son, Alexandre Hogue, had grown up on a relative's ranch not far from Dalhart, left for the city, then returned with a plan to paint what he saw. Hogue was a careful student of the land, studying the way a grove of trees he remembered from his youth now looked like standing skeletons, or how farm animals gnawed on fence posts, or what happened when their eyes were hardened wide open with dust, and the pained expressions on their faces. He saw death on the plains like a black plague. Hogue painted starving animals, drifts that covered tractors and homes, a surfeit of predatory snakes and bugs, a landscape of rotting hell. *Life* magazine ran his paintings in 1937, calling him "the artist of the Dust Bowl." The painting that drew the most attention was an oil-on-canvas piece named *Drouth Survivors,* a portrait of an agrarian nightmare, with surreal touches. It showed two dead cows face-planted into a drift, the top of a leafless tree buried by dust, a tractor half-smothered by sand, a fence drifted. After *Life* ran the painting, it hung in the Pan-American Exposition in Dallas.

McCarty railed against the painting, backed by his Chamber of Commerce. It was bad enough that *The Plow That Broke the Plains* was still playing in some theaters, but now here was this fancy-pants ar-*teest* making the High Plains of Texas out to be like an open-faced cemetery. McCarty pushed a plan through the Chamber to buy the painting, bring it back to Dalhart, and burn it to the cheers of his Last Man Club. The town sent an emissary to Dallas with fifty dollars. The painting couldn't be worth any more than that, they figured. But in Dallas, the Exposition wanted at least two thousand for *Drouth Survivors.* This here painting had been featured in *Life* magazine, after all. The Dalhart representative returned home empty-handed. The painting was later purchased by the Galerie Nationale du Jeu de Paume, a museum in Paris, and burned in a fire.

In early summer, a couple of decent storms visited, and the rain didn't fall in a fury, like the kind that caused flash floods. It was just simple rain at intervals in the middle part of the growing season. It wasn't pure and clean — there was dirt in the downpour — but it was steady enough to do some good. Parched earth that had been planted in grass, hay, and corn looked spongelike for the first time in years. We finally got our break, folks said. Bam White's little patch of green grew to a blanket of green by early July. Doc Dawson's beaten-down sections also had a little blush going and rows of healthy corn stood tall.

Even the grass planted on Andy James's ranch went from a nice start to ankle-high carpet. It seemed like a miracle, and people gave God and Franklin Roosevelt equal credit. God had brought the rain, and FDR showed people the way to bring the land back. Dallam County had the largest soil conservation project in the nation; and in the summer of 1937, it was a trophy. Most of the county was still a wasteland. But on the sections where dunes had been moved, the ground furrowed, and the conservation restrictions put in place, it looked alive — a resurrection. Hugh Bennett came back for another visit and posed for pictures in fields of waist-high alfalfa. Big Hugh was cautious and urged people not to read too much into this little spurt of life. Again, he nagged them all about holding together a sea of conservation districts, not just a small patch of cooperation here and there.

In July the rains gave out and the heat returned, pushing the mercury well past 110 degrees. The ground burned in the big areas that were barren or drifted, and blast-furnace winds browned the crops to a crisp. The corn was not ready for harvest, but maybe some of the grass and hay could be cut and stacked for feed before it crumbled. Some people decided to wait, hoping for one more soaker, gambling that they could outlast the heat or another big duster.

Melt White was outside in early evening, temperature still above a hundred, when he heard a buzz like the electricity of a snapped power line. He poked around and could not find anything that would cause the noise, just a soft breeze at the end of a clear, oppressively hot day. The buzz grew louder. He looked up at the sky and saw a strange-looking cloud, about three times the size of a football field, moving toward him. At first he thought it was an odd duster, some new type of dirt cloud. This mass was thick and dark, and it moved quickly, erratically, the sunlight filtering through as it flickered. The buzz sharpened as the cloud approached, a whirring sound. It scared the boy. He called out for his daddy. Bam White ambled outside, his bowlegs moving slowly in the heat.

What is it, boy?

That cloud. Funny-looking duster, making that noise.

Bam crinkled his eyes and shaded his brow, taking in the moving, buzzing cloud.

Damn! That ain't no duster. It's hoppers.

The cloud dispersed in a few minutes' time, descending on Bam White's grass, latching on to his hay, smothering the garden. Melt was scared — an uncountable swarm of grasshoppers had invaded his home. They consumed everything the family had grown. The grass was gone in minutes. The hay disappeared in a hurry. Melt took a broom and tried to swoosh the hoppers off the grass, but it was no use. Some of them attacked him, chewing on his clothes. They swallowed every cell of fiber in the ground until nothing was standing, and the field looked dead and brown again, and then they lifted off, fortified by the White family's season of labor.

When the grasshoppers hit Doc Dawson's fields, they chewed the corn down to thin stalks and then sucked up the standing strands as well. Grasshoppers are eating machines, each bug consuming up to half of its body weight in a single day. The insects took out all Dawson's grass, all his corn, all his maize, and moved on to the wooden handles of his farm tools. The Doc had left a few shovels, some pitchforks, and a rake lying out. In their feeding frenzy, the hoppers crawled over the polished wood and tried to consume it too. Then they were on the fence posts. His acreage looked like a solid layer of moving, munching hoppers, and his hope for any income in 1937 was destroyed. He had nothing. The Doc's wife said it was like the Biblical Exodus and they were the Egyptians, coping with one plague after another.

The grasshoppers were not selective. The insect clouds moved from county to county, looking for any living thing, leaving not a flower or leaf or a sprig of grass standing. In No Man's Land, they chewed all the turf on the irrigated Kohler ranch, and in the shaded draws on the Lujan spread, and in fields where people had felt encouraged enough to try and nurse wheat through to harvest. The buzzing clouds dropped down on Fred Folkers's place and gnawed his garden to dirt, a plane of winged, bent-legged omnivores. His orchard was long gone, but he had some knee-high wheat planted in furrows. The hoppers got it all. The county ag man, Bill Baker, said he had never seen a bigger surge of insects in his lifetime. He estimated there were 23,000 grasshoppers per acre, fourteen million per

square mile. A farmer with two sections faced twenty-eight million of
the voracious creatures.

Nature was out of whack. In place of buffalo grass, prairie chickens, and mourning doves were black blizzards, black widows, cut-
worms, rabbits, and now this — a frenzied sky of grasshoppers. They
had come out of the dry Rocky Mountains, the government men said,
locusts that laid eggs in the flatlands and multiplied during dry years
without predators. A wet year would usually produce a fungus that
killed many of them. Birds that used to populate the High Plains year-
round or descend on its stubble during the migrating season had disappeared. Same with rattlesnakes. A farmer used to fill a bucket in the
spring with all the rattlers he shot on his half-section. But no more.
For five years, people had rarely seen a rattler. Snakes and birds ate
grasshoppers. When they were taken out of the prairie life cycle, the
hoppers metastasized. That much, people could see; it was obvious.
The early ecologists in Bennett's soil service were only beginning to
examine how much life had frayed below the surface, among the small
world of insects and microorganisms.

The National Guard was called out and instructed to exterminate
the grasshopper plague by any means necessary. The troops tried
burning fields. They tried crushing the insects, using tractors to drag
big rollers over the ground. They brewed up tanks of poison and
spread it over the land, as much as 175 tons of toxins per acre. If there
was anything still alive in the ground, it would die under the blanket
of poison. CCC crews were diverted from their furrowing and dune-
reshaping projects and put on the poison campaign. In No Man's
Land, eighty trucks from the state highway department joined National Guard troops in mixing and hauling grasshopper poison
around the clock. A combination of arsenic and bran was settled on as
the best method, and it was sprayed from the air and distributed by
seeding machines. In places where it killed the grasshoppers, roads
were slick with dead, squashed bugs. But the poison killed everything
else as well. After the promising rains, the growing season had turned
in a few days' time to another disaster.

Just as the hoppers were piling up dead in the fields, the dusters
kicked up again. By the fall the tally was put at half a billion dollars'

worth of lost crops — to dust, grasshoppers, or drought. The southern plains were in no better shape than at the start of the drought five years earlier.

In Dalhart came a surprise announcement: John McCarty was leaving town. The founder of the Last Man Club, the Dust Bowl cheerleader, the Empire Builder, the director of the Dalhart Chamber of Commerce, the editor and publisher of the *Texan* was pulling up stakes and moving south to the city of Amarillo. Nothing personal, he explained to slack-jawed friends around the DeSoto. Nothing against Dalhart, this fine town, full of Spartans, he told Dick Coon and Doc Dawson and all the people who had signed a pledge to never leave, a virtual marriage contract with a town. McCarty wanted a divorce. Nothing against Dallam County. It was just that a man had to follow opportunity when it called your tune. He had had a good job offer in Amarillo and could not afford to turn it down. Nothing against the other members of the Last Man Club. He said good luck and goodbye and turned his back for good on a town he swore he would never leave. The betrayal lingered through the last years of the dust storms.

So Dalhart lost its biggest booster and the *Dalhart Texan* was without its unique voice. The promising crop was ruined by hoppers. The land was on the move again, worse than any time since the start of the black blizzards. Children were dying of dust pneumonia; it seemed like one death every ten days. Uncle Dick was the only community pillar left in town. The survivor of the Galveston hurricane looked around at his shriveled, humbled town, coated in grime, as colorless as the inside of a gopher hole. The First National Bank had folded and never reopened. The pool hall was gone, taken by Dick himself in reluctant foreclosure. Herzstein's was gone, also lost in foreclosure. The DeSoto could barely hold on. Bennett's project had brought a payroll to town and provided rental income for folks who opened up their houses to the CCC workers who didn't want to bunk in the camps outside town. But when Operation Dust Bowl folded its tents, what would be left for Dalhart? Coon found his answer at the card table, where he looked into the weather-creased, sun-blasted faces of

XIT cowboys playing their hands and spitting tobacco into cups. Dalhart had a resource after all: this history, the biggest ranch in the state, the spread that built the capitol, the largest grass under fence in the world, the boys of original Texas.

"We oughtta have ourselves a barbecue," said Uncle Dick. "A reunion, all the XIT cowboys, get 'em here in Dalhart and hold a barbecue."

The idea was an easy sell, especially since Dick said he would pay for the chow. That first week of October, they gathered up as many cowboys as they could find, after a call went out near and far, and held a big feast, with spits of pork ribs and sides of chicken and slabs of beef, grilled in the open air, on a day when the dirt clouds kept their distance. Bam White brought his fiddle, and he was joined by other cowboys. They played all afternoon and danced into the evening, the finest time in Dalhart since the start of this dirty decade. Cowboys gave speeches and toasted the great ghost — the grassland of the XIT. Old-timers told their stories of riding herds and sleeping on the good, soft sod of the Llano Estacado, and how this place was so green in the spring you would have thought it was Ireland. They could not put a stopper in the stories; they just kept coming, late into the night: about how Doc Dawson's sanitarium was a cowboy refuge for a man carved up by barbed wire after a drunk, about all the antelope running over grass, about lightning killing a horse during a thunder-boomer, about how you could ride from sunup to sundown and never get out of the XIT, about snowstorms that came down the prairie lane from Canada, northers so cold they froze your piss in midstream. People laughed late into the night, danced to fiddle music, sang, and ate bread pudding with corn whiskey sauce poured over it. Everyone felt they had something good here with this reunion, that they should not let these stories go.

A few days later, Uncle Dick was leaning against a rail in front of the DeSoto when he spotted a young cowboy and his family drifting through town. For five years now, Dick had watched a steady parade of jalopies and wagons float through Dalhart, the people staying only a night or two, and then moving on to some place where there might be work or stable land. California had turned its back on the

Exodusters. A billboard posted outside of Tulsa told people traveling west on Highway 66 to stay away.

"NO JOBS IN CALIFORNIA
IF YOU ARE LOOKING FOR WORK — KEEP OUT"

Dick rolled a cigarette from the plug of tobacco he kept in a vest pouch, staring all the while at one cowboy and his family. He overheard part of the conversation, the man telling his kids he knew they were hungry but would have to hold on a little longer, maybe at the next town they could get something to eat. The cowboy had wandered into town with the XIT reunion. He thought with all those old saddle-riders around, somebody might know of a place to get work.

"You there," Uncle Dick called out to him.

"Yes, sir?"

"Wha'cha doing here?"

"Fixing to leave, sir. I came hoping to find something on a ranch."

"You know how to ride?"

"Yes, sir. And rope. Fix a fence line. Mend a windmill. I can do it all."

"What's holding ya back?"

"No jobs around here."

"Nothing?"

"No, sir."

Uncle Dick reached into his pocket and pulled out his hundred-dollar bill. He handed the money to the cowboy, told him to take it — it was his. The young man was stunned.

"Are you sure?"

"You take it," Uncle Dick said. "Get yourself situated. Good luck."

The cowboy broke down in tears, sobbing on the dusted streets of Dalhart. Later, when the cowboy asked around about his benefactor, people told him it was Dick Coon, the richest man in town. He owned everything. But they were surprised to see him give up the C-note. He probably had another hundred-dollar bill to replace the one he gave to the cowboy. Only Coon's closest friends knew the truth: Uncle Dick was broke. All his properties were mortgaged and not bringing in any income. He had four dollars left in his bank account. And he was sick. The Doc told Dick Coon he had placed himself in peril by staying on the High Plains. But he had signed the Last Man pledge and took his oath seriously. The Doc said people would understand if he pulled up stakes and said goodbye to Dalhart. It wasn't like that hypocrite John McCarty leaving to take a better job after getting everybody worked up into a froth and pledging to stick around. Dick had to leave in order to stay alive. Okay, then. He moved into the Rice Hotel in Houston and died with little more money than he had when he came into the world, the son of penniless parents.

Lizzie White's great fear was starvation; it kept her up at night and made her weep. After the grasshoppers ate everything that Bam White had put into the ground, he was forced to go on relief. The family got government clothes and government food to go with a government mortgage on the shack. That winter was not easy. Northers blew down and drove the temperature so low that Bam's handlebar mustache froze stiff, just like the water inside their place. The boys would get up early and get the stove going to melt enough water for coffee and washing. Bam seemed to have lost his spirit. He did not want to go outside or kick around with cowboys. He looked rusted.

"Get me that fiddle, boy."

In the winter, trapped for days in the enclosure of cold and darkness, a little music could change the mood inside the White shack. But Bam didn't often feel good enough to play. His hands were cracked, chipped and arthritic; he could barely close them. Melt brought his daddy the instrument and Bam started in. He winced at the pain of moving those cracked hands, but the music came, and as it did, Bam's fingers started to bleed. Melt told his daddy he should stop, but the cowboy kept at it, playing soft fiddle music for his family in the drafty shack, blood trickling down onto the cold, dusted floor.

A few days later, on a Saturday during the first week of February 1938, Bam did not get out of bed. He groaned and wailed, said his stomach was killing him. He was burning with fever. The boys were sent to town to get something for him and rushed back with a pink fluid, like Pepto-Bismol. Bam White drank the bottle of pink liquid, but it did not still the pain. He held his stomach and groaned so loudly his cries could be heard outside. Sunday brought no improvement. He tried to hold it in, to keep his children from seeing him in such agony. The pain was sharp and persistent, like he had a cat inside him clawing to get out. On Monday he died.

They buried Bam near the old XIT, a small service, just family and some cowboys. It was noted that even though Bam White had been shunned by people in town for being a part of that film and had not been asked to join the Last Man Club, he never gave up on the High Plains; he stayed longer than McCarty himself, stayed till his last breath. A few days later, the Resettlement agency came out and sold everything the family had left — a cow, a couple of hogs, every bird in the henhouse, a pair of horses, a mule — to satisfy the debt on the house. When they were done, they told Lizzie White that the family still owed the government $2,300. She had nothing. Resettlement took title to the shack and its dirt patch. Lizzie moved the family south, as she had always wanted to, settling in with her sister in a part of Texas that was not so dusted and torn. They found work picking cotton. Melt could not stand it. He needed freedom, open space, just like his daddy. One day he said he'd had enough. He would never pick cotton for a living. A boy of seventeen, Melt packed a few things and said he was going home.

Home? His mama was taken aback. Where's home?

Melt said he missed the old place where his daddy was buried and that he was born to horses and the open range. He was going to get back to Dalhart and find some way to work a ranch. His mama tried to dissuade him, this headstrong boy, and asked him why he could possibly want to go back to that place of horrors. Melt didn't know himself, at first. He said later his Indian blood was calling him back to the Llano Estacado because it was a place that belonged to Indians and grass, and one day both might be restored.

Dalhart was a lonely town for Doc Dawson in his last years. He missed Dick Coon's generosity, John McCarty's blustery boosterism, Bam White's fiddle. A lot of the faces he did not know; they were strangers, working for the CCC on the big soil conservation project north of town. People had started bringing water up with deep wells, reaching into the Ogallala Aquifer, in a hurry to get that water out of the ground and running. If only they could get the soil to settle, folks said, the Panhandle would be back on its way, for now it had its own liquid gold. But Dawson was done with the land. He had tried for nearly a decade to raise a decent crop — first cotton, then wheat, corn, sorghum, anything — on his couple of sections, but it was a cursed piece of dirt. Through cycles of drought and black blizzards, grasshoppers and blue northers, he had nothing to show but tumbleweeds snagged on a fence line. As his strength faded, he gave up his duties at the soup kitchen. He still kept a little office in town where he saw patients every now and then, but most of them could not pay for his services. More often, people came by just to talk. He spent one afternoon helping a woman with her domestic troubles, and by the end of the day, she had decided not to seek a divorce. But he felt bad because "this may be taking a shingle off the lawyer's roof," he wrote to his son.

The winter of 1938 lingered well into April, a white blizzard entombing the town one day, a black blizzard smothering Dalhart the next, and in between a snuster, followed by a three-day blow of midnight dirt that blocked out the sun almost as bad as the dust of Black Sunday.

"Never in all the 31 years we have lived in the West, have we seen the thing continued for three days and nights without a stretch, without one minute between violent gusts and lambasting dirt deluging us unceasingly," wrote Willie Dawson in a letter to her son John.

On a rare clear day in early May, the Doc went into town. He found the entrance door to his office had blown open and the floor buried by dust. A small dune had formed in his little doctor's office. It took him and a friend most of a day to shovel it out. The Doc decided it was time for him to move as well. But his thoughts were stuck in a loop of despair: he had come to the Texas Panhandle for his health, and now it was one of the unhealthiest places on the planet.

"We are all so discouraged and ready to go," he wrote his son.

How could he leave? His fine house was worth little in a town where one in five people had packed up and rolled away. And how could he stay? If the dust had defeated Dalhart's most vocal cheerleader, and its richest man, and its toughest cowboy, how could an ailing, aged doctor expect to hold on? Dalhart, like Boise City, was closed to the outside world for days on end as dusters buried roads in and out of town, covered the railroad tracks, and made it impossible to see. Some days, the only thing on the Doc's calendar was a visit from an old friend. Even that small joy was taken from him in the spring of 1938 as the black blizzards kept people off the roads.

A massive brain hemorrhage killed Dr. G. Waller Dawson. Going through his belongings, his son John found a tattered, crumbled card inside the Doc's wallet. It was his Last Man Club card, signifying Dawson as the fourth person to join, with his familiar doctor's signature attached to the pledge that he would be the last man to leave the High Plains and that he would always be loyal to it.

24

Cornhusker III

THROUGH SEVEN CENTURIES, a single tree grew in a fold of the land in Nebraska. After it was cut down in 1936, the rings were counted and examined, each circle telling a story of a season on the plains. Dry years were thin rings, when the tree itself barely grew but held on, a still life; wet years were thick, when the tree fattened up with fiber. An examination of the tree found that Nebraska had been through twenty droughts over the previous 748 years. At stake for Don Hartwell was whether he could survive the twenty-first. At the start of August 1937, when he put his thermometer into the ground, it registered a temperature of 151 degrees.

"Rain just doesn't fall in Inavale," Hartwell wrote.

Hartwell was a nudge short of being washed out among the hoboes. His farm was down to three lame horses and a single hog. He still played music in town at night, though the crowds were thin as Webster County hollowed out. His wife took in other people's clothes to iron and sew, but the odd jobs did not bring enough money for seed. The bank had been harassing Hartwell with a flurry of notices that he was well behind on his mortgage. He picked up rumors of work in Leadville, Colorado, or Phoenix, but he seemed paralyzed to move. Though he was only forty-eight years old, he was often sick, forced into bed. He felt tired and stiff. On the arid plains, he noted in his diary, people got old early.

Aug 9

Today is a combination of killing heat, scattered dusty clouds, gusts of burning wind & a few drops of rain. Verna got a letter from Sarah Points at Ward, Colo wanting her to come out there and go into the restaurant business. It is certain we will have to do something . . .

Aug 27

Verna and I were married 25 years ago today. It would be foolish to say that we have never had trouble. One would have trouble even by himself in that length of time . . . Today is terribly hot, dry S. breeze, a few scattered clouds.

Aug 31

Practically all the corn in this country & most of the state has been destroyed by hot winds and drouth this month. This makes the 4th total failure in succession here.

Sept 6

Today is Labor Day. Holidays mean very little here, as in this country it is a sort of distinction NOT TO observe them.

Sept 21

I have not felt right for some time. I always did live intensley [*sic*]. Perhaps it might be a nervous reaction — I hope nothing worse.

Oct 10

Fair and pleasant today. Verna and I listened to the World Series baseball game. The N.Y. Yankees beat the Giants, 4-2, the Yankees winning and ending the series. We have listened to these World Series games for several years now, but I believe that this is the last one we will ever listen to here in Inavale — we shall see.

Nov 8

I burned some Russian Thistles on the W. place. I cut down a dead tree W. of our house. I set out this tree more than 20 years ago, it was a Norway poplar & it seemed that when it turned green that

spring had really come. But the drouth of the last few years got it —
the same as it has us.

Nov 19

Today is very cold & mean, a continuous N. wind. We have no hogs
at all now, it is the first time I can remember in my entire life when
there haven't been either hogs or cattle on the place. In fact — we
have nothing left. We literally have no place to go if we are not 'all
dressed up.'

The communities around Hartwell's farm were dying fast. A village four miles north of his home fell empty, the school abandoned,
the houses and farm buildings deserted, tumbleweeds pressed against
the sides. This could not possibly be the same land Lewis and Clark
had seen in 1804, "well calculated for the sweetest and most nourish-
ing hay," the bluestem twelve feet high. Clark had marveled at the
grass as the Corps of Discovery moved up the Missouri River, staring
west at the plains of Nebraska. "So magnificent a scenery," he wrote,
"one of the most pleasing prospects I ever beheld."

One of Hartwell's best friends left for Wyoming, saying he planned
to return, but Hartwell was sure he would never see him again. Another friend turned on him, becoming cold, "as impersonal as an election notice on a telegraph pole," Hartwell wrote. The frozen air killed
drifters or forced others to steal. Someone threw a rock through the
window of a lumberyard, "so that he could go to jail & get something
to eat & keep from freezing to death," Hartwell wrote.

Around Thanksgiving, a letter arrived from a friend in Denver,
urging the Hartwells to move west. To a middle-aged farm couple,
Denver was a strange city, big and uncertain. Hartwell felt cornered by
his circumstances. He tucked away his pride and appealed to the Red
Cross for a relief grant but was rejected. Now he felt he had no luck
left; he was on a path to sure collapse. He still had a working car but
no money for gas.

"I guess we have reached the end of the trail in Nebraska," he
wrote at year's end.

He spent much of early 1938 begging the bank to let him keep the farm after failing to make a payment for nearly half a year. As a stop-gap measure, the bank agreed to stretch out the interest payments, which lowered the monthly bill but did nothing to move the pile of debt off Hartwell. By habit, he still tried to think like a farmer, using the winter months to plan for the coming year's crop, and to act like a farmer, pruning trees, and clearing out drainage ditches. But his motions were faint and halfhearted. He could not afford seed for the crop, and the bank would not extend him a penny. Another horse died, a mare named Bell. He mourned the loss for months. His body ached and his stomach made strange noises; without money to see a doctor, he had no idea what ailed him.

"I haven't felt right for a year."

People continued to leave Webster County, chased away by dust and dead ground. Some shuttered their houses and moved without notice; others held big home sales, weepy parties, and departed on ceremony. Hartwell scrounged around his family farmstead looking for something of value. The piano was an obvious choice, but he could not bring himself to give it up. He took his land roller, a big metal cylinder used to flatten dirt, to Red Cloud and got five dollars for it. There was a crowd in town, pawing over the possessions of people who had given up. It was mostly junk, Hartwell wrote, but it was the only way most people could shop.

Apr 5

Verna has been doing a little sewing for different ones & I have been doing principally nothing. No income, only 2 horses left, 95 acres of mortgaged land, unpaid taxes & interest and $0 in cash. That is the outlook that faces us after I have lived more than 40 years in Nebr.

Apr 6

Electric lights have been off all day, the first time for a long time. But I think ours will soon be off for good.

Apr 8

Verna got $2 for fixing Miss Bloom's coat.

Apr 18
Well here it is Monday again & I haven't done a bit of farm work yet
& I don't know if I ever will. With only 2 horses, not a cent to our
name, not a cent of income for the last 4 years I just don't know exactly where to turn.

A friend loaned him some seed, on the condition that he pay
it back in corn or money. Hartwell disked the fields and planted
twenty-two rows of corn. Off and on during the planting in May,
he was harassed by "dust showers," rain and dirt falling together.
He also planted Sudan grass, which the CCC was pushing as a
drought-tolerant plant that would take easily to the wind-raked
land. The corn no sooner came up than grasshoppers descended
on his fields. He spread poison. Verna found work washing sheets
and towels at a hotel in town, and after a while they were allowed to eat there in the laundry room, dining on the hotel's leftover
food.

July 12
Today is a terrible day. A glaring sun, a few little clouds & a deliber-
ate, deadly S.W. breeze which has set out to destroy every thing
again this year. I had hoped to live long enough to see one more decent year in this country.

July 20
I wonder if in the next 500 years — or the next 1,000 years, there
will be a summer when rain will fall in Inavale. Certainly not as long
as I live will the curse of drought be lifted from this country.

July 24
Today is just common hell, death and destruction to every growing
thing. A dry, deadly S.W. wind, a dead clear sky & a vicious blazing
sun make up the picture of destruction. God in his infinite wisdom
might have made a more discouraging place than Webster Co,
Nebr., but so far as I know God never did.

July 25

I have felt lost since the horses are gone. There is not much I can do. It is the first time in nearly 40 years that I have not had a team to use. I walked up through the corn and cane in the forenoon. It is being hurt every day by drought.

Aug 17

Bad luck — destingy [*sic*] — (call it what you will) has seemed to follow us since 1932 & this year will be little better. We could not pay back taxes & interest & as the horses are all gone now & we have no income and not one cent in reserve — So what?

The next week, Hartwell and his wife set off for Denver to find work. The money Verna made washing at the hotel was not enough to keep them on the farm. In the city, they stayed with friends who had lined up a job for Verna as a maid at a doctor's house. There was no work for Hartwell and no room for him at the doctor's house. The farmer said goodbye to his wife and returned to Inavale. The separation was supposed to be temporary. The dust, the drought, the fractured farm had broken the last thing they had: their bond. It was the first time they were apart in twenty-six years of marriage. Hartwell moped around his farm, talking to himself and writing in his diary, without even a horse or hog to keep him company. He played music, and at times he was so low he cried at the sight of one of Verna's dresses or a half-opened can of peaches.

"I can hardly call it home anymore. I can't write how I really feel about that."

Oct 7

I wrote to Verna. It seems so long since she was here. Yet it is only a week! How will it seem if the days go on into weeks, the weeks into months, the months into . . .

Nov 2

I did a rash thing today & started for Colo & when I got as far as McCook I changed my mind & came home. I just didn't have the money to go on.

Nov 24

The first thanksgiving since 1912 when Verna & I haven't been to-gether. Will we ever live together again?

Dec 19

I never saw fields any drier. Everything is filled with dust.

Dec 21

I went up & took some pictures of abandoned farms N. of here (I in-tend to put them in a book) in the forenoon. Little is left up there of a once prosperous country. Drouth has all but obliterated a fairly prosperous farming region. Vacant houses, tumble-down buildings, weed-grown fields are all that remain.

Dec 24

Very dry everywhere. I raked the N. side of our yard in the forenoon. I swept and dusted in the afternoon. I trimmed the tree and lighted it in the evening, so it was lighted when Verna came up from the de-pot. She got home at 10 p.m.

Verna stayed a week, then returned to Colorado and her maid's job at the doctor's house. She made forty dollars a month and sent her husband five dollars every two weeks. Hartwell started 1939 still on the farm in Inavale but alone, without seed, horses, cattle, or hogs. To stave off foreclosure, he sold his farm machinery — getting nineteen dollars for a two-row lister, his biggest sale. He sometimes thought of going to town to play music, or even to dance, but he never did. Once, he took a train to Kansas City and saw a burlesque show.

"The girls danced and posed with nothing on," he reported. "But 4H can do that."

The tug of failure was too strong; his life was on a course he could not reverse. But he was still not ready to give up. A friend loaned him a mule and some seed, and he made plans to plant corn again. His heart was torn by loneliness.

"We lived here 26 years together before Nebraska weather & economic conditions finally ruined and separated us," he wrote at year's end.

Feb 3

I used to look forward to spring this time of year, but now — I don't know what to do. I never have been cornered like I am now.

Feb 4

A cold mean wind all day . . . I doubt very much if Verna & I will ever have a home of our own again. I wouldn't even guess what is ahead of us.

Feb 5

I have felt lost lately — not knowing where to turn or what to do. In fact, if one hasn't 'got' anything, there is not much he can do.

Feb 23

I got a letter from the Federal Land Bank saying they were foreclosing on our place. So our last place will soon be gone.

May 27

A chilly, driving N.W. wind. I finished planting corn on the W. bottom in the afternoon, (probably for the last time). An outdoor picture show in the evening but pretty cool to sit out and watch it.

July 10

The same clear, glaring sky & vicious blazing killing sun. Cane is about dead, corn is being damaged; it will soon be destroyed. Those who coined the phrase 'There's no place like Nebraska' wrote better than they thought. In Nebraska, you don't have to die to go to hell.

Aug 4

Practically no one comes here now. Of those who used to ask so diffidently 'Is Verna here?' not one comes around any more. They have vanished like last year's crop of turnips.

Aug 5

Nearly everything is destroyed.

Sept 13

Today is a terrible day of S.W. wind, dust & heat. One can't really do much afternoons owing to the blast of wind & dust. I raked up what little cane there was worth cutting, but there is very little.

Sept 18

There are no dances here anymore — nothing but silence, emptiness, 'respectability.'

Sept 30

September, 1939 was one of the driest ever known, the Weather Bureau says in 40 years. Almost continuous hot winds. . . . there is less corn even than last year. . . . Hitler, Russia, France and England are now supposed to be at war.

Oct 13

Well today is my birthday again. They seem to come altogether too often. Verna sent me a dollar & I went to the hotel to get my dinner.

Nov 14

Everything is a reek of dust. It is in your clothes, you taste it; feel it.

Dec 12

Well, there is not a great deal to report. Winter, in Inavale, is just staying, just living. But I don't look for or expect anything going on any more.

The bank took the land that Hartwells had owned since 1909. Hartwell was allowed to stay in the house for another year, as a rent-paying tenant. He found part-time work on a government road crew. Verna stayed in Denver, still working as a maid. After being apart from her husband for two years, she returned for Christmas. Hartwell ended his diary with a poem, attributed to a woman from Ridgewood, New Jersey, Eleanor Chaffee. He attached the poem to the last page of his diary, without additional comment.

We had a crystal moment
Snatched from the hands of time,
A golden, singing moment
Made for love and rhyme.

What if it shattered in our hands
As crystal moments must?
Better than earthen hours
Changing to lifeless dust.

25

Rain

THEY WORKED THROUGH the hottest days of summer, stitch-
ing a flag forty-nine feet long by twenty-nine feet high, the biggest in the world. Every musician in the Texas Panhandle was
summoned to fall in line, forming another superlative: the largest single marching band ever assembled on American soil — 2,500 instruments. Amarillo had never looked so good. All was in place on the
afternoon of July 11, 1938, for President Roosevelt's visit to the southern plains. He chose Amarillo, headquarters for Operation Dust
Bowl, because it was the only city of any size in the broken land and
because Bennett had told him to go out, have a look, see how farmers
were holding the land down, taking what he had started and making it
their own.

The crowd was enormous, nearly a hundred thousand people in a
city with less than half that population. They jammed into Ellwood
Park under uncertain skies and lined the streets for three miles back
to the station. At 6:45 P.M., a train pulled into Amarillo from the east.
Word went out: he's here! The crowd stirred and a ripple of cheers
followed. The wind was gathering force, and the light seemed to fall
out of the sky sooner than it should have. The heat dissipated quickly.
As clouds thickened, Amarillo's leaders worried that a duster was
about to dump a load on the leader of the Western World.

Some people had driven for two days on drifted roads to get a
glimpse of the president. He was not one of them, but many felt that

this crippled man from New York had kept his promise: he had not forgotten them. The flatland was not green or fertile, yet it seemed as if the beast had been tamed. The year had been dry, just like the six that preceded it, and exceptionally windy, but the land was not peeling off like it had before, was not darkening the sky. There were dusters, half a dozen or more in each of April and May, but nothing like Black Sunday, nothing so Biblical. Maybe, as some farmers suggested, Bennett's army had calmed the raging dust seas, or maybe so much soil had ripped away that there was very little left to roll. Amarillo had begged the government to send its CCC soil-saving and tree-planting crews to the Panhandle, and when they came, they were greeted like firemen arriving at a blaze. Rows of spindly trees — little more than sticks in the ground — now ran through the land, nearly forty million saplings, 3,600 miles of living hope, planted within the most tattered parts of Texas, Oklahoma, and Kansas. In addition, farmers were paid a stipend to list their soil and plant grass alongside the work done by the CCC. Nearly a million acres were under contract as part of Bennett's blueprint to rescue the land. Bennett hoped that seven million acres would eventually be replanted in grass, a prairie reborn in "that delicate miracle the ever-recurring grass," as the poet Walt Whitman called it.

Elsewhere in 1938, the recovery and the energy of the New Deal had run out of steam. More than four million people lost their jobs in the wake of government cutbacks, and the stock market fell sharply again. Some of the gloom that enveloped the country at midterm in President Hoover's reign was back. In the Dust Bowl, the fuzz of a forced forest and the re-tilling of tousled dirt did not stop the wind or bring more rain, but it was a plan in motion — *something* — and that was enough to inspire people to keep the faith. As Will Rogers said, "If Roosevelt burned down the Capital we would cheer and say, 'Well, we at least got a fire started, anyhow.'" The High Plains had been culled of thousands of inhabitants. In No Man's Land, the plague, as nesters called it, had killed or forced out nearly one family in three. It was almost as bad in the Texas Panhandle. But as the dirty decade neared its end, the big exodus was winding down. The only way that folks who stayed behind would leave now, they said, was horizontal, in a pine box.

Melt White had found his way back to the place where his daddy was buried, next to the old XIT on the outskirts of Dalhart. He bought a colt with his savings from picking cotton and took his horse out for a run every day, scouting for a place where he could dig himself a toehold. There was going to be water available soon, all over the Llano Estacado, water from below. People were drilling deep and tapping into the main vein of that ancient, underground reservoir of the Ogallala Aquifer, as big as the grassland itself, they said. These new boomers, a handful of men in town, wanted no part of Bennett's soil-conservation districts. They wanted money to pump up a river of water from the Ogallala, pass it through a tangle of pipes, and spit it out over the sandpapered land. They would grow wheat and corn and sorghum, and they would make a pile, using all the water they wanted, you just wait and see. They talked as if it were the dawn of the wheat boom, twenty years earlier. Melt thought they had not learned a thing from the last decade. The High Plains belonged to Indians and grass, but few people in Dalhart shared his feelings.

Could the soul be returned to a corpse left to the winds? Could Comanche ever ride free again, lords of the tattered plain? Could bison ever find a home on land that had given up its grass? Could the turf that evolved over eons, tailored by nature's calibrations to take fire, drought, eternal wind, and cold into its life cycles, ever be re-stitched to sterile ground?

The land all around Roosevelt's parade route showed signs of terminal disorder. How to explain a place where black dirt fell from the sky, where children died from playing outdoors, where rabbits were clubbed to death by adrenaline-primed nesters still wearing their Sunday-school clothes, where grasshoppers descended on weakened fields and ate everything but doorknobs? How to explain a place where hollow-bellied horses chewed on fence posts, where static electricity made it painful to shake another man's hand, where the only thing growing that a human or a cow could eat was an unwelcome foreigner, the Russian thistle? How to explain fifty thousand or more houses abandoned throughout the Great Plains, never to hear a child's laugh or a woman's song inside their walls? How to explain nine million acres of farmland without a master? America was passing this land by. Its day was done.

Roosevelt had first tasted prairie dust in 1934, when it blew into the White House. Now he was at the source. The rain started just after the president's train pulled into Amarillo. What are the odds of that? Hundred-to-one, local reporters said. It came in showers at first, the tight clouds frayed at the bottom, and then developed into a downpour. People strained to hold the big flag in place, but it grew heavy as it took on the weeping skies. They wanted the president to see the biggest flag in the world before it broke under the weight of water. Roosevelt rode slowly in an open car, through the rain, down the three-mile length of town to the park. He was hatless, and water splattered off his glasses and ran down his nose, but he kept his political face forward, jaw out, smiling and waving. The rain pooled in the streets, and people stood in fast-rising puddles, their shoes wet, to get a glimpse of the president. When he passed by the big flag, Roosevelt ordered the car to stop. He saluted the seamstresses standing near their creation, and the young men trying to hold the flag above ground. Music still poured forth from the world's biggest marching band, even as the instruments were pelted. Now the giant flag began to sag; the young men could not keep it from drooping. The stars and stripes bled away from the 150-square yards of cloth onto the wet street, bled purple.

At Ellwood Park, there was no shelter for the honored guest. It had been dry for six years; no one expected a downpour in mid-July. No one even brought an umbrella. Roosevelt was helped out of the car and up to a grandstand. He stood, using the heavy metal braces to lock his knees in place. The crowd roared, everyone on their feet. He was their savior, and he did not betray their trust in him. Some of his experts had told him that it had been a monumental failure to settle this part of the world and that all the conservation measures and tree planting could not bring life back. People had killed this land by their own greed and stupidity — and, yes, hubris — and it could not be restored. Let it die. If Roosevelt believed this, he never let on. Standing in the rain, hair wet and suit drenched, he looked radiant.

"I think this little shower we have had is a mighty good omen."

Thunderous cheers rose, lasting several minutes. It could have been the Texas high school football championship, for the roar. Yes, sir, a good omen. What else could this land throw at them? What fresh hell could there still be? The rain pounded the crowd as the last of the big flag's color leaked onto the street, purpling the water like food dye in a creek. After the cheers and applause settled, Roosevelt resumed his speech. As he got into it, he took on the nester's chip, the righteous anger of the victim.

"I wish more people from the South and the East could visit this plains country," he said.

Yes, sir, Mr. President — we're not all dead, people said to each other. Damn straight. Tell it to the world!

"If they did you would hear less talk about the great American desert. You would hear less ridicule of our efforts to conserve water and restore grazing lands and to plant trees." He told the crowd how their topsoil had blown all the way to his family home on the Hudson and how people in the East did not understand these nesters, but he would never give up on them.

Roosevelt had always believed in the power of restoration. He was also starting to believe that the Dust Bowl could have been prevented. He had taken to heart some of the conclusions of the Great Plains committee, and he saw a way out in Operation Dust Bowl and his own tree-planting design. What happened on this hard ground was not a weather disaster at all; it was a human failure. A year earlier, in a speech at the dedication of Bonneville Dam on the Columbia River, Roosevelt said if only Americans had known as much thirty years ago as they knew today about care of the arid lands, "we could have prevented in great part the abandonment of thousands and thousands of farms in portions of ten states and thus prevented the migration of thousands of destitute families."

The president said nothing about hindsight on this day, however: he was all sunshine in the rain. "We seek permanently to establish this part of the nation as a fine and safe place which a large number of Americans can call home."

He praised the nesters for their guts and sprinkled half a dozen compliments on local pols before departing with a wave and one last flash of the smile and strong chin. Then it was back to the train, a quick ride to get out of the rain, and away, never to return to the High Plains, away to a world war, fought by some of the same young men straining to hold the flag on the wet streets of Amarillo, away to a day when the Dust Bowl would be forgotten, the flat land left to the winds, the towns shriveled and lost, the last survivors bent and broken, telling stories of a time when the sky showered the land down on them, not knowing if people believed them but not giving a damn if they did.

Epilogue

T HE HIGH PLAINS never fully recovered from the Dust Bowl. The land came through the 1930s deeply scarred and forever changed, but in places it healed. All told, the government bought 11.3 million acres of dusted-over farm fields and tried to return much of it to grassland. The original intent was to purchase up to 75 million acres. After more than sixty-five years, some of the land is still sterile and drifting. But in the heart of the old Dust Bowl now are three national grasslands run by the Forest Service. The land is green in the spring and burns in the summer, as it did in the past, and antelope come through and graze, wandering among replanted buffalo grass and the old footings of farmsteads long abandoned. Some things are missing or fast disappearing: the prairie chicken, a bird that kept many a sodbuster alive in the dark days, is in decline, its population down by 78 percent since 1966. The biggest of the restored areas is Comanche National Grassland, named for the Lords of the Plains, which covers more than 600,000 acres, much of it in Baca County. Plans are underway to reintroduce bison to the shortgrass prairie, as was done in tallgrass preserves in other parts of the Great Plains.

The Indians never returned, despite New Deal attempts to buy rangeland for natives. The Comanche live on a small reservation near Lawton, Oklahoma. They still consider the old bison hunting grounds between the Arkansas River and Rio Grande — "where the wind blew free, and there was nothing to break the light of the sun," as Ten Bears said — to be theirs by treaty.

The trees from Franklin Roosevelt's big arbor dream have mostly disappeared. Nearly 220 million were planted, just as the president envisioned. But when regular rain returned in the 1940s and wheat prices shot up, farmers ripped out the shelterbelt trees to plant grain. Other trees died in cycles of drought over the last half a century. Occasionally, a visitor comes upon a row of elms or cottonwoods, sturdy and twisted from the wind. It can be a puzzling sight, a mystery, like finding a sailor's note in a bottle on an empty beach.

The United States was founded as a nation of farmers but less than 1 percent of all jobs are in agriculture now. On the plains, the farm population has shrunk by more than 80 percent. The government props up the heartland, ensuring that the most politically connected farms will remain profitable. But huge sections of mid-America no longer function as working, living communities. The subsidy system that was started in the New Deal to help people such as the Lucas family stay on the land has become something entirely different: a payoff to corporate farms growing crops that are already in oversupply, pushing small operators out of business. Some farms get as much as $360,000 a year in subsidies. The money has almost nothing to do with keeping people on the land or feeding the average American.

Only a handful of family farmers still work the homesteads of No Man's Land and the Texas Panhandle. To keep agribusiness going, a vast infrastructure of pumps and pipes reaches deep into the Ogallala Aquifer, the nation's biggest source of underground freshwater, drawing the water down eight times faster than nature can refill it. The aquifer is a sponge, stretching from South Dakota to Texas, which filled up when glaciers melted about 15,000 years ago. It provides about 30 percent of the irrigation water in the United States. With this water, farmers in Texas were able to dramatically increase production of cotton, which no longer has an American market. So cotton growers, siphoning from the Ogallala, get three billion dollars a year in taxpayer money for fiber that is shipped to China, where it is used to make cheap clothing sold back to American chain retail stores like Wal-Mart. The aquifer is declining at a rate of 1.1 million acre-feet a day — that is, a million acres, filled to a depth of one foot with water. At present rates of use, it will dry up, perhaps within a hundred years.

In parts of the Texas Panhandle, hydrologists say, the water will be gone by 2010.

During a three-year drought in the 1950s, dusters returned. There were big storms covering roads and spinning over towns but nothing like Black Sunday. Droughts in 1974–1976 and 2000–2003 made the soil drift. But overall, the earth held much better. Why no second Dust Bowl? In 2004, an extensive study of how farmers treated the land before and after the great dusters of the 1930s concluded that soil conservation districts kept the earth from blowing. There was also irrigation water from the Ogallala to compensate for drought, but it was not available in many parts of the dry farming belt. What saved the land, this study found, was what Hugh Bennett had started: getting farmers to enter contracts with a soil conservation district and manage the land as a single ecological unit. By 1939, about 20 million acres in the heart of the Dust Bowl belonged to one of these units. Hugh Bennett died in 1960 at the age of seventy-nine. He is buried in Arlington National Cemetery. His legacy, the soil conservation districts spread throughout America, is the only New Deal grassroots operation that survives to this day.

Dalhart still stands, a windblown and dog-eared town at the crossroads of three highways. It never recovered its population from pre-1930; barely six thousand people live in Dallam County now. At the entrance to town is a striking monument: an empty horse saddle, dedicated to the XIT cowboys. Every year, Dalhart holds a celebration for the old XIT ranch and the ghosts of cowboys who ran through its grass during the glory years. After moving out of Dalhart, John McCarty, the town's biggest booster, never returned. In his later years, he took up painting, concentrating on art that depicted dust storms as heroic and muscular. Born in 1900, the same year as Dalhart, McCarty died in 1974. In a home he built at the edge of town, Melt White lives with his wife of more than sixty years, Juanita. He worked as a house painter and paperhanger, though he still considers himself a cowboy by trade and inclination. He keeps a couple of horses out back on land next to the old XIT. He curses the day farmers came to the Panhandle and tore up the grass.

Boise City is alive — but barely. With just three thousand people,

Cimarron County has lost nearly half its pre–Dust Bowl population. Fred Folkers was ten thousand dollars in debt at the start of the war. But four-dollar wheat got him out of it, in the same way that wartime factory production finally got the United States out of the Depression. In 1948, at age sixty-six, Fred had a heart attack. He continued to farm right up until his death in 1965. His wife, Katherine, outlived him by ten years. She died at the age of ninety. The children, Faye and Gordon, still own the homestead, land where Katherine ironed centipedes in the walls of the dugout. Hazel Lucas Shaw had another child, Jean Beth, to go with her son, Charles, Jr. Hazel's husband, Charles, died in 1971, of heart disease. After surviving the Dust Bowl and two subsequent tornadoes, Hazel outlived all her friends from Boise City. She died in 2003 at the age of ninety-nine. Though she never returned to live there, she told her grandchildren she always missed No Man's Land.

Inavale, Nebraska, where the Hartwells lived, is a ghost town. Webster County, with four thousand people, has lost more than 60 percent of its population from the 1930s. Years ago, a neighbor found Verna Hartwell burning her late husband's diary. The diary was rescued and after Verna's death turned over to the Nebraska Historical Society in Lincoln.

Approaching his ninetieth birthday, Ike Osteen lives with his wife, Lida Mae, not far from the dugout where the family of nine children passed their days in a hole in the ground. After leaving Baca County, Ike worked on the railroad and road projects, and then joined the Army. By the time Hitler's forces occupied most of Europe, Osteen was in boot camp. The soldier from the dugout landed in France on D-Day, June 6, 1944, fought the Germans through hedgerows, saw friends bleed and die. When the war was over, he thought about his place in the world and was drawn back to Baca County. It takes a certain kind of person to make peace with land that has betrayed them, but that is the way with home. Ike's mother died at the age of ninety-two. Most days, Ike puts in a full day's work around the house and usually spends some part of an afternoon sorting through the living museum of his life on the High Plains. He loves it still.

NOTES
AND SOURCES

———◆◆———

ACKNOWLEDGMENTS

———◆◆———

INDEX

Notes and Sources

INTRODUCTION

The quotes and descriptions of Dalhart, Boise City, and Baca County come from interviews conducted by the author and reporting trips to the High Plains. Ike Osteen was interviewed at his house in Springfield, Colorado, on April 25, 2002. Jeanne Clark was interviewed in Lamar, Colorado, on April 22, 2002, with follow-up phone conversations on April 3, 2003, and June 1, 2003. Melt White was interviewed at his home in Dalhart on November 21, 2002, with follow-up phone conversations on August 3, 2003, and September 12, 2003.

The figure on percentage of the population that left the Dust Bowl versus the number who stayed is from the U.S. Census Bureau population surveys, 1930 and 1940, www.census.gov.

Donald Worster is quoted from his book *Dust Bowl: The Southern Plains in the 1930s* (New York: Oxford Univ. Press, 1979).

1: THE WANDERER

The story of the White family migration comes from Melt White, as told to the author, November 21, 2002, Dalhart, Texas.

Descriptions of the XIT ranch from the author's visit to the XIT Museum, Dalhart, Texas, and *Six Thousand Miles of Fence: Life on the XIT Ranch of Texas,* Cordia Sloan Duke and Joe B. Frantz (Austin: Univ. of Texas Press, 1961).

Early years in Dalhart and the Dawson family story from *High Plains Yesterdays: From XIT Days Through Drouth and Depression,* John C. Dawson (Austin, Texas: Eakin Press, 1985).

John McCarty's story is from the Amarillo Public Library John C. McCarty Collection, Introduction to the collection, no title, Amarillo Public Library, Amarillo, Texas.

Quotes from the newspaper are from the *Dalhart Texan,* May 1, 1930.

Property records and civil cases came from the public records on file in the Dallam County Courthouse, Dalhart, Texas.

The early history of Dalhart from *The Book of Years: A History of Dallam and Hartley Counties,* Lillie Mae Hunter (Hereford, Texas: Pioneer Book Publisher, 1969).

Comanche tribal history came from a variety of sources:

Author interviews with Comanche tribal elders, among them Lucille Cable of Lawton, Oklahoma, and Ray Niedo of Indianola, Oklahoma, conducted on October 2 and 5, 2003.

Being Comanche: A Social History of an American Indian Community, Morris W. Foster (Tucson: Univ. of Arizona Press, 1991).

Comanches: The Destruction of a People, T. R. Fehrenbach (New York: Alfred A. Knopf, 1974).

The New Encyclopedia of the American West, Howard R. Lamar, ed. (New Haven, Conn.: Yale Univ. Press, 1998).

Museum of the Great Plains, Lawton, Oklahoma, author visit May 15, 2003.

Comanche Nation, Comanche Tribal Home Page, www.comanchenation.com.

Grasslands and ranches, in part from United States Forest Service files on history of the national grasslands, La Junta, Colorado, provided to the author by the Forest Service. Also, "The Panhandle of Texas," Frederick W. Rathjen, Handbook of Texas online at www.tsha.utexas.edu/handbook; Rathjen's *The Texas Panhandle Frontier* (Austin: Univ. of Texas Press, 1973); and *The Grasses of Texas,* Frank W. Gould (College Station: Texas A&M Univ. Press, 1975).

Wesley L. Hockett's quotes are from his oral history on file in the Special Collections of the Amarillo Public Library, Amarillo, Texas.

2: NO MAN'S LAND

Descriptions of Boise City from author trips to the town and from interviews, notably Norma Gene Butterbaugh Young, interviewed at her home in Boise City, Oklahoma, on September 8, 2003.

Early description of fraud from the *Cimarron News,* various editions, and records provided by the Cimarron Heritage Center, Boise City, Oklahoma, September 9, 2003.

How people lived in part from *Commerce of the Prairies,* Josiah Gregg, Max W. Moorhead, eds. (Norman: Univ. of Oklahoma Press, 1990).

Early Boise City descriptions and family histories from *The Tracks We Followed,* Norma Gene Butterbaugh Young, ed. (Amarillo, Texas: Southwestern Publications, 1991).

Early Panhandle homestead stories in part from author visit to Oklahoma Historical Society, Oral History Program, Oklahoma City, Oklahoma, September 9, 2003.

Anecdote on preacher and postal worker from Young, *The Tracks We Followed,* previously cited.

The Hazel Lucas Shaw story and larger story of the Lucas family from author interview with Charles Shaw, Hazel's son, on September 21, 2003, and from *Sunshine and Shadows* (1984), a self-published family history written by Hazel Shaw, given to the author by Mr. Shaw in 2002, as well as personal correspondence from Mr. Shaw to author, September 22, 2003.

The Folkers family story from author interviews with Faye Folkers Gardner, on April 30, 2002, and Gordon Folkers, on May 2, 2002, as well as Mrs. Gardner's self-published family history, *So Long, Old Timer!* (1979), given to the author by Mrs. Gardner in 2002.

Descriptions of mid-1920s life in No Man's Land from author interview with Imogen Glover at her home in Guymon, Oklahoma, on April 29, 2002.

Farming statistics from the annual *Yearbook of Agriculture,* United States Department of Agriculture (Washington, D.C.: Government Printing Office, 1926, 1927, 1928, 1929).

Oklahoma settlement in part from *It's Your Misfortune and None of My Own: A New History of the American West,* Richard White (Norman: Univ. of Oklahoma Press, 1991).

Information on windmills, dugouts, and first homes in No Man's Land from author interview with Janie Harland of Texhoma, Oklahoma, on September 3, 2003, and her oral history on windmills in *Panhandle Pioneers,* compiled and edited by the Texhoma Genealogical and Historical Society, vol. 7.

The Government Bureau of Soils and John Wesley Powell's *Report on the Arid Lands* (Washington, D.C.: U.S. Geological Survey, 1878) provided early description of aridity and potential for agriculture in the High Plains.

3: CREATING DALHART

The White family travails from author interviews with Melt White on November 21, 2002, at home in Dalhart, Texas.

Town-building years from the *Dalhart Texan,* various editions on file at the XIT Museum in Dalhart, Texas, and from previously cited Hunter, *Book of Years.*

Dawson family details are from Dawson's previously cited book, *High Plains Yesterdays.*

Kansas details are from *Kansas: A Guide to the Sunflower State,* Federal Writers Project of the WPA (New York: Viking, 1939).

Story of early southern plains town-builders from oral history, Federal Writers Project, 1936–1940, public records, Library of Congress, www.loc.gov/ammem/wpaintro/wpahome.html.

4: HIGH PLAINS DEUTSCH

Ehrlich family history taken in part from author interview with Juanita Ehrlich Thompson of Albuquerque, New Mexico, on July 18, 2003, and from Willie Ehrlich's oral history audiotape on file at the Oklahoma Historical Society, Oral History

Program, Oklahoma City, Oklahoma, recorded July 17, 1986, as well as from an un-published family history, *Seventy-Eight First Cousins* (1990), compiled by Yvonne Fortney Jones and Georgia Ehrlich Fortney and given to the author.

Borth family story from author interview with Rosa Borth Becker, of Shattuck, Oklahoma, on September 12, 2003.

Information about early German settlement in the High Plains from author in-terview with Mildred Becker, curator, Wolf Creek Heritage Museum, Lipscomb, Texas, and from exhibits at the museum during author visit September 10, 2003.

Details on home life, food, and routine of Russian Germans in High Plains in part from oral history archive of tape recording with George Hofferber, Oral History Pro-gram, Oklahoma Historical Society, Oklahoma City, Oklahoma.

The story of the Volga Germans is drawn from several sources:

Conquering the Wind: An Epic Migration from the Rhine to the Volga to the Plains of Kansas, Amy Brungardt Toepfer and Agnes Dreiling (Lincoln, Neb.: American Historical Society of Germans from Russia, 1966).

The Czar's Germans, Hattie Plum Williams (Lincoln, Neb.: American Historical Society of Germans from Russia, 1975).

Displays at the Wolf Creek Heritage Museum, Lipscomb, Texas, author visit September 7, 2003.

American Historical Society of Germans from Russia, Lincoln, Nebraska, au-thor visit June 22, 2003.

"The Migration of Russian-Germans to Kansas," Norman E. Saul, *Kansas His-torical Quarterly,* Spring 1974, vol. 40, no. 1.

Population gains in the High Plains from the United States Census, 1870, 1890, 1900, 1910, and 1920, www.census.gov.

Story of Scandinavians from *Oslo on the High Plains,* Peter L. Petersen, Norwe-gian American Historical Association, vol. 28, p. 138, 1979.

5: LAST OF THE GREAT PLOWUP

Early tree-planting from *Plains Folk,* Jim Hoy and Tom Isern (Norman: Univ. of Oklahoma Press, 1987).

Homesteading details in part from Homestead National Monument of America, Beatrice, Nebraska, author visit April 10, 2003.

Kansas details from previously cited WPA guide, *Kansas: A Guide to the Sun-flower State.*

Size of the federal budget from *The Great Depression: America in the 1930s,* T. H. Watkins (Boston: Little, Brown and Co., 1993).

Dawson family details from previously cited Dawson book, *High Plains Yester-days.*

Folkers details from author interview with Faye Folkers Gardner, April 30, 2002, and her previously cited book, *So Long, Old Timer!*

Osteen family narrative from author interview with Ike Osteen, April 25, 2002, and his previously cited book, *A Place Called Baca.*

Description of Boise City at the time from the *Cimarron News,* various editions, 1930.

Early twentieth-century American life in general, in part from *America in Mid-passage, Vol. III: The Real Rise of American Civilization,* Charles A. Beard and Mary R. Beard (New York: MacMillan Co., 1939), and *This Fabulous Century: Sixty Years of American Life,* Volume III, 1920–1930 (New York: Time-Life Books, 1969).

6: FIRST WAVE

Bank closure from the *Dalhart Texan,* various issues, 1931, on file at the XIT Museum, Dalhart, Texas.

Depression details in general, in part from several books:

The Great Depression, Robert S. McElvaine (New York: Times Books, 1984).

Watkins, *The Great Depression,* previously cited.

The Great Crash: 1929, John Kenneth Galbraith (Boston: Houghton Mifflin, 1954).

Hard Times: An Oral History of the Great Depression, Studs Terkel (New York: Random House, 1970).

White family troubles from author interview with Melt White, November 21, 2002.

Dalhart details from previously cited Hunter, *Book of Years.*

Dalhart collapse from letters, archives, and newspapers on file at the XIT Museum, Dalhart, Texas.

Information on the Herzstein family came from a variety of sources:

Author visit to the Herzstein Museum in Clayton, New Mexico, June 4, 2003.

Author interview with Mortimer H. Herzstein on October 2, 2003.

Herzstein family archives, on file at the Zimmerman Library, Lerzstein Latin American Reading Room, University of New Mexico, Albuquerque, New Mexico.

Author interview with Isabel Lord, daughter of Simon Herzstein, on February 20, 2002.

7: A DARKENING

Weather records are from federal weather bureau records, available online, www.nws.noaa.gov/, and from archives at the National Drought Mitigation Center in Lincoln, Nebraska, author visit June 22, 2003.

Hazel Shaw story from author interview with her son, Charles Shaw, September 21, 2003.

Folkers details from Faye Folkers Gardner's previously cited book, *So Long, Old Timer!*

Information on William Murray in part from *Alfalfa Bill Murray,* Keith L. Bryant Jr. (Norman: Univ. of Oklahoma Press, 1968) and William H. Murray Collection at Oklahoma University, Carl Albert Center archives, author visit, September 9, 2003.

Sheriff Hi Barrick and his story from oral history interview with Barrick, recorded January 7, 1983, on file at the Oklahoma Historical Society, Oral History Program, author visit September 6, 2003.

First dust storm details from federal government's Monthly Weather Review, January 1932, www.history.noaa.gov.

Approaching storms and social conditions from *The Dust Bowl: An Agricultural and Social History,* R. Douglas Hurt (Chicago: Nelson-Hall, 1981).

White family details from author interview with Melt White, November 21, 2002.

Reaction in Boise City from *Boise City News,* various editions, 1932 and 1933.

Farming troubles from *An Empire of Dust,* Lawrence Svobida (Caldwell, Idaho: Caxton Printers, 1940).

8: IN A DRY LAND

Dawson family descriptions of bugs from Dawson's book, *High Plains Yesterdays,* previously cited.

White family from author interview with Melt White, November 21, 2002.

Story of Black Jack's grave in part from pages of the *Dalhart Texan,* various editions, 1932, and from author interviews with Herzstein family members, February 20, 2002, and October 2, 2003.

Weather bureau reaction to early storms in part from *The Dust Bowl: Men, Dirt and the Depression,* Paul Bonnifield (Albuquerque: Univ. of New Mexico Press, 1979).

Information on Oklahoma Panhandle reaction from author interview with Gerald Dixon at his home in Guymon, Oklahoma, on November 21, 2002.

Details of drought, social, and agricultural life from author interview with Dr. Ken Turner, curator, No Man's Land Historical Museum, Guymon, Oklahoma, on November 20, 2002.

Lujan family details from family history on file at Boise City Public Library, Boise City, Oklahoma, and from Young, *The Tracks We Followed,* previously cited.

County agricultural agent, William Baker, and his actions in part from *Boise City News,* various editions, 1932–1934.

Hispanics and how they lived in part from oral history of Joe Garza, on file at Oklahoma Historical Society, Oral History Program, Oklahoma City, Oklahoma.

Hugh Bennett from United States Department of Agriculture official biography, www.nrcs.usda.gov/about/history/bennett.html, and *Big Hugh: The Father of Soil Conservation,* Wellington Brink (New York: MacMillan, 1951).

Farming troubles from Svobida, *An Empire of Dust,* previously cited.

9: NEW LEADER, NEW DEAL

White family details from author interview with Melt White, November 21, 2002.

Bill Murray decline from Murray archives, William H. Murray Collection at Oklahoma University.

Depression information in general from previously cited McElvaine, *Great Depression*, and *The Age of Roosevelt: The Crisis of the Old Order, 1919–1933*, Arthur M. Schlesinger, Jr. (Boston: Houghton Mifflin, 1957), as well as *Franklin D. Roosevelt: A Rendezvous with Destiny*, Frank Freidel (Boston: Little, Brown, 1990).

Details of Boise City from *Boise City News*, various editions, 1933–1934.

Farm income from *Yearbook of Agriculture 1934*, United States Department of Agriculture (Washington, D.C: U.S. Government Printing Office, 1934).

General plains details from *Heaven's Tableland: The Dust Bowl Story*, Vance Johnson (New York: Farrar, Straus, 1947).

Bennett quotes from previously cited USDA biography and Brink, *Big Hugh*.

10: BIG BLOWS

Weather details from *Boise City News*, April 1 and 14, 1933, and from No Man's Land Historical Museum, Guymon, Oklahoma, author visit November 20, 2002.

Weather history from *History of United States Weather Bureau*, Donald R. Whitnah (Champaign: Univ. of Illinois Press, 1961).

Dalhart details from the *Dalhart Texan*, various editions, 1933.

Hazel Shaw information from her previously cited book, *Sunshine and Shadows*, and from author interview with her son, Charles Shaw, September 21, 2003.

Lindbergh landing from *Dalhart Texan* and *Boise City News*, various editions, 1933.

Eyewitness accounts of early storms from Oral History Program, Oklahoma Historical Society, author visit September 6, 2003.

Cable sent to Washington from *Boise City News*, various editions, 1933.

Hazel Shaw's pregnancy from her book, *Sunshine and Shadows*, previously cited.

11: TRIAGE

Government checks and government plans in Boise City from *Boise City News*, various editions, 1934.

Hazel Shaw details from author interviews with son Charles Shaw, September 21, 2003, and her previously cited book, *Sunshine and Shadows*.

Description of area, as quoted, from *New Outlook* magazine, May 1934.

McCarty writings from his column, *Dalhart Texan*, various editions, 1934.

Information on the Kohler ranch and how the Kohler family coped from Robert Kohler interview, recorded March 14, 1983, on file at Oral History Program, Oklahoma Historical Society, Oklahoma City, Oklahoma, author visit September 5, 2003.

Description of storms from "The Dust Bowl," Michael Parfit, *Smithsonian*, June 1989.

Big dust storm hits New York, from the *New York Times*, various editions, 1934.

Caroline Henderson writings from "Letters of Two Women Farmers," *Atlantic*

Monthly, August 1933, and collected in *Letters from the Dust Bowl,* Caroline Henderson, Alvin O. Turner, eds. (Norman: Univ. of Oklahoma Press, 2001).

12: THE LONG DARKNESS

Birth of Shaw child and travails from Hazel Shaw's previously cited book, *Sunshine and Shadows.* More Shaw details from author interview with Charles Shaw, September 21, 2003.

Hi Barrick from oral history recorded January 7, 1983, on file at Oral History Program, Oklahoma Historical Society, Oklahoma City, Oklahoma, author visit September 5, 2003.

Depression era birthrate from U.S. Census, www.census.gov.

Government plans and payouts from *Boise City News,* various editions, January 1935.

Kohler ranch from oral history, Oral History Program, Oklahoma Historical Society, Oklahoma City, Oklahoma, author visit September 6, 2003.

Lowery family canning and eating Russian thistles from Odalee Lowery Bohn's story in *Footsteps: Family Histories of Cimarron County, Oklahoma,* Norma Gene Butterbaugh Young, ed. (Amarillo, Texas: Southwestern Publications, 1989).

Ehrlich family details from Willie Ehrlich oral history at Oral History Program, Oklahoma Historical Society, Oklahoma City, Oklahoma, recorded July 17, 1986.

Borth family details from author interview with Rosa Borth Becker, Shattuck, Oklahoma, September 12, 2003.

13: THE STRUGGLE FOR AIR

Osteen illnesses and life in dugout from author interview with Ike Osteen, April 25, 2002.

Osteen land and descriptions of family struggle from Osteen's previously cited book, *A Place Called Baca.*

Dr. Blue on dust pneumonia from *Boise City News,* April 1935.

Red Cross hospitals from *Boise City News,* April and May 1935, and Osteen recollections, author interview, April 25, 2002.

Stories of Baca County during 1930s from Baca histories on file at the Baca County Public Library, Springfield, Colorado.

Stories of Red Cross and other dust-related emergency measures in southeast Colorado from *Prowers County Heritage,* the county history, on file at the Lamar Public Library, Lamar, Colorado.

Weather history, *From Weather Vanes to Satellites,* Herbert J. Spiegel and Arnold Gruber (New York: John Wiley & Sons, 1983).

14: SHOWDOWN IN DALHART

Arrest of blacks from *Dalhart Texan,* various issues, Spring 1935.

Lunacy trials from records on file in Dallam County Courthouse, Dalhart, Texas, and from previously cited Dawson, *High Plains Yesterdays.*

Details of Dalhart decline from previously cited Hunter, *Book of Years.*

White family chores and challenges, author interview with Melt White, November 21, 2002.

Big Dalhart meeting from *Dalhart Texan,* various issues, Spring 1935.

McCarty comments from his column in the *Dalhart Texan,* various issues, Spring 1935.

Rainmaking from *Dalhart Texan,* various issues, Spring 1935.

15: DUSTER'S EVE

Baby's illness and death, from Hazel Shaw's previously cited book, *Sunshine and Shadows,* and from Hi Barrick oral history, recorded January 7, 1983, on file at Oral History Program, Oklahoma Historical Society, Oklahoma City, Oklahoma, author visit September 5, 2003.

Other details and family reaction to tragedy from author interview with Charles Shaw, September 21, 2003.

Folkers troubles from Faye Folkers Gardner's previously cited book, *So Long, Old Timer!* and from author interviews with Gordon Folkers, May 2, 2002, and Faye Gardner, April 30, 2002.

Boise City life just before Black Sunday from author interview with Norma Gene Butterbaugh Young, September 8, 2003, and her book, *Footsteps,* previously cited.

Kansas State professor's estimate of volume of dust, as reported by *Amarillo Daily News,* April 22, 1935.

Hi Barrick's duties from his oral history on file at Oral History Program, Oklahoma Historical Society, previously cited.

Descriptions of rabbit clubbings from *Boise City News* and oral history of Verdela Harriman Fry, on file at Oral History Program, Oklahoma Historical Society, Oklahoma City, Oklahoma, author visit September 6, 2003.

16: BLACK SUNDAY

Description of weather that morning, author interviews with Ike Osteen, Melt White, and Norma Gene Butterbaugh Young, all previously cited, and newspaper accounts.

Osteen activities, from author interview with Ike Osteen, and Mr. Osteen's book, *A Place Called Baca,* previously cited.

Description of storm hitting Dodge City from *Black Sunday: The Great Dust Storm of April 14, 1935,* Frank L. Stallings, Jr. (Austin, Texas: Eakin Press, 2001).

Lucas funeral from Hazel Shaw's previously cited book, *Sunshine and Shadows,* and *Boise City News,* various editions, April 1935.

Trucks in ditch and sky black in Boise City from remembrance of Louise Fairchild, as told to Natalie Weaver and Andrew Randolph in Boise City Language Arts class, 1999, on file at Cimarron Heritage Center, Boise City, Oklahoma.

Folkers's experience from Faye Folkers Gardner's previously cited book, *So Long, Old Timer!*

Story of Joe Garza and saving the child from interview with Garza, recorded 1985 (no month), on file at Oral History Program, Oklahoma Historical Society, Oklahoma City, Oklahoma, author visit September 8, 2003.

The Associated Press team, from AP dispatches, chiefly the one sent the day after Black Sunday, April 15, 1935, printed in the *Amarillo Daily News*, April 15, 1935.

When storm hit Denver from photos and records on file at Denver Public Library, Western History Department, Denver, Colorado, author visit May 12, 2004.

How the Germans fared from author interviews with Ehrlichs, July 18, 2003, and Borths, September 12, 2003.

What happened to Ehrlich, from Willie Ehrlich oral history, Oral History Program, Oklahoma Historical Society, Oklahoma City, Oklahoma, recorded July 17, 1986.

Black as night from Berenice Jackson, Oral History Program, Oklahoma Historical Society, Oklahoma City, Oklahoma, author visit September 6, 2003.

When the storm hit Texas Panhandle from *Amarillo Daily News*, April 15, 1935.

Woody Guthrie account from a recording made March 21, 1940, between Guthrie and Alan Lomax, as presented on "Woody Guthrie on Weekend Edition, Oct. 20, 1996," from the transcript.

17: A CALL TO ARMS

Bob Geiger dispatches from Associated Press filings, previously cited.

Hugh Bennett waiting for storms to call for aid from previously cited USDA biography and Brink, *Big Hugh*, and news accounts, as well as government booklet, "The National Grasslands Story," United States Department of Agriculture — Forest Service (Washington, D.C.: U. S. Government Printing Office, 1964).

Land "essentially destroyed," from USDA, *Yearbook of Agriculture 1935*, previously cited.

Beginnings of conservation plans from *The Soil Conservation Service*, D. Harper Simms (New York: Praeger Publishers, 1970).

Odalee Bohn Lowery recollections, from oral history on file at Boise City Public Library, Boise City, Oklahoma, and from previously cited Young, *Footsteps.*

Dalhart stirrings from John L. McCarty Collection, Amarillo Public Library, Amarillo, Texas.

Formation of Last Man's Club from *Dalhart Texan*, April 22, 1935.

Rainmaking from the *Dalhart Texan*, April 29, 1935, and Dawson, *High Plains Yesterdays*, previously cited.

Roosevelt actions, in part, from *Franklin Roosevelt and the New Deal*, William E. Leuchtenburg (New York: Harper & Row, 1963), and *The Age of Roosevelt*, 3 vols., Arthur M. Schlesinger (Boston: Houghton Mifflin, 1957–1960).

Harold Ickes, in part, from *Righteous Pilgrim: The Life and Times of Harold L. Ickes, 1874–1952*, T. H. Watkins (New York: Henry Holt, 1990).

Ickes quote on idealism from *New York Times Magazine,* May 27, 1934.
Bennett from previously cited USDA biography and Brink, *Big Hugh.*
McCarty quotes from his columns in the *Dalhart Texan,* April, May, June, 1935.
Cimarron County telegram from *Boise City News,* April 1935.

18: GOINGS

Osteen breakup, all from author interviews with Ike Osteen and Mr. Osteen's book, previously cited.

Resettlement activity in Baca, from records on file at Springfield Public Library, Baca County Library, Springfield, Colorado.

Osteen graduation, mother comments, from author interviews with Mr. Osteen, previously cited.

19: WITNESSES

Donald Hartwell's writings are from his unpublished diary, on file at the Nebraska State Historical Society, Lincoln, Nebraska, and provided to the author. Copyright holder unknown.

Rothstein information, from Farm Security Administration public records, www.loc.gov/ammem/fsahtml, and *The Depression Year,* Arthur Rothstein (New York: Dover Publications, 1978).

Pare Lorentz, "The Plow That Broke the Plains" from the film itself (U.S. Government short film, produced by Pare Lorentz, 1936), and from *Pare Lorentz and the Documentary Film,* Robert Snyder (Norman: Univ. of Oklahoma Press, 1968).

Panhandle reaction to film from *Amarillo Daily News,* June 1, 1936.

Dorothea Lange from *An American Exodus: A Record of Human Erosion,* Dorothea Lange and Paul Schuster Taylor (New York: Reynal & Hitchcock, 1939).

Bam White watching film from author interviews with Melt White, previously cited.

20: THE SADDEST LAND

Hazel Shaw pregnant, from her previously cited *Sunshine and Shadows.*

Statistics on volume of dirt, from the *New York Times,* March 31, 1935.

Statistics on out-migration from United States Census Population Survey, www.census.gov, and *American Exodus: The Dust Bowl Migration and Okie Culture in California,* James N. Gregory (New York: Oxford Univ. Press, 1989).

Caroline Henderson letters from letters published in the *Atlantic Monthly,* previously cited.

Hazel Shaw details from author interview with son Charles Shaw, September 21, 2003, and her previously cited book, *Sunshine and Shadows.*

Weather statistics on Oklahoma, from a chart entitled "Oklahoma Weather Timelines," courtesy of the State of Oklahoma.

Ehrlich details from family history, *Seventy-Eight First Cousins,* and Willie Ehrlich oral history, both previously cited.

Borths from Rosa Borth Becker interview, September 12, 2003, and family history on file at Wolf Creek Heritage Museum, Lipscomb, Texas.

New York Times story from March 31, 1935, edition.

Another *New York Times* story, May 27, 1934, edition.

McCarty singing and Guymon visitors from *Dalhart Texan,* various editions, Spring 1936.

21: VERDICT

Quotes from report are direct from public file, "Report of the Great Plains Drought Area Committee, Aug., 1936," www.newdeal.feri.org.

Second report directly quoted from "The Future of the Great Plains," 1937, public record, www.newdeal.feri.org.

Roosevelt thoughts from Harold Ickes's diary, *Secret Diary of Harold L. Ickes: The First Thousand Days, 1933–1936,* Harold L. Ickes (New York: Simon & Schuster, 1953).

22: CORNHUSKER II

Donald Hartwell's writings are from his unpublished diary, on file at the Nebraska State Historical Society, Lincoln, Nebraska, and provided to the author. Copyright holder unknown.

23: THE LAST MEN

White family details from interviews with Melt White, previously cited.

Dick Coon and the hundred-dollar bill, and the barbecue from Hunter, *Book of Years,* previously cited.

XIT reunion barbecue from displays at the XIT Museum, Dalhart, Texas.

McCarty leaving, from *Dalhart Texan,* 1936.

Migration statistics, from Gregory book, *American Exodus: The Dust Bowl Migration and Okie Culture in California,* previously cited.

Death of Bam White, from author interviews with son Melt, previously cited.

Dick Coon broke, from Hunter, *Book of Years,* previously cited.

Death of Doc Dawson from Dawson, *High Plains Yesterdays,* and from Hunter, *Book of Years,* both previously cited.

24: CORNHUSKER III

All of Hartwell's writings are from his unpublished diary, on file at the Nebraska State Historical Society, Lincoln, Nebraska, and provided to the author.

25: RAIN

FDR visit from *Amarillo Daily News,* various editions, July 1938, and from FDR archives, www.newdeal.feri.org.

Trees, "Forestry on the Great Plains, 1902–1942," R. Douglas Hurt, Kansas State University, archive, History Department, www-personal.ksu.edu/~jsherow/lesintro.htm.

EPILOGUE

Information on grasslands from author interview with Michelle Stevens, archaeologist with United States Forest Service grasslands division in La Junta, Colorado, on August 10, 2003, and Forest Service history of grasslands, previously cited.

Information on farm subsidies, and exporting of cotton, from USDA, author interviews, December 2, 2004, and subsidies list published at www.ewg.org.

Trees, from Hurt paper, previously cited, and author visit to southern plains, April 24–26, 2002.

Population crash from United States Census figures.

Ogallala Aquifer from variety of sources: *Water Follies: Groundwater Pumping and the Fate of America's Fresh Waters,* Robert Glennon (Washington, D.C.: Island Press, 2002); Kansas Geological Survey, report of the Ogallala, 2002; Kansas State Research Office, January 14, 2003.

Study on soil conservation districts and their impact on curbing future dust storms, from 2004 study by Zeynep K. Hansen and Gary D. Libecap, "Small Farms, Externalities, and the Dust Bowl of the 1930s," *Journal of Political Economy,* June 2004, vol. 112, no. 3.

Other Bennett information from previously cited USDA biography and Brink, *Big Hugh,* and Soil Conservation Service records, provided by U.S. Forest Service, La Junta, Colorado.

Folkers family details from author interviews with Faye Gardner, April 30, 2002, and Gordon Folkers, May 2, 2002.

Hazel Shaw's last years from author interview with her son, Charles Shaw, September 21, 2003.

Osteen epilogue from author visit to Ike Osteen's house, April 25, 2002.

Acknowledgments

During a reporting trip for this book I arranged to meet a man about town in Guymon, Oklahoma, one of the little communities in No Man's Land that was hammered during the Dust Bowl. Gerald Dixon was well past eighty, a vigorous and bright-eyed man with a droll sense of humor and a quick step. We met in his cluttered office, a museum in itself, where he dabbles in just about every business in Guymon.

"Get in the car," he said at the start of the lunch hour. "I'm taking you to the finest dining establishment in town — the country club."

We rode in his big Buick out to the edge of Guymon, passed a few wheat fields, turned off the main road, went past trailers and some abandoned farmhouses and onto a narrow, rutted dirt road. I could not see another car or another human. The wind was shrieking, the same tune I heard during most of my days on the plains, and tumbleweeds rolled by the car. The sky was white and warm and empty. I began to think that Gerald was lost or that he was playing a trick on me.

"You sure there's a restaurant out here?" I asked.

"'Nother couple of miles."

Finally we descended into a little draw to a shed with some cars parked around it. There were about a dozen guys, most of them Gerald's age, and a handful of women. They were cooking burgers over a big outdoor grill, drinking beer and pop, and talking up Sooner football. Gerald introduced me to his posse, Guymon lifers, and said I was looking for stories about the Dust Bowl. Over lunch, they gave me terrific leads and true-life details to flesh out what I'd only read about the Oklahoma Panhandle during the Dirty Thirties. These old folks were all kids then, teenagers mostly, but they remembered the dusters and the hunger as if they had happened last Friday.

"Now here's a treat," Gerald said. "Hope you saved some room for cobbler."

All morning, they had been cooking peach cobbler in a pit. Fresh peaches, honey, brown sugar, a rich pie dough — all blended into a big vat of cobbler cooked around hot coals set in the ground. I never tasted a better thing at midday, and it was typical of the kind of hospitality I found on the High Plains. It also gave me an inkling as to why people stuck around, even when they faced "the hate of all nature," as John McCarty put it.

That part of the country was like another planet to me. I'm a son of the Pacific Northwest. I grew up with wraparound green, water everywhere, and a horizon always interrupted by mountains. The Gerald Dixons of the flatlands made me feel at home in a brown land. So, for Gerald and his boys out at the burger shack, for the peach cobbler and all the rest, my deepest thanks.

About thirty miles west, in Boise City, I found an invaluable tour guide to the past in Norma Gene Butterbaugh Young. My thanks to Norma for her help and memory, and for her service to the region's history. Hundreds of family stories would have slipped away without her.

Every town has at least an attic that holds the local secrets, usually a small museum. Among the bigger facilities, the Oklahoma Historical Society was very useful, especially the oral history department. Mildred Becker, curator of Wolf Creek Heritage Museum in tiny Lipscomb, Texas, was one of the best of a breed. I would also like to thank the staff of the XIT Museum in Dalhart.

Further thanks are due Charles Shaw, for his generosity of heart in sharing stories about his mother; to the wonderfully effusive Jeanne Clark, who helped to launch this project by bringing together a number of witnesses from her hometown of Lamar, Colorado; to Melt White, maybe the last true cowboy left on the Texas Panhandle; and to Ike Osteen, Baca County's greatest living resource.

For the idea, the direction, the patience, and for keeping his hand on the wheel whenever I wanted to steer the other way, I owe everything to Anton Mueller at Houghton Mifflin. My agent, Carol Mann, saw the match and nudged me into it. And a final bow to Joni, Sophie, and Casey — a family that has never stopped being curious or thrilled by the magic of bookmaking.

Index